A People's History of Catalonia

'Catalonia's aspiration to cut loose from the Spanish state is often dismissed as the whim of a self-interested merchant class. The truth is more complicated. As Michael Eaude's sharp, engrossing, and comprehensive historical narrative makes clear, the centuries-long push for Catalan independence is closely entwined with the peasant- and working-class struggle for social justice and democratic government.'
— Sebastiaan Faber, author of *Exhuming Franco*

'This well-written study takes us on a much-needed historical journey from below, eloquently capturing the rebellious traditions of Catalonia's assertive and proudly defiant popular classes from medieval times to today. By combining broad strokes and intricate detail, he establishes crucial connections between past and contemporary struggles to produce a vivid picture of the class war in a fractured and divided society that produced, in many respects, the most far-reaching social revolution in European history.'
— Chris Ealham, author of *Anarchism and the City*

'This timely and impressive book not only dispels the myths and prejudices about the Catalan people's struggles, so prevalent in Spain and elsewhere, but demonstrates the constant intertwining of the battles for national rights with peasant and working-class revolt "from below". A thoroughly recommended read.'
— Andy Durgan, historian and author of *Voluntarios por la revolución*

'Gives a voice to one of the most rebellious people in Europe whose insurgency reached a pinnacle in 1936 with working-class revolution in Catalonia and continued through the ending of the Franco dictatorship through to today's fight to gain independence in the face of Spanish repression and nationalism. Michael does the Catalan people proud.'
— Chris Bambery, author of *Catalonia Reborn* and Public Point of Enquiry for the All-Party Parliamentary Group on Catalonia

People's History

History tends to be viewed from the perspective of the rich and powerful, where the actions of small numbers are seen to dictate the course of world affairs. But this perspective conceals the role of ordinary women and men, as individuals or as parts of collective organisations, in shaping the course of history. The People's History series puts ordinary people and mass movements centre stage and looks at the great moments of the past from the bottom up.

The People's History series was founded and edited by William A. Pelz (1951–2017).

Also available:

A People's History of Tennis
David Berry

A People's History of the Russian Revolution
Neil Faulkner

Long Road to Harpers Ferry
The Rise of the First American Left
Mark A. Lause

A People's History of Modern Europe
William A. Pelz

A People's History of the German Revolution, 1918–19
William A. Pelz
Foreword by Mario Kessler

A People's History of the Portuguese Revolution
Raquel Varela

A People's History of Europe
From World War I to Today
Raquel Varela

A People's History of Catalonia

Michael Eaude

PLUTO  PRESS

First published 2022 by Pluto Press
New Wing, Somerset House, Strand, London WC2R 1LA

www.plutobooks.com

British Library Cataloguing in Publication Data
A catalogue record for this book is available from the British Library

ISBN   978 0 7453 4212 2   Hardback
ISBN   978 0 7453 4213 9   Paperback
ISBN   978 1 786808 58 5   PDF
ISBN   978 1 786808 59 2   EPUB

This book is printed on paper suitable for recycling and made from fully
managed and sustained forest sources. Logging, pulping and manufacturing
processes are expected to conform to the environmental standards of the
country of origin.

Typeset by Stanford DTP Services, Northampton, England

Simultaneously printed in the United Kingdom and United States of America

This book is dedicated to the memory of two dear and brave comrades, both of whom continued to fight for revolutionary change despite debilitating ill health:

Mike Polley, 1954–2015, who taught me patience

Pedro Serrano Lobato, 1957–2019, who showed me boldness

Contents

Acknowledgements

Many more people than I mention here have enriched my knowledge of Catalonia in 30 years of residence. In particular, I have been taught by the political culture and creative militancy of the activists of *En lluita* and *Anticapitalistes*.

Conversations with the following and/or information from them have contributed specifically to this book. Needless to say, responsibility for all errors and stupid remarks is mine alone. Many thanks to:

Jordi Amat i Tarruella, Brian Anglo, Chris Bambery, Aníbal Besora, Arnau Barquer, Óscar Blanco, Pere Comellas, Chris Ealham, Mike Gonzalez, Angelina Llongueras, Nick Lloyd, Leo Magrinyà, Dámaso Martín, Fernando Palomo, Maria Rovira i Lastra, Elena Sagristà, Professor Josep Maria Salrach, Joel Sans Molas, Teresa Solana and Robin White.

I am especially grateful to Paul Ambrose, Marisa Asensio, Andy Durgan, David C. Hall and Óscar Simón Bueno, who read various chapters and corrected loose syntax, undigested ideas and several embarrassing mistakes. The suggestions of David Castle of Pluto Press have also greatly improved the book.

Authors should explain their prejudice. I'll opt for the late actor Pepe Rubianes' succinct summary of the Catalan question:

'A mí la unidad de España me suda la polla por delante y por detrás.'

A polite translation might be: 'I don't give two fucks for the unity of Spain.'

Figures

Abbreviations and Acronyms

ANC   Assemblea nacional catalana: Catalan National Assembly
BOC   Bloc obrer i camperol: Workers' and Peasants' Bloc
CCMA   Central Anti-Fascist Militia Committee
CDR   Committees for the Defence of the Republic
CEDA   Spanish Federation for Autonomous Rights (Gil Robles' party, close to fascism)
CiU   Convergència i Unió: Convergence and Union (Pujol-led Conservative coalition)
CNT   Confederació Nacional de Treball: National Labour Federation (anarchist-led)
CUP   Candidatures d'Unitat Popular: Popular Unity Candidacies
ERC   Esquerra Republicana de Catalunya: Republican Left of Catalonia
FAGC   Front d'Alliberament Gai de Catalunya: Gay Liberation Front of Catalonia
FAI   Federation of Iberian Anarchists
FOC   Front obrer català: Catalan Workers Front
FOUS   Workers' Federation for Unity (POUM trade union)
ICE   Izquierda Comunista de España: Communist Left of Spain (1930s followers of Trotsky)
IWA   International Workers Association
JSU   United Socialist Youth
LCR   Revolutionary Communist League
LOAPA   Organic Bill to Harmonise the Autonomic Process
(1982)
ORT   Organización Revolucionaria de Trabajadores: Workers' Revolutionary Organisation
PCE   Communist Party of Spain
POUM   Partit obrer d'unificació marxista: Workers' Party of Marxist Unification
PP   Partido popular: People's Party (right-wing)

PSAN   Partit Socialista d'Alliberament Nacional: Socialist Party for National Liberation (independentist)

PSC   Partit dels Socialistes de Catalunya: Catalan Socialist Party

PSOE   Partido Socialista Obrero Español: Spanish Workers' Socialist Party

PSUC   Partit Socialista Unificat de Catalunya: Unified Socialist Party of Catalonia (Communist Party)

UCD   Unión del Centro Democrático: Union of the Democratic Centre

UGT   Unió general de treballadors: General Union of Workers (Socialist)

Glossary

This is a Glossary of Catalan words used; some Castilian words included are indicated by (*cast.*)

Abat: Abbot
¡A por ellos! (*cast.*): Go get 'em!
Aiguardent: firewater, coarse brandy
Alianza obrera (*cast.*): Workers Alliance
Almogàvers: medieval Catalan and Aragonese wild warriors
(Los) amargados (*cast.*): The embittered
Assemblea de Catalunya: Assembly for Catalonia
Assemblea de Pau i Treva: Sanctuary and Truce Assembly
Associacions de veïns: Residents' Associations
Ateneu: Athenaeum – cultural centre
Barretina: traditional red floppy cap
Barri: neighbourhood
Biga: beam
Botifler: Catalan who sides with Spanish nationalism
Bruixa (pl. bruixes): witch
Bullanga: tumult, riot
Busca: splinter
Cadastre: property tax
Cadells: Pups (sixteenth–seventeenth-century armed gangs defending
   the Spanish monarchy)
Cafè per a tots: coffee for everyone
Call: Jewish quarter
Casa pairal: patriarchal home (traditional peasants' house)
Catalunya Nord: North Catalonia
Comissions obreres/Comisiones obreras (*cast.*): Workers' Committees
Comunero (*cast.*): commoner
Consell de Cent: Council of a Hundred (Barcelona City Council)
Conseller/era: minister in Catalan government
Consolat de mar: Sea Consulate

Constitucions: constitutions and laws
Coronela: Barcelona's volunteer defence force
Cortes (*cast.*): Spanish parliament
Corts: Catalonia's parliament
Criollo (*cast.*): Creole; local ruling class in Spanish America
¡Desperta ferro!: Iron, awake!
Diada: 11 September, Catalonia's national day
Diputació: Regional Council
Drassanes: shipyards
Eixample: Expansion
Escola catalana: Catalan school
Escoles concertades: publicly subsidised private schools
Escola moderna: modern school (anarchist schools)
Estat català: Catalan state
Estatut: statute
Estelada: Catalan independence flag
Euskadi: Basque Country
Front d'esquerres: Left Front (1936 Popular Front in Catalonia)
Front català d'ordre: Catalan Front for Order
Furs (fueros, *cast.*): charters
Generalitat: Catalan government
(Els) grisos: The greys (Franco's police)
Hereu: male heir, oldest son
Hez del pueblo (*cast.*): dregs of the people
Indià (pl., Indians): someone who returned rich from America
Insaculació: election of City Councillors by placing candidates' names
    in a bag
Junta: council, committee
Latifundio (*cast.*): Large estate
Mals usos: bad practices
Mancomunitat: Commonwealth
Maquis: anti-Franco guerrilla fighters
Margalló: squat palm
Mas (pl. masos): large farmhouse
Maulets: Valencian peasant rebels
Miquelets: armed rural militia
Miserables: wretched (unemployed)
Modernista: Modernist, Catalan art nouveau

Mossos d'esquadra: Catalan police force
Mujeres Libres (*cast.*): Free Women
Nova cançó: New Song
Nueva planta (*cast.*): Felipe V's 'New Plan', suppressing Catalan and
  Valencian rights
Nyerros: sixteenth–seventeenth-century guerrilla fighters defending
  Catalan rights
Ocell: bird
Operaris: workers
Països Catalans: Catalan lands
Palau: palace, mansion
Pàtria (patria, *cast.*): fatherland
Patuleia: gang
Pistolerisme: gun law
Pistoleros (*cast.*): gunmen
Porciolisme: corrupt building practice
Privado (*cast.*): King's favourite
Pronunciamiento (*cast.*): military coup declaration
La quinta del biberón (*cast.*): The Children's Levy
Rabassaire: grape farmer
Reconquista (*cast.*): reconquest
Remença (pl., remences): redemption
Renaixença: rebirth, resurgence
Rosa de foc: Rose of fire
(Els) segadors: The reapers
Selfactines: automatic ('self-acting') looms
Senyera: official flag of Catalonia
Setmana tràgica: Tragic Week
Setze jutges: Sixteen Judges
Sindicats Lliures: free unions (violent bosses' union)
Sindicat únic: single union
Sometent: local militia
Tercios (*cast.*): Spanish army battalions
Terra de pas: thoroughfare, strategic crossroads
Treintistas: 'Thirty-ists'
Usatges de Barcelona: Observations (laws limiting feudal nobles'
  power)
Vigatà (pl. vigatans): inhabitant of Vic

¡Visca Catalunya!: Long Live Catalonia!
¡Visca el rei!: Long Live the King!
¡Visca la terra!: Long Live our Land!

Timeline

1659	Treaty of the Pyrenees: North Catalonia lost
1687–1689	Revolt of the *barretines*
1700	Felipe V comes to Spanish throne
1701–1713	War of the Spanish Succession
1702	*Corts* with Felipe V
1705	Archduke Carles takes Barcelona. *Corts* with the Archduke
25 April 1707	Battle of Almansa
October 1707	Felipe V's army besieges and sacks Lleida
1713–1714	Siege of Barcelona
January 1716	New Plan Decree
1808–1814	French occupation of Catalonia
2 May 1808	Insurrection in Madrid against French
June 1808	Victories at the Bruc pass
May–December 1809	Third siege of Girona
1812	Spanish liberal Constitution agreed at Cadiz
1814	Restoration of Fernando VII
1820–1823	Liberal triennium, inspired by the revolt of Rafael de Riego
1833–1840	First Carlist War
1835–1843	*Bullangues*, revolts in Catalonia's cities
July 1835	Sacking of monasteries
5 August 1835	General Bassa killed and Bonaplata factory burnt
3 December 1842	Espartero shells Barcelona
1843–1844	*Jamància* revolt: Prim shells Barcelona
November 1843–1844	Slave revolt in Cuba, led by Carlota
1855	First General Strike in Catalonia. 'Unions or Death'
1868	Overthrow of Queen Isabel. Arrival of Bakunin's agent Fanelli
June 1870	Spanish Federation of the First International founded in Barcelona
1873–1874	First Spanish Republic
July 1873	Workers' Government in Alcoi
July 1873–January 1874	Canton of Cartagena

1889–1892	Autonomous Working Women's Association
1892	Bases de Manresa
7 November 1893	Liceu bomb
7 June 1896	Corpus Christi bomb
February 1902	General strike
25 November 1905	Military trash *Cu-cut* offices
20 May 1906	Mass demonstration in Barcelona against militarisation of justice
April 1907	Electoral triumph of *Solidaritat catalana*
July 1909	Uprising against conscription. 'Setmana tràgica'
October 1909	Execution of Francesc Ferrer and closing of the *escola moderna*
October 1910	CNT founded
1914–1925	*Mancomunitat de Catalunya*
August 1917	General strike
February–March, 1919	La Canadenca strike
June 1919	Layret wins Sabadell election to the Spanish *Cortes*
1919–1923	Police and *Sindicats Lliures* murder at least 250 working-class militants
30 November 1920	Murder of Layret
10 March 1923	Murder of Salvador Seguí
November 1926	Macià's failed invasion of Catalonia
14 April 1931	Second Spanish Republic proclaimed
July–September 1931	Strike wave
July–December 1931	Barcelona rent strikes
January 1932	Attempted insurrection at Fígols
19 November 1933	The right wins the Spanish elections
October 1934	Workers' Alliance takes over Asturias. Crushed by Franco
6 October 1934	Catalan state declared. *Generalitat* suppressed
29 September 1935	POUM founded
16 February 1936	Popular Front electoral victory. *Front d'Esquerres* wins in Catalonia
19–20 July 1936	In Catalonia, mass mobilisation defeats military coup

26 September 1936	Anarchists and POUM join Catalan government
February 1937	POUM and anarchist youth organisations form Revolutionary Youth Front
3–7 May 1937	May Days fighting
5 May	Autonomy Statute of 1932 suppressed
15 May 1937	Fall of Largo Caballero's Spanish government
16 June 1937	POUM illegalised
July–November 1938	Battle of the Ebre
26 January 1939	Fall of Barcelona
January–February 1939	circa 465,000 people leave the Spanish state through Catalonia
October 1944	Communist invasion of the Vall d'Aran
8 May and 15 August 1945	Workers' protests against dictatorship
January 1946	Strike at Bertrand y Serra, Manresa
March 1951	Barcelona tram boycott and strike
1956	Unrest in universities
12 March 1956	Engineering strikes
19 May 1960	Christian protest in the *Palau de la Música*
20 November 1964	*Comissions obreres* founded in Sants
1969 onwards	Rise of Residents' Associations
October 1971	Occupation at SEAT
November 1971	Assembly for Catalonia set up
20 November 1975	Death of Franco
May 1976	Founding of Autonomous Women's Movement
8 November 1976	Start of 95-day strike at Roca Radiadores
15 June 1977	Statewide general election. Workers' parties win in Catalonia
1 and 8 February 1976 and 11 September 1976 and 1977	Mass demonstrations for Catalan autonomy
6 December 1978	Vote in favour of new Constitution
1980–2003	Jordi Pujol, President of Catalonia
23 February 1981	Tejero's attempted *coup*
30 July 1982	LOAPA approved: *cafè per a tots*
June 2001	World Bank meeting in Barcelona cancelled

15 February 2003	Biggest of many demonstrations against invasion of Iraq
18 June 2006	New statute proposal approved in Catalan referendum
10 July 2010	Mass demonstration against Constitutional Court's rejection of statute
13 September 2009– 25 April 2011	Local independence referendums
9 November 2014	Consultative referendum on independence
1 October 2017	Binding referendum on independence
3 October 2017	General strike against repression
27 October 2017	Independence declared. Spanish state sacks Catalan government
Late 2019	*Tsunami democràtic*. Mass protests against jail sentences for Catalan political leaders
14 February 2021	Pro-independence parties win 52 per cent of the vote in Catalan election
June 2021	PSOE Government pardons jailed independence leaders

Introduction

People who live outside the Spanish state are often astounded when they learn of the anti-Catalan vitriol poisoning Spanish social media, television and press. This book aims to explore the background to this alarming hostility, fostered today by the Spanish ruling class to oppose the Catalan struggle for independence. This anti-Catalanism is not some new reaction to troublesome secessionists, but has roots deep in history. The notorious Spanish police assault on Catalans voting in a referendum on 1 October 2017 (see Chapter 12), which hit headlines all round the world, was only the latest incident in a centuries-old conflict.

The conflict can be traced right back to the fifteenth century when, in 1412, a Castilian king acceded to the throne of the Crown of Aragon after the line of the Counts of Barcelona died out. Conquering and trading along the Mediterranean coast and across the sea, Catalonia had evolved differently from landlocked Castile. The former developed a tradition of internal 'pacting' and negotiation between the Count of Barcelona and his upper-class subjects in a quite different political system from Castile's, where absolutist kings reigned.

The book gives a chronological account of the centuries-long and successful struggle of Catalonia to survive as a nation. Chapter 1 explains how it began to form as an entity in the eleventh and twelfth centuries. What some historians call the 'aristocratic revolution' to impose feudalism on a land-owning peasantry from about 1000 CE was answered forcefully by the Church-led movement of Sanctuary and Truce. This led, in the following decades, to legislation ordering the relationships between monarch, peasants and nobles. A series of laws and practices – in particular a parliament (*Corts*) of the three ruling estates, or 'arms', (church, nobles and military, and 'honourable' merchants in the cities) – meant that the Count of Barcelona was controlled in part by the *Corts*.

As Chapter 1 focuses on Catalonia's medieval development as a Mediterranean power, so Chapter 2 focuses on three great class conflicts of the fifteenth century. These were the Civil War between the king and the new Catalan government, known as the *Generalitat*, flexing its muscles against absolutist desires; a city uprising of lesser merchants, artisan workshops and liberal professions against the wealthy 'honourable citizens'; and third, a peasants' revolt that shook the country to its foundations and broke the back of feudal oppression.

In the diabolical year 1492, the Spanish state came into being under Ferdinand of Aragon and Isabella of Castile. The last Moorish kingdom, in Granada, was defeated, the Jews were expelled or forced to convert and Columbus reached Hispaniola. There was no room for an independent Catalonia in this new Spain, which in the sixteenth century built – through military conquest – the greatest empire Europe had yet seen, extending from America to Flanders, Italy and the Philippines. Yet, paradox that has exercised generations of historians, the Spanish Empire under the Hapsburgs was unable to unite the peoples of Iberia. Though part of the new Spain, Catalonia continued to raise its own taxes and be governed by its own parliament. The Holy Roman Emperor Charles V, Spain's first Hapsburg king (1516–1556), crushed brutally the Spanish *Cortes* (parliament) but did not attempt to suppress the rights of Catalonia. He had to negotiate with Catalans if he wanted to raise cash from them.

This underlying tension between an absolutist monarchy and a nation within its state that practised negotiation between the monarch and the estates could not rest in an eternally stable relationship. Chapters 3 and 4 deal with the two wars waged by the Spanish monarchs against Catalonia.

When Olivares came to power in Madrid in 1621, he began to press hard for a unified administration, army and taxation throughout Spain. His pressure led to the Catalan revolution of 1640–1641, when Catalonia came close to winning an independence that Portugal, on the other side of the Iberian Peninsula, did achieve at that time.

Chapter 4 discusses the year-long siege of Barcelona in 1714. After promising support to Catalonia in the War of the Spanish Succession, England ('perfidious Albion') abandoned it. Catalonia was reduced to a province of Spain, with all its distinctive characteristics suppressed: laws, governing bodies, language, university etc. This defeat is a scar that has failed to heal. The day that the Bourbon Felipe V's forces took Barcelona, 11 September, is Catalonia's national day, when those who died in the siege are honoured. In recent years of rising independence struggle, 11 September demonstrations have mobilised over a million people – some 14 per cent of the country's population.

Chapter 5 focuses on another devastating war: Napoleon's occupation of Spain in 1808–1814, including Catalonia's integration into the French state for two years. Catalan popular resistance was widespread and Catalan intellectuals played a leading part in drafting Spain's 1812 liberal constitution. This generation of enlightened Catalans aspired to lead Spain out of its backwardness to become a capitalist democracy, but their hopes were dashed by the return of the absolutist Fernando VII.

These first five chapters chart the medieval glory of Catalonia and its long decline. Part II of the book is dominated by working-class struggle. In the nineteenth century, Barcelona developed a justified reputation as the most militant city of Western Europe. Chapter 6 describes the constant, fierce rebellions against poverty and wage slavery of the 1830s and 1840s, as capitalism's cotton mills were built on the basis of the profits from trade and from slave plantations in Cuba. At the same time as these first working-class revolts, the Carlists, who wanted a return to absolute monarchy, were fighting the Spanish army in the Catalan countryside. To add to the complexity, the Catalan rebirth (*renaixença*) of national spirit was recovering the memory of its glorious past, first in culture and language and then, towards the end of the nineteenth century, in political organisation. Catalonia's modern history is best understood through the intertwining of national and class demands, or often their failure to intertwine. There was a serious fault-line between the political capital in Madrid and the economic centres on the northern and eastern coasts, between military and semi-feudal agricultural interests and the needs of industrial capitalism.

Chapter 7 explains the overthrow of the Bourbon Queen Isabel in 1868 and the explosion of freedom that led to the 1873 First Republic. Anarchism began to organise in these brief years of free expression, but its strategies of boycotting political action and arguing for immediate revolution meant it had little impact on the working and middle classes fighting for a Republic. In 1874, the Republic was overthrown and the Bourbons restored. The greatness of the anarchist movement was seen in the following decades in its educational work among an ignorant peasantry and proletariat and in its efforts to build militant, non-bureaucratic unions oriented towards revolutionary general strikes.

Chapter 8 explains the founding of the mass, anarchist-led union, the CNT, in 1910 and its great victory in the six-week Canadenca strike in 1919. The bosses responded to the strength of the revolutionary movement by organising squads that murdered hundreds of CNT activists. Chapter 9 focuses on the Second Republic, proclaimed on 14 April 1931, opening a pre-revolutionary period in which Catalonia recovered its self-government. The Spanish Revolution erupted in response to the military coup of 18 July 1936. Chapter 10 discusses this revolution, the counter-revolution led by the Communist Party and the Civil War defeat in 1939. Of the three great European workers' revolutions, the Paris Commune of 1871 and Russian Revolution in 1917 being the other two, the Spanish Revolution took place in the most advanced country. And it was in Catalonia where the most far-reaching and profound social changes took place. Many readers will know of the revolution's defeat through *Homage to Catalonia*, George Orwell's report on his months fighting with the POUM militia and the 1937 May Days. Ironically, it shows little understanding of Catalonia, fine book though it is.

Chapter 11 discusses the terrible years of the Franco dictatorship (1939–1977), which treated Catalonia as occupied territory, disbanded all Catalan institutions and banned the language in an even more ferocious rerun of 1714. Resistance to Franco was long, up-and-down and hard. In the 1970s, a new working class organised in the factories and neighbourhoods forced the ruling class to dismantle the dictatorship. The chapter suggests how the mass mobilisations of this 'Transition' could have achieved a better deal for the working class.

Chapter 12 concentrates on the nature of the post-Franco democracy and the independence movement that flowered after 2009 to challenge an immobile Spanish state. Spanish centralists deny that Catalonia is a nation. This is the basic justification for the refusal of Spain's main political parties to permit a referendum on independence, or even to discuss the possibility of one. They defend this intransigence with a number of distortions of history. The most obvious sleight of hand is to insist that Catalonia never was an independent state, as medieval Catalonia was part of the Crown of Aragon and thus the conquests of the Mediterranean and trading successes were Aragonese, not Catalan.

Such arguments may seem recondite. One cannot base today's fight for independence on ancient history, we are told. Yet, history is a live presence in the mind, especially for those who suffer its hammer-blows.

The years 1641, 1714 and 1939 are dates engraved in blood on Catalan brains, when the Spanish state slaughtered tens or hundreds of thousands and wrecked Catalan aspirations to freedom.

*   *   *

The French historian Pierre Vilar (1906–2003) is much loved by Catalan nationalists today for his authoritative 2,000-page *La Catalogne dans l'Espagne modern*, which includes this quote:

> Between 1250 and 1350 the Principality of Catalonia may be the European country to which it would be least incorrect and least dangerous to apply the apparently anachronic terms of political and economic imperialism and nation state ... This creation is remarkable, therefore, especially on account of its precociousness. Language, territory, economic life, the shaping of a mentality, a cultural community – the fundamental conditions of a nation – are already fully present as early as the 13th century.[1]

Such sentences drive Spanish nationalists up the wall. Note Vilar's caution: 'least incorrect' and 'least dangerous'. Like any serious historian, he is well aware that to talk of nation-states in the thirteenth century is anachronistic.

The nation only became a political concept in the nineteenth century, following the Enlightenment and the Romantic movements, and at much the same time as the Industrial Revolution. The relation between nation and class is thorny and complex. Though Marx and Engels did not develop a full theory of the national question, the later, great European revolutionary generation of activist-theorists did. Stalin was commissioned by the Bolshevik Party in 1912 to compose theses on the national question. Rosa Luxemburg opposed Stalin's rather schematic definition. She believed that the right to self-determination of a nation had little to do with working-class struggle: nationalist movements merely reflected the economic requirements of the bourgeoisie.

Lenin built on Stalin's theses and his was the classic position followed in the 1930s by the POUM (Workers' Party of Marxist Unification): that revolutionaries should support the self-determination, though not necessarily the independence, of oppressed nations. The Marxist Joaquín Maurín, leader of the BOC (Workers' and Peasants' Bloc), took this a step further and argued at the start of the 1930s that the working class should support the independence struggles of all the oppressed nations of the Spanish state and that the national independence of these would help smash the state, a position close to that of the CUP (Popular Unity Candidacies) – the anti-capitalist formation that is driving forward the struggles for independence and social justice in Catalonia today.

The demand today for a referendum on Catalonia's independence from the Spanish state is a quite simple democratic one, supported by 70–80 per cent of Catalonia's population. Independence supporters and many opposed to independence want a referendum to settle the issue. Spanish nationalist politicians block this, bound by their own centralist history and terrified of the effects of Catalan independence on Spain's economy (Catalonia, with about 16 per cent of Spain's population, contributes about 20 per cent of Spain's GDP) and international influence.

While explaining Spanish nationalists' arguments and rebutting their attacks on Catalonia, this book also challenges the founding myths and falsifications of the Catalan ruling class. When you read Catalan nationalist histories, the glories of the past are often exaggerated while the sins are skipped over lightly. You would not know that Catalonia was once the 'lord and terror of the Mediterranean', as the nineteenth-century traveller Richard Ford put it. Nationalist historians prefer to highlight the pacts between the various Catalan estates in medieval times, that is, negotiation instead of fighting, democracy in embryo, and tend to gloss over the 'terror' of imperialism. A good example is the conquest of Mallorca in 1229–1232, presented by Ferran Soldevila as 'the expansion of Catalonia's national territory and the start of its Mediterranean expansion. Populated by Catalans, it was an extension of Catalonia through blood, language and culture'.[2] True enough, but the account omits the slaughter, enslavement or expulsion of the previous Moorish population (see Chapter 2). No democratic 'pacting' in the invasion of Mallorca! This said, modern Catalan nationalism is not an imperialist, ultra-right nationalism. It is a reactive nationalism, in defence of Catalan rights and identity against a more powerful Spanish state. And the modern independence movement is a coming together of sections of a bourgeoisie fed up with the lack of political influence consonant with its economic strength and a working-class/petit bourgeois movement fighting for socialism or, at least, a more just state.

The Spanish state is in a deep crisis of legitimacy today. All its institutions are questioned, in a context of multiple crises: of the economy (mass unemployment and poverty); of the monarchy (the former king in exile fleeing corruption investigations); of political efficacy; of the judiciary; of corruption, without mentioning the failure to tackle climate change and how COVID-19 exposed the murderous consequences of neoliberalism, that is, cut-backs, precarious jobs, privatisation and low wages, old people's homes run for profit etc. The crises are most likely to deepen, which means that poverty, injustice and insecurity will intensify Catalan desire to leave this sinking ship.

But would independence bring serious progressive change or just a neoliberal reshuffle? The big question has no sure answer. One thing we can be sure of, though, is that an independence movement driven from below radicalises wide sections of the population. The intertwining of the class and national questions is dynamite.

* * *

Perry Anderson wrote nearly 50 years ago:

> History writing in the proper sense is inseparable from direct research into the original records of the past – archival, epigraphic or archaeological. The studies below have no claim to this dignity.[3]

The two sentences apply precisely to this book. I have done no direct research into original records. Though I have striven to get the facts right, this is a book of interpretation. I have relied on others, real historians, with the exception of the last two chapters on the 1970s Transition and the 40-plus years since of parliamentary democracy. For these I have both talked extensively with activists and participated in the struggles: against NATO in 1985–1986, in the anti-globalisation rebellions of the 2000s and in the independence movement of recent years.

It is a truism that a people's history should rescue from oblivion the silenced voices of the oppressed. For the most part, this has not been possible, as for many centuries the lives of women, peasants or workers were unrecorded. Only occasionally do we get a flash of feeling, of focus, as in the case of the peasant rebellion led by Pere Joan Sala or in in the trials of women accused of witchcraft. The nearest I have come is in the accounts of the Napoleonic invasion and the Spanish Civil War, thanks in both cases to the monumental work of Ronald Fraser (1930–2015), who wrote histories based on detailed local research in the former and extensive interviews in the latter.

When writing about the French, Russian or Portuguese Revolutions, a 'history from below' is more obvious, as history speeds up: the masses are in ferment and propel events forward throughout the brief period under scrutiny. Writing about the thousand-year history of a country is different. My first impulse was to scour history books for accounts of revolts and rebellions. Luckily, in Catalonia, there are many turning points when the weight of mass struggle on events was felt. A 'People's History', though, is not just a list of revolts. These result in political decisions and it is the Counts of Barcelona, the monarchs of the Spanish state or the Catalan *Generalitat* that took these decisions. Here's a clear example: in the fifteenth century (see Chapter 2), at the end of the long struggle of the *remença* peasants to loosen their bonds, some 400–500 men and women led by Pere Joan Sala rose in an armed onslaught on feudal power. The desperate and brave peasant fighters were defeated and their leaders executed in 1485 but, in 1486, King Ferran (Ferdinand in English), in the famous 'Sentence of Guadalupe', stopped the *mals usos* (bad practices). His decision, which ended or reduced feudalism in Catalonia (interpretations vary), is not fully understandable without the long history of peasant organisation and struggle of 1448–1485, culminating in Sala's uprising. The decisions of kings are best understood when the struggles of the poor are included.

Map 1   Map of Catalan-Speaking Lands (Marisa Asensio)

PART I

From Empire to Province

Figure 1   Abat Oliba's monastery at Ripoll (Dámaso Martín)

1

Rise and Fall of the Crown of Aragon

We, who are as good as you, swear to you, who are no better than us, to accept you as our king and sovereign lord, provided you observe all our liberties and laws – but if not, not.[1]

On 24 October 1971, the world's most famous cellist Pau Casals addressed the United Nations General Assembly. Casals, aged 94, had been awarded the UN Peace Medal in recognition of his lifelong commitment 'to truth, to beauty and to peace'. The award was a slap in the face for the Franco dictatorship (1939–1977), which had driven Casals into exile. The cellist opened by saying that he loved peace and continued:

> …I am a Catalan, today a province of Spain, but what has been Catalonia? Catalonia has been the greatest nation in the world … I will tell you why. Catalonia has had the first Parliament, much before England. Catalonia had the beginning of the United Nations. All the authorities of Catalonia in the eleventh century met in a city of France, at that time Catalonia, to speak about peace, in the eleventh century, peace in the world and against, against, against wars.[2]

In his moving speech, Casals was quite right that Catalonia had been reduced from its former glory to a mere province of Spain, but, Catalan nationalist as he was, he exaggerated his country's status as the first democracy. This chapter attempts to explain what Casals was referring to. It describes the period when the area known in the eighth–tenth centuries as the Hispanic March developed into the feudal state of Catalonia, a name whose earliest surviving written use was in 1198, somewhat later than Casals' date.

The Hispanic March extended from just south of Barcelona to what is now the Roussillon in southern France. It had been established by Charlemagne after his troops had expelled the Moors in 801 as a buffer zone between al-Andalus, the Muslim Moorish kingdom based in Cordoba that controlled most of the Iberian Peninsula, and the Christian Carolingian Empire to the north. Charlemagne and his descendants offered military protection against possible Moorish invasion to the counts of this area, of which the Count of Barcelona was the first among equals. The brevity of the Moorish occupation left the Hispanic March much less affected by Islamic culture than most of the Iberian Peninsula.

In the ninth and tenth centuries, the peasants in the Hispanic March were mostly free men and women who lived off the land's produce, as in many parts of Europe. Peasants made their own clothing and ate bread and gruel. They might hunt rabbits, wild boar or even a bear. These were self-sufficient societies. Pre-feudal peasants were 'free' only in the sense that they were not slaves or serfs and that they held their land in freehold. Though Moorish invasion and Christian 'reconquest' had not ravaged the Hispanic March, the peasants were not free from hunger, disease or the abuse of local nobles. Historians calculate that famine was constant: crops failed at least once a decade.

For 200 years, the Hispanic March was the southernmost outpost of the Carolingian Empire, which was based on the Roman idea of state: rights and justice were dispensed in exchange for taxes. In the Hispanic March, authority was invested in the counts and local magistrates appointed from Aachen by the Empire.

In the Pyrenees, on both sides of today's border between Spain and France – a frontier at that time non-existent and not even thought of – a series of Romanesque churches and monasteries were constructed in the ninth and tenth centuries. The Church built in these remote mountain valleys because they were of difficult access to potential Arab invaders, the land was fertile and stone was plentiful.

The most powerful of these magnificent Pyrenean monasteries was at Ripoll, founded in 880 by Guifré *el Pilós* or Wilfred the Hairy. Guifré is a bit like King Arthur in Britain, a semi-mythical founding father of the nation. Guifré was a real enough historical figure, but his deeds merge into legend. Count of Ripoll, Guifré was created Count of Barcelona by Charlemagne's grandson, Charles the Bald, in 874. By conquest, marriage and inheritance, Guifré managed to combine several Pyrenean counties, and his will left the counties of Barcelona, Girona and Vic undivided, making Guifré's descendants the dominant counts in the Hispanic March and laying the basis for a united country. The legendary bit is that, when he died in battle in 897 on a raid against the Moors, the Carolingian general dipped his fingers in Wilfred the Hairy's blood and traced four red lines on his golden shield. These lines became the four red stripes on the yellow flag of Catalonia, which today flies over every public building. This official flag is known as the *senyera*; the independence supporters' flag is the *estelada*, with a star on a blue triangle added.

In 985, Al-Mansur's army sacked Barcelona. The Arabs did not have the resources to occupy the area and withdrew, though not without slaughtering many and bearing off others as slaves. The last Carolingian king, Louis V, was too weak to react and, in 988, Count Borrell of Barcelona withdrew the tribute paid to the Frankish kingdom and did not renew his oath of allegiance. More or less from this point, one can begin to talk of the independence of the area, though it was not yet Catalonia, but a mosaic of small baronies, religious communities and free peasants, dominated by the Counts of Barcelona.

Feudalism and Sanctuary Assemblies

Round about the turn of the millennium, a feudal revolution overthrew the existing legal framework, altering class relations. The end of Carolingian control meant that local counts no longer paid allegiance and tributes to Aachen. These and the officials appointed by the empire were able to become owners of the goods and lands. They were no longer appointees governing on behalf of the emperor. In this 'aristocratic revolution', nobles began to appropriate free peasants' land and create serfs. The free peasants who had paid taxes to the empire were now obliged to pay half of their crops to local nobles. Over time, they were squeezed more and more. The strings of the corset of poverty in which they lived were drawn tighter.

It is in this context that a social movement to halt the nobles' violence led to the *Assemblees de Pau i Treva*, Sanctuary and Truce Assemblies. In 1027, a conference was organised by Oliba, a great-grandson of Guifré and Abbot of Ripoll and Bishop of Vic, to protect ecclesiastical property, agriculture and clergy against attacks. The Church's main weapon was the threat of excommunication. Even evil nobles believed in Heaven and Hell, so excommunication was a serious business.

The Pope sanctioned this conference, as he had a previous one in Charroux (near Poitiers) in 989. He supported too a subsequent meeting in 1033 in Vic, also organised by Abbot Oliba. However, the most famous Sanctuary Assembly was the 1027 one held at Toluges (a monastery and village near Perpinyà – Perpignan – not to be confused with Toulouse). This is the meeting to which Pau Casals referred in his address to the United Nations Assembly. Here, the days of the week when arms could be used were restricted and sanctuary from violence or pursuit within a church and for 30 steps around it was stipulated. The Sanctuary Assembly was dominated by clergy, but also attended by a large number of peasant farmers. The protection debated and approved was not just for the clergy's benefit, but also included widows, public highways and those who travelled on them, and peasants' houses and possessions. The time of 'no violence', formerly just on Sundays, was extended from Wednesday sunset to dawn on Monday. The movement was not wholly original: rights of asylum from authority or sanctuary from criminals in temples and churches were common in Ancient Greece and Anglo-Saxon England. In Catalonia, it was a strong defensive response to the violence of the aristocratic revolution.

Oliba (c. 971–1046) was the most famous priest and scholar of his time. The monastery at Ripoll attracted students from all over Europe. By the time of Oliba's death, its library contained 246 volumes. Ripoll was one of the main conduits through which Arabic learning passed into more backward Europe. The Hispanic March was not just a buffer but also a thoroughfare, a *terra de pas*. Scholars at Ripoll translated medical and philosophical texts from Arabic to Latin. The astrolabe, pharmaceutical formulae, algebra and the manufacture of paper were some of the fruits of Arabic technology and learning that passed through the Hispanic March. The concept of zero and Arabic numerals, the ones we use today, reached the rest of Europe by way of Ripoll.

Such was the atmosphere of violence in 1027 that the Count of Barcelona did not dare travel to the Council at Toluges, but he did attend the Vic meeting six years later. At first, his ability to impose his law on other nobles was tenuous. The following Count of Barcelona, Ramon Berenguer I (ruled 1035–1076), managed to enforce his authority in two principal ways. First, like many weak rulers, he resorted to war to increase his prestige. The Caliphate of Cordoba had collapsed in 1031, fragmenting into warring kingdoms. Through successful raids south and exaction of tributes from neighbouring Moorish areas, Ramon Berenguer I distributed loot and coined money, so purchasing the loyalty of the nobles.

Second, he convened several Sanctuary Assemblies during his reign. The movement, designed to defend the Church and that incidentally assisted the peasantry, was transformed into an instrument of royal power. The Count of Barcelona consolidated his position at the cost of the peasantry, submitted to a feudal regime of servitude. 'The count abandoned the pretence of being a sovereign above the system to become the head of the system.'[3]

In the 1060s, the *Usatges de Barcelona*, or *Observations*, were developed. Often these are wrongly and anachronistically referred to as a Bill of Rights. They were a series of laws that ordered society under the new mode of production and limited the power of nobles. Catalan nationalists like Pau Casals argue that it preceded Magna Carta, the English Charter of 1215. They are partly right, for Ramon Berenguer I did start on the definition of the rights and duties of the ruling count and the nobles. However, this legal document of checks and balances was not completed until the time of Jaume I 'the Conqueror' in 1251, when the *Usatges* defined executive, legislative and judicial power, penalised feudal excesses and eventually became something like the Constitution of the new state. The Roman law that the Carolingian Empire adopted and parts of Visigothic law were incorporated. The *Usatges* granted all free men (not women, not slaves) equality before the law. In practice, equality was not real, but the *Usatges* did mean that gross injustices committed by a noble could, in theory, be taken by a peasant to arbitration. The *Usatges* also codified 'emphyteusis', a system of leasehold originating in Roman practice. This was a perpetual lease, whereby the male peasant had the right to continue living and working on the land as long as the land's tithes were properly paid and half his produce (or a negotiated lesser amount) was paid to the noble. The lease was inherited and brought stability. Without emphyteusis, there would have been no motivation to keep improving the land. Peasants felt they 'owned' their land. With the *Usatges*, a distinct Catalan identity began to form. And from the *Usatges*' first drafts in the 1060s, the Counts of Barcelona became pre-eminent in the area soon to be known as Catalonia: buying allegiance with wealth obtained from raids on the Moors, founding a new legal system and placing themselves at the head of the new feudalism.

In this reshaping of class relationships, the nobles could not afford to over-oppress the peasants (an economic truism that Stalin failed to appreciate). In a highly localised economy, nobles depended on peasants working the land. If not, both peasants and nobles starved. This happened in years of crop failure. And to work the land, there had to be a certain degree of peace. No farmer is going to plant seed if some heavily armed lout is going to come along and burn his house or seize his crops.

Half-Naked Raiders

The authority of the Counts of Barcelona grew quickly. By 1154, the frontiers of modern Catalonia were defined to the south, including the present-day Spanish provinces of Lleida and Tarragona, conquered from the Moors and known as New Catalonia. To the north, through marriage in 1112, the Count of Barcelona gained control of Provence. The most important event, though, was the union of Catalonia and Aragon through Ramon Berenguer IV's pact of marriage with Petronella of Aragon in 1137 (marriage agreement rather than actual marriage because Petronella was only one year old). Thus, the Crown of Aragon, led by the Count of Barcelona (king in all but name), was founded.[4]

Feudalism was not a static system of domination, but as dynamic as any other set of class relations. The feudal nobles were interested in expanding the lands under their control, so were prepared to finance the clearance of forests and drainage of swamps. In Catalonia, as in much of Europe, production of food doubled from 1000 to 1300, which led both to greater wealth for the nobles (the construction of houses and castles, and the purchase of food, furniture and silk clothing) and to better tools for the peasantry. Watermills and windmills were developed at this time; blacksmiths shaped iron into tools. Horseshoes meant that horses could be used for heavier work; ploughs became stronger.

From 1225 to about 1315, Catalonia (again, like most of Europe) lived a century of prosperity. Hunger disappeared for generations. In this time of expansion south and into the Mediterranean, Jaume I 'the Conqueror' (ruled 1213–1276) evicted the Moorish ruling class from Mallorca, Menorca and Eivissa (Ibiza) in the 1230s and Valencia in the 1230s and 1240s. The Moors working on the land continued as serfs. Valencia became a third kingdom, alongside Catalonia and Aragon, in the Crown of Aragon. Wealthy Sicily was conquered in the 1280s.

Sardinia was occupied in 1323–1326. Both these islands were important producers of cereals, which Catalonia's several coastal towns and the dominant city of Barcelona imported.

The nineteenth-century romantic invention of Catalan nationalism promoted the famous 'pactism' of Catalans, a supposed willingness to negotiate pragmatically. This dovetails with Pau Casals' exaltation of Catalan democracy, but conveniently ignores these imperial conquests.

> What happened in Sardinia and Minorca … was as bad as anything the Castilians inflicted on the Peruvians and Incas, and far worse than anything they later did to the Catalans themselves. It verged on cultural genocide.[5]

Sardinians were sold as slaves and the inhabitants of Alghero, a small city on the island's west coast, were killed or exiled in 1354 by Pere III 'the Ceremonious'. Alghero (L'Alguer in Catalan) was repopulated by Catalans, some of whose descendants still speak the language. Alfons 'the Liberal' had most of Menorca's male population killed or enslaved in 1287. As Richard Ford wrote: 'It [Catalonia] was always prosperous under its native princes; and during the middle ages, like Carthage of old, was the lord and terror of the Mediterranean.'[6]

The conquest of Mallorca in 1229–1230 was equally bloody and even more badly organised. After four months of fighting, the Catalan troops, who took the capital on 31 December 1229, killed so many Moors that thousands of bodies lay unburied. This extraordinary negligence caused an epidemic that killed many in the conquering army. The nobles took advantage to keep the spoils of war for themselves, instead of sharing them out among the soldiers. This led to a revolt within the army, finally settled by the sharing of the spoils in April 1230. Meanwhile, given the epidemic and squabbling among the Catalans, the Moors had been able to reorganise in the hills and fought on for two more years. The surviving Moors were enslaved. Finally, ending this sorry story, Mallorca was integrated into the Crown of Aragon as a kingdom dependent on Catalonia.

The most remarkable event in Catalonia's imperial expansion was the expedition to the east, well documented by the contemporary chroniclers Ramon Muntaner and Bernat Desclot. After the conquest of Sicily in 1282 and the subsequent peace treaty in 1302, several thousand soldiers of the Crown of Aragon were unemployed and restless. Andronicus II, the emperor of Constantinople (1282–1328), asked Frederic II, the Catalan king of Sicily, for help in the war he was losing against the Muslims. Frederic was only too glad to pay the passage to Asia Minor for 4,000 of these soldiers, known as *almogàvers*, on 39 ships. Here is the famous description of this Catalan strike-force by Desclot:

> These men called *almogàvers* live only from carrying arms. They do not inhabit the cities, but the mountains and forests, and wage war without truce against the Saracens, entering their territory for a day or two to steal and take prisoners. They live from these earnings. Few people could support their lives. They can go two days without eating if need be or eating grasses from the fields … Each one is armed with a good knife, a good spear and two darts. On their backs they carry a leather bag with food for two or three days. They are very strong men and light for hunting and fleeing. They are Catalan and Aragonese.[7]

The *almogàvers* originated in the Pyrenees, where life as shepherds made them hardy. Throughout the Iberian Peninsula, they operated on the shifting borders of the Christian and Muslim worlds. Life as a guerrilla raider was for many better than being a shepherd or working the land. The *almogàvers* struck their short swords on the ground before battle, shouting ¡*Desperta ferro!* (*Iron, awake!*). They were filthy and half-naked, inspiring fear in their opponents before battle commenced. Desclot continues: '[the *almogàver*] wore only an animal-skin tunic tied with a cord, without a shirt, he was black from the heat of the sun, his beard was very long, his hair black and long…'[8]

Roger de Flor, the impoverished son of a German nobleman, was born in Brindisi in 1266. Roger became a soldier and joined the Knights Templar, with whom he fought in the last crusade in 1291. This adventurer was no exemplary knight, though, and was expelled from the order for stealing from the very Christians he was evacuating from Acre. Roger's reputation for ruthlessness led Frederic to appoint him commander of the *almogàvers*. The expedition to the east was successful. From their base at Gallipoli, the *almogàvers* drove the Muslims out of the western part of modern Turkey. Roger de Flor was not content with the titles and marriage to his niece that Andronicus offered as reward and demanded to be named king of the territories he had conquered. No fool and as ruthless as his ally, Andronicus invited Roger with 130 of his commanders to a banquet at Adrianopolis to discuss terms and, after splendid food and wine made everyone content, had them all slaughtered at the table on 4 April 1306.

Roger de Flor's *almogàvers*, even without their leaders, yet pillaged their way through the Emperor's lands. Their slaughter and rapine earned the name the 'Catalan vengeance'. Athens and Neopatras (modern Ypati) became Catalan possessions for 70 years. Count of Barcelona Pere 'the Ceremonious' (ruled 1336–1387) boasted of his most far-flung possession: 'There is no jewel in the world more beautiful than the Parthenon.'

Contemporary with the scoundrel Roger de Flor's imperialist adventures were the books and preaching of the Mallorcan philosopher Ramon Llull (1232–1315), often called Raymond Lully in English. Llull believed that reason was a better way to persuade Muslims of the true faith than conquest. He appealed to the Pope to abandon the holy wars. With impeccable logic, he maintained that, since Christianity is the true religion, then logical argument would win round the Muslims. He is believed to have been killed by a crowd while preaching outside a mosque in Tunis, aged 83. If only Llull's way had prevailed! History, though, advances through class and national struggles, not through good intentions.

Even before the imperial expansion of the thirteenth century, Barcelona was fast becoming a centre of trade throughout the Mediterranean. This represented an important point of divergence with landlocked Castile, whose towns at the time were predominantly military emplacements and whose trade was in wool and little else. By the end of the thirteenth century, Catalonia had consulates in at least 100 Mediterranean towns and cities.

Barcelona exported to Naples, Sicily, Crete, Cyprus, Rhodes, Byzantium and Beirut: gold and silver jewellery, swords and knives (highly regarded due to Catalan iron-work); also sheep-, rabbit- and wild animal-skins from the Pyrenees; along with leather, ropes and textiles of all kinds, musical instruments and tradesmen's tools.[9]

Catalan ships returned from Constantinople and Alexandria with spices, 'pepper, incense, cinnamon, and ginger (a mania for spices pervaded medieval Europe – strong flavours drowned the rancid tastes of meat in a time that had no refrigeration).'[10] These luxury goods might then travel inland to Toulouse or Saragossa. The ships also brought wheat from Sicily, alum (used in dyeing as a fixative) and slaves.

The Crown of Aragon's ships reached Flanders and England, and even what is now Senegal according to Pierre Vilar. Catalans competed with Genoese traders for domination of the Western Mediterranean. Barcelona's role is seen not just in conquest and trade, but also in its development of regulations to control maritime affairs, through the *Consolat de Mar* (Sea Consulate). These regulations were adopted throughout the Mediterranean.

> However spectacular the foreign policy of the Crown of Aragon seems to be in the thirteenth century, the historian finds it is much less remarkable than the liveliness and bustle of its constituent countries. Maritime expansion is backed by a trading frenzy.[11]

Arab and Asian societies were much more developed at this time than Europe. Until the eleventh century, there was very little commodity production in Europe. Towns existed for administrative and military purposes. Imports, though, began to encourage local production for exchange and export. As Abram Leon argued: 'The development of trade thus stimulates native production. The production of use values progressively gives way to the production of exchange values.'[12]

The *Corts catalanes*, the Catalan 'Parliament', reflected the rise of this merchant class. With its roots, like the *Usatges*, in the *Pau i Treva* assemblies, the *Corts* became institutionalised towards the end of the thirteenth century – Catalonia's century of prosperity. The *Corts* had three arms (or 'estates'): the ecclesiastical, the noble (including military) and the towns (known, confusingly, as the royal arm). Peasants and artisans were not represented. Pere 'the Great' (ruled 1276–1285) had been excommunicated for his capture of Sicily and was facing imminent French invasion, which inclined him towards making concessions. At the *Corts* held in Barcelona in 1283, he undertook to convene the *Corts* once a year and to submit any legislative initiative or statute to the approval and agreement of the prelates, nobles, knights and 'honourable citizens' (mainly rich merchants) at the meeting.

In the same decade, at the 1289 joint Aragonese and Catalan *Corts* held at Montsó (or Monzón: town between Saragossa and Barcelona), a Standing Committee was set up to collect the taxes ceded by the 'arms' to the Count of Barcelona. This committee would develop, at the *Corts* of 1358–1359, held in Barcelona, Vilafranca and Cervera, into the *Generalitat* of Catalonia, the forerunner of the body that governs Catalonia today. The Bishop of Girona, Berenguer de Cruïlles, appointed the first president of this tax-gathering body, is usually considered the first president of the *Generalitat*.

Barcelona also developed a City Government during these ebullient years of prosperous trade. From 1274, the *Consell de Cent*, Committee of a Hundred, was chosen from among aristocrats and merchants to run the affairs of the city. The *Consell de Cent* was renewed each year. Ingeniously, election was by *insaculació*, by which candidates' names were drawn from a *sac*, a bag. This lottery defused rivalries for election, but did not solve the controversy of how wide representation should be: should the *sac* include the city's poorer merchants, shopkeepers and artisans? This was a class conflict that would erupt violently in the mid-fifteenth century (see Chapter 2).

Thus, it is only internally, within Catalonia, that 'pactism', that is, settling conflicts by negotiation, was born. These early forms of participatory democracy for the upper classes are often cited by nationalists as indicating Catalonia's long democratic tradition. It is more correct to say that all parties were weak and forced to negotiate with each other. Catalan nationalist insistence that Catalonia practises 'pacting' (political negotiation) rather than 'imposing' is false, as the descriptions of feudal oppression and imperial conquest above show. However, it is certainly true that the relative strengths of the three arms meant that the Count of Barcelona could not impose his will, fully freely, within Catalonia. This was a major divergence with Castile, where there was a weaker merchant class and where the king could enact whatever laws he wanted.

Certain Italian city-states of the time also saw the benefits of non-absolutist government. John Payne summarises the system neatly:

> Catalans are rightly proud of their democratic traditions, limited and disputed as they may have been ... They limited the autonomy of the king while granting him sufficient power to hold the Aragonese–Catalan federation together. The system gave the Monarchy a strong

vested interest in good government ... The oath of allegiance still rings impressively in the ears of Catalans...: 'We, who are as good as you, swear to you, who are no better than us, to accept you as our king and sovereign lord, provided you observe all our liberties and laws – but if not, not.'[13]

In all the struggles of later centuries, right down to today, that resonant and resolute *If not, not* has legitimised and encouraged Catalan struggles against Spanish monarchs trying to centralise the state.

Collapse

The fourteenth century saw Catalonia's collapse after the prosperous century. This was part of a Europe-wide crisis. Hunger returned. Historians attribute this to various causes: population growing faster than agricultural production was one. Second, a cycle of colder weather damaged crops. The failure of the 1333 wheat crop caused the death by starvation of thousands in Barcelona.[14]

The Black Death, which reached Barcelona in May 1348 with the fleas on the rats on its trading ships, was a key factor. Population fell by at least one-third: some say it was halved. A Catalan population of about 500,000 before 1348 fell to under 300,000 by 1400. The plague struck several times during the century: in 1362, 1371 and 1396. Catalonia came to a standstill during these outbreaks. Towns were covered by choking blankets of ochre smoke rising from the bonfires burning the dead and their clothes. John Elliott maintains that Catalonia never recovered: the pandemic decisively swung power away from the Crown of Aragon to Castile.

The Black Death was decisive in Catalonia's impoverishment, but social contradictions should not be overlooked. Growth from the eleventh to thirteenth centuries concentrated power and wealth in fewer nobles and increased social inequality. These nobles invested less in improvement as they became more removed from the land. More and more of them were idle, living in newly built castles or absent in city mansions. Peasants unhappy at this growing inequality left the land to fight in the imperial wars, often enticed by the promise of booty or land in a conquered territory, or to learn a trade in the growing cities.

About a fifth of Catalan society consisted of the Jews who had lived in the area since the Diaspora of the first century CE. Jews, mainly though not exclusively urban dwellers, had been pioneers in importation of goods. As Catalonia took shape under the Counts of Barcelona, Jews were important as moneylenders and doctors, trades considered impure by Christians. These were in no respect Jews' only professions: many worked as jewellers or weavers. Some were farmers, too. They became key in trade with North Africa, as they were permitted to reside there, whereas Christians were not, because Christian monarchs waged holy wars against Muslims. The Catalans were never able to conquer this tantalisingly nearby coast, but merchants prospered from the cotton, dyes, gold and dates of Tunis; while woven cloth, Valencian rice, Tarragona nuts and dried figs returned to North Africa.

As urban industry began, with commodities for exchange produced, Christian traders began to form a new commercial class in the cities. There, the social surplus was not only used to acquire consumer goods, that is, luxury products for the court and the nobles, but also to invest in production. 'With the development of exchange economy in Europe, the growth of cities and of corporative industry, the Jews are progressively eliminated from the economic positions which they had occupied.'[15]

On 20–24 July 1263, what is known as the Disputation of Barcelona took place. The renowned Jewish scholar Nachmanides debated with Pau Cristiani, a converted Jew, before the Count of Barcelona, prelates and nobles whether Judaism or Christianity was the true religion.[16] Several such public debates were organised throughout Europe in this period. In no way were these free debates for intellectual pleasure or due to a thirst for knowledge. The Church organised them in order to humiliate the Jewish representatives and force Jews to convert. However, Barcelona's has the reputation of being the most open Disputation. In all others, Jewish representatives had to speak with great caution, to avoid accusations of heresy. Nachmanides demanded the freedom to say what he thought without consequences. In one of several versions of the event, this freedom was guaranteed by Jaume I 'the Conqueror', which allowed Nachmanides to argue, *inter alia*, that Jesus was not a divine being and that the Virgin Mary could not be both mother and virgin. It is said that, after the debate, Count Jaume attended the synagogue and awarded Nachmanides a prize for 'so nobly defending an unjust cause'. His liberal attitude towards the Jews was doubtless conditioned by the loan he received that same year from the Jewish banker Jehuda de Cavallera, with which he equipped an entire fleet to fight Arab revolts in recently conquered Valencia.[17] The Counts of Barcelona had to balance between protecting the Jews and complying with the demands of the Church. The Catalan bishops and the Pope campaigned to have Nachmanides arrested for heresy. Jaume I did not comply, but finally, in 1267, expelled Nachmanides, who died in Haifa, far from home.

Jewish people were the direct property of the Counts of Barcelona, which meant they were not subject to nobles or to feudal rules and were taxed separately. They had to wear a distinctive disc. They were nominally protected by the Counts of Barcelona, who relied on Jewish moneylenders to finance the court and wars. Interest was high on loans – as much as a remarkable, to our ears, 30 per cent, though this figure for Catalonia is lower than in much of Europe at the time. Nobles and the monarch were so indebted to Jewish usurers for money borrowed for luxury or war that they alternately persecuted the Jews to free themselves from debt or embraced them because they needed the cash. The decline of Jewish pre-eminence in commerce and the ensuing fierce competition with Christian merchants undermined the Jews' position still further.

The Black Death allowed the Jews' antagonists to scapegoat them. These Christ-killers had become the poisoners of wells. Illiterate peasants and urban dwellers, terrified by death all around and famine stalking the land, were easy prey for anti-Semitic campaigns. Apocalyptic preachers such as the Dominican friar Vicent Ferrer used his eloquence to urge the slaughter of Jews and the burning of their houses, which reached its apogee throughout Spain in 1391.[18] The Jewish quarters of Girona, Besalú and Barcelona were sacked. The Barcelona *call* was destroyed, about 3,000 Jews were forcibly baptised and 300 who refused conversion were murdered.

With the memory of 1391 still a vivid wound, Benedict XIII (1328–1423), known as 'Papa Luna' and the last Avignon Pope, who was in exile at Peníscola, organised another Disputation at Tortosa, a port on the River Ebre in southern Catalonia. The debate lasted for 67 sessions over 21 months in 1413–1414. The outcome was severe. The city's Jews were forced to convert, signing a document on the errors of their faith. After the arrival of the Black Death, the Jews' position had become increasingly untenable. Many emigrated to North Africa, where Muslims accepted the Jews' religious practice more readily than Christians did.

Despite the reduction of Europe's population by 33–50 per cent in the fourteenth century, civilisation did not collapse. Farmland was abandoned, guilds of skilled workers ceased to function and villages were left empty, but recovery was rapid. In the chaos in Catalonia, migration to the cities or death due to pandemic led to abandoned farmhouses and land. Neighbouring peasants took over these deserted lands and grew wealthier, sometimes becoming a threat to the feudal nobles. The latter fought to reinforce their control through a whole number of measures, known generically as the *mals usos* (bad practices). One can get an idea of the complexity of the legal context by naming these *bad practices*. They included *intestia* (loss of the property lease if the peasant died without making a will), *eixorquia* (compensation to be paid if the peasant died without sons), *eugeia* (in case of adultery of the peasant's wife, the noble could seize her goods), *arsina* (in case of fire, the peasant had to compensate the noble), *firma d'espoli* (tax on weddings) and *remença* ('compensation' to the noble if a peasant left the land). Several of these *mals usos* show the position of women, who were essential to work the land and to produce children, but who were seen as men's property. Thus, adultery was perceived as theft.

> Among the poor, because illegitimate birth meant a dependent mother and child, … the peasant girl had to pay a fine if she became pregnant. But the lord's authority and responsibility was not just an economic relationship. The concept that a woman had the right to dispose freely of her person was completely alien to feudalism.[19]

Pau Casals is excessive in claiming that Catalonia had the earliest parliament in Europe: there were similar movements in many European countries whereby monarchs allied themselves with peasants and/or the Church to limit nobles' power. Nevertheless, the *Usatges* were certainly central to the development of a national consciousness. In the polemic today over whether Catalonia was ever a nation, the Spanish nationalists who oppose Catalan independence blur the reality of the federation of Aragon, Catalonia and Valencia that made up the Crown of Aragon. This is often achieved by an able elision of the 'Crown of Aragon' into the 'Kingdom of Aragon'. In fact, the Kingdom of Aragon was one of the three components of the Crown of Aragon. Valencia and Catalonia were the other two countries in this federation, whose undisputed leader during nearly three centuries was the Count of Barcelona, king of the Crown of Aragon in all but name.

Each of the three parts had different laws and taxation systems, only coming together in the figure of the Count of Barcelona. And, from 1137 to 1410, when Martí 'the Humane' died and the line came to an end, the Crown of Aragon was ruled from the complex of buildings around Barcelona's Plaça del Rei. One of these buildings houses today the Archive of the Crown of Aragon, symbolic representation of how Barcelona was the central city of the Crown of Aragon and the Count of Barcelona, its ruler.

The Sanctuary and Truce Assemblies and the *Usatges*, along with the powers of the *Corts* and the *Generalitat* accepted by the monarchs in the thirteenth century, known collectively as *constitucions* (charters), represent fundamental milestones in the creation of Catalonia's national identity. In Castile, the medieval monarchs, then the Hapsburgs and (after 1700) the Bourbons wielded absolute power. The internal pacts that characterised the Crown of Aragon and the agreements between the monarch and the estates moulded Catalonia into a society that was very different from Castile. The classic difference has much to do with geography. While land-locked Castile continued its wars against the Moors for another 200 years, Catalonia directed its expansive energies across the Mediterranean, to conquest too, but also and ultimately to trade.

2

The Three Great Class Struggles of the Fifteenth Century

...in the Realm of Aragon, there was to be found perhaps the most sophisticated and entrenched Estates structure anywhere in Europe.[1]

Peasant revolts were a common response to feudal oppression in Europe throughout the Middle Ages, but were crushed with relative ease. The French *jacquerie* of 1358 flared up as war, plague and famine ravaged Europe. In Britain, Wat Tyler's 1381 uprising still echoes today, with John Ball's *When Adam delved and Eve span, who was then the gentleman?* Catalonia had several local rebellions in the fourteenth century, but its extraordinary *remença* rebellion took place a century later.

It's a truism that peasants, that is, people farming the land, did not have the power to remould society or develop a clear ideology. Even though peasants tended to live in villages and had common interests, they had less collective power and less knowledge of the world than city dwellers. Nevertheless, they were able to change specific situations. Peasant struggle could open cracks in the feudal edifice. In particular, as in the *remença* peasants' rebellion, they could take advantage of divisions in the ruling class. The revolts of the fourteenth and fifteenth centuries typically respected the monarch. The peasants accepted the feudal framework, the only one they knew, and appealed to the monarch to force the nobles to return from some abuse to the status quo ante. This was the fatal error of Wat Tyler: *if only the King knew about us, he would improve our lot.* However, the fifteenth-century peasants' revolts in Catalonia succeeded, like few others in Europe, in overcoming the difficulties of organisation and defeating the nobles on a whole series of questions. Key to their success was Pere Joan Sala and his followers' understanding of the real role of the king, that is, the monarch was not neutral.

A *remença* (pl. *remences*) was a redemption, the payment that a peasant had to make to the feudal noble if he (not she) wanted to leave the land. Peasants had to buy their freedom of movement. By extension, the peasants bound by this 'bad practice' were known as *remences*. Without this limitation, many more would have left backbreaking exploitation to try their luck with the armies of conquest or look for work in the city. *Remença* peasants were concentrated in 'Old Catalonia', the northern part of the country that had been the Hispanic March. By the fifteenth century, they made up some 100,000 people on 15,000–20,000 farms, about a quarter of the total population of Catalonia.

The context to the revolts of the *remences* was the economic collapse mentioned in Chapter 1: Barcelona's trade in 1450 was just one-fifth of what it had been in 1333. Genoa took over much of Barcelona's Mediterranean business. The city's population fell from 50,000 in 1333 to 20,000 by 1477.[2] The court of the Crown of Aragon moved to Valencia, which had suffered much less from the Black Death (less trade meant fewer plague-infected ships) and was sustained by the huge market garden surrounding the city. Thus, the fifteenth became Valencia's 'Golden Century', in architecture, trade and literature.

Catalan is also the language of Valencia (and the Balearic Islands). The writers mentioned below of the Golden Century all wrote in Catalan, which started as a literary language with Ramon Llull and was consolidated by the fifteenth century. Though these three main Catalan-speaking areas have often turned their backs on each other since the end of the Crown of Aragon, the common language (naturally, with its dialects and variations) has led minorities in all three areas to argue for the unity of the *països catalans*, the Catalan lands.

The first printing press in the Iberian Peninsula was installed in Valencia in 1474 and the two greatest writers of the age in Catalan were both Valencians, the poet Ausiàs March (1397?–1458) and one of Europe's earliest novelists, Joanot Martorell (1413?–1465). March wrote anguished poetry, breaking from the courtly love tradition that idealised inaccessible women. March is earthy. He wonders if he and the woman he loves will go to Hell because they revel in animal passion. He admits that he fears God more than he loves him.

Martorell's novel *Tirant lo Blanc* drew a picture of the Constantinople court (based on the Valencian one) and showed the private lives of sexual intrigue behind the images of religious dignity and political stability that the monarch and his family projected in public. Admired by Cervantes, *Tirant lo Blanc* is something new, that is, a *novel*, showing the real human relationships underlying the simulacrum of power. Like March, Martorell was a trailblazer: they were originals, realists moving beyond the moralising formalities of the poetry and prose that preceded them.

The Trastámara Kings and Civil War

While Valencia's upper class flourished and its writers produced in Catalan some of the greatest medieval literature, three major subversive movements, overlapping and at times occurring at the same time, dominated Catalonia's fifteenth century. Peasants rebelled against their nobles. The feudal nobles rebelled against the king, which led to the Civil War of 1462–1472 (with the king in alliance with peasant rebels). And third, the lower classes in the cities fought rich merchants in the 1450s and 1460s. This chapter will look at each of these: first, the great peasant revolt.

The *remença* peasants reacted strongly against the *mals usos* (bad practices) as early after the arrival of the Black Death as 1353, when a crowd attacked the presbytery at Palau, a church dependent on the monastery of Ripoll, and burnt all the land deeds. In 1388, peasants presented a petition to the Count of Barcelona to abolish the *mals usos*. Maria de Luna, wife of Martí 'the Humane', appealed on their behalf to the Pope to abolish *mals usos* on Church-owned lands. The appeal was rejected, but showed that the peasants could organise themselves and gain support in high quarters.

In 1410, Count Martí died with no heir – and with the misfortune that his four legitimate children and their mother all died before him. The *Compromís de Casp* (Compromise of Casp) in 1412 brought to the throne of the Crown of Aragon – after clashes between the Aragonese and Catalan candidates and against the votes of at least two of the three Catalan representatives at the conference – a Castilian king, Fernando de Trastámara (Ferran in Catalan). At the *Corts* held in 1413, the feudal nobles took advantage of this foreign king, more accustomed to absolutist ways, to insist on stronger measures against the peasantry. It was agreed that the peasants had to live as they had always done 'with no right to proclaim their freedom'. Those who had taken over abandoned lands in the preceding decades had to cede them to the local noble.

Figure 2   King Martí's Tower, Plaça del Rei, Barcelona
(Marisa Asensio)

These victories of the nobles under the new dynasty not only crushed peasant aspirations, but also threatened the power of the new kings. This was an additional reason why, uncomfortable with Catalan restrictions on his freedom to do what he wanted, the second Trastámara monarch Alfonso 'the Magnanimous' (ruled 1416–1458) moved his court to Valencia in 1432. He then left his wife Maria in Valencia as regent, while he moved to Sicily and then his newly conquered kingdom in Naples, never to return.

The Neapolitan court became a famous centre of Renaissance luxury and culture. To maintain his style of life and reputation for generosity, Alfonso needed cash. The increasing confidence of Catalonia's feudal nobles in his absence threatened his position and income, which was a prime reason for his support of peasant demands as a counter-balance to the nobles. In 1448, he authorised peasant assemblies (the tradition of the *Pau i Treva* meetings was not dead) to discuss grievances. From 13 October 1448 to 10 March 1449, 553 peasant assemblies were held throughout most of Old Catalonia, from Elna in Rosselló to Urgell, near Lleida. The meetings were controlled: no more than 50 people could attend and a royal official had to be present to take the minutes.[3] The express purpose of the meetings was to elect delegates to take the *remença* peasants' demands to the king.

For the next 35 years, Alfonso and his successors played off the peasants against the nobles. In 1452, the *Corts*, representing the nobles, offered the king 400,000 florins if he returned from Naples and, it is supposed, acceded to their demands. The peasants could not match this sum. However, Alfonso refused the nobles' overture and, in 1455, on the peasants' payment of 100,000 florins (3 florins per farm), decreed the end of the *mals usos*, including the *remença*.

After Alfonso died suddenly in 1458, his brother and heir Joan II (Joan is John in Catalan, a man not a woman) reaffirmed the abolition of the *mals usos* in 1460. The tension with the nobles moved quickly to armed conflict. Joan and his son Carlos de Viana were in dispute over the throne of Navarre. In 1460, Joan had his son arrested, a 'clumsy error' in Vicens Vives' phrase. In 1461, the *Generalitat* forced Joan to free Carlos. Then, on the popular Carlos' sudden death and the spread of rumours of foul play (now thought to be unfounded), the *Generalitat*, representing the two arms (or estates), often in conflict but now in concert, of the nobles and the wealthy merchants, saw their opportunity and deposed Joan, who fled into exile to muster troops to retake his throne. His wife Joana and his heir, the seven-year-old Ferran, took refuge in Girona, where they were besieged by the forces of the *Generalitat*.

In this situation of civil war, the *remença* peasants saw an opportunity and rebelled, led by a charismatic leader, Francesc de Verntallat. A minor noble, he had married a *remença* peasant and himself worked the land. Queen Joana entered into contact with Verntallat, who assisted her by drawing off the *Generalitat*'s troops besieging Girona. Fighting

33

under the royal standard, Verntallat and his peasants cannily kept to the mountains, knowing they could not defeat the *Generalitat*'s army on open ground. These guerrilla fighters organised themselves in groups of three farmers, so that one of them fought with Verntallat while the other two worked the land of all three. The coordination and contacts won through the experience of the assemblies fifteen years earlier were paying dividends. Verntallat's soldiers survived in the mountains for two decades.

Finally, in 1472, Joan II won the Civil War. Wisely, he settled the conflict without revenge on those who had supported the *Generalitat*, which included the Barcelona City Council. This magnanimity has two sides to it. In one respect, the war was an intra-class rather than inter-class conflict. Against both the city artisans and the *remença* peasants, king and *Generalitat* had the same interest. It also reflected Joan's weakness. The *Generalitat*, originally merely the tax-gathering arm of the *Corts*, had grown in influence and shown its ability to govern during the Civil War. This home-grown Catalan body had proved popular as representing Catalan interests against the 'foreign' Trastámara king of the Crown of Aragon. Of course, the *Generalitat* was no democratic body, but it showed that the nobles and wealthy merchants could create an alternative power to the king, an alternative power that could appeal to Catalan law and Catalan sentiment for its legitimacy. The nationalist historian Jaume Sobrequés wrote: 'In the 1462–1472 civil war, the *Generalitat* came of age. It became all-powerful and won extraordinary prestige throughout Catalonia.'[4]

Peasant Rebellion

The Civil War won, Joan disappointed his *remença* allies. He vacillated on the question of the *mals usos*. Indignant at betrayal, many peasants now stopped paying tithes. The nobles, naturally enough, refused to accept this situation. In these years of conflict, the *remença* movement split and a smaller radical wing emerged, led by Pere Joan Sala, formerly Verntallat's second-in-command. Sala and his followers moved towards a programme of abolishing not just the *mals usos* but also the whole feudal system. They questioned Verntallat's continuing loyalty to the king, who had so signally failed to deliver. Finally, after years of peasant unrest, in 1481, Ferran (Ferdinand in English) – the infant prince besieged with his mother in Girona 20 years previously and king since Joan's death in 1479 – proved Sala's analysis right. Pressured by the nobles, Ferran formally reneged on the agreements with the *remença* peasants by restoring the *mals usos*, 26 years after their abolition by Alfonso.

Following the royal decision, nobles zealously began to collect back-payments from rebel peasants, with mass evictions – now in the king's name – of peasants who refused to pay. In March 1482, a tax collector, Joan Desvern, was killed by an arrow in the Amer valley west of Girona. At the start of June, Sala and another peasant leader Joan Serinyà were arrested for killing Desvern. However, such was the ferment in the countryside that their trial, and almost certain execution, was delayed. In the autumn, they were released to avert the outbreak of a new uprising. It is hard to see the faces and behaviour of the poor so many centuries ago, as their voices and feelings are unrecorded. Just sometimes, an action pokes up above time past's anonymity. So it is with Sala shooting his arrow at Desvern. Geography helps. I do not know his face, but can see Sala stepping out from the forest and taking that momentous decision in the fertile, beautiful, secluded Amer valley.

The nobles continued pressing. In September 1484, the king's soldiers were supporting an official called Salbà in mass evictions for non-payment in the Mieres area. On 22 September, several dozen peasants led by Sala attacked Salbà and his armed escort. Salbà lost an eye and one of his soldiers was killed. Sala and his followers had become outlaws. The second *remença* war had begun.

Verntallat and his moderate forces did not support Sala's movement. Jaume Vicens Vives wrote:

> Abandoning Verntallat's moderate policy, Sala stoked as best he could the fire of discord, with the fanatical and demagogic spirit of born revolutionaries ... it was he who, by attacking the royal official Salbà, ... would unleash the people's passions held back for over 20 years.[5]

One can see that Vicens Vives was no friend of this rebellion, but his words enable us to intuit the organisation and courage of Sala and his followers.

Sala's army marched through the Vic and Empordà areas, arousing the peasants by the promise of their becoming owners of their land.

Though Sala had broken with the king, he still used the cry ¡*Visca el rei! Long Live the King!* – both because explicit opposition to the king was a capital offence and because the rebels believed that, as the king had been pressured by the nobles to restore the *mals usos*, so he could be pressured back. On 14 December, Sala attacked Girona, but failed to take the city. Neither Verntallat nor King Ferran were inactive. While Sala's forces roamed the countryside, Ferran rubber-stamped a peace proposal composed by Verntallat. Ferran was absent in Seville; the letter from him dated 12 January 1485 reached Barcelona on 31 January. Sala met on 2 February with moderate *remença* representatives who urged him to accept the peace proposal. Sala had little option but to reject it: there was no guarantee of the rebels' personal safety other than Ferran's 'magnanimity' and Ferran was only proposing the abolition of some *mals usos*.

The day after the meeting, on 3 February, Sala's 400 armed peasants defeated the *Generalitat*'s army at Montornès and took the town of Granollers. This 'gateway to Barcelona' was sacked and a number of people were killed. Sala pressed on into the Maresme and Vallès counties adjacent to Barcelona, occupying the towns of Terrassa and Sabadell. Granollers was reconquered by the *Generalitat* and, on 10 March, Sala failed in an attempt to take it again: the people of Granollers may well have sympathised with Sala's cause at first, but were not pleased at his army's slaughter and theft. He moved on to capture Mataró on the coast north of Barcelona, but time was running out.

Over-confident after their victories or desperate for a decisive victory to open the road to Barcelona, Sala's peasant army was defeated on open ground at Les Franqueses on 24 March 1485. Two hundred were killed. Sala and other leaders were captured and executed four days later in Barcelona. This was the defeat of the rebellion, but not the final defeat for the *remença* peasants. The canny Verntallat had maintained his forces active in the hills and, with the defeat of the radical abolitionists, King Ferran, Verntallat and the *Generalitat* entered into negotiations. 'Pactism' was not dead.

In April 1486, the king dictated his decision at Guadalupe, in Extremadura. This 'Sentence of Guadalupe' has caused controversy among historians. Vicens thought that the sentence only punished the radical peasants and ended the *remença* system, leading to a post-feudal system of lands held permanently by farmers. This was the basis for a wealthy and independent peasantry that flourished in its *masos* (large farmhouses) well into the twentieth century. The Catalan Renaissance of the nineteenth century (see Chapter 6) exalted this peasantry as the backbone of the country, a conservative unit based round the *casa pairal* (patriarchal home) embodying the values of hard work, family, religious observance and dogged defence of their rights. However, Josep Fontana's recent history maintains that the Sentence of Guadalupe only abolished *mals usos* that were already being ignored by wide sections of the *remences* and reimposed royal and feudal authority by insisting that the peasants pay to the nobles both compensation for their revolts and the moneys owed from years of non-payment. These fines and 'debts' were only ever collected in part.[6]

Though Sala, his family and other leaders lost their lives and properties, the peasant uprising contributed to the defeat of the most reactionary parts of Catalan society. Retrograde social relations in the country were altering, which was preparing the way for a new mode of production.[7] Ferran, now not only monarch of the Crown of Aragon but King of Spain through his 1469 marriage to Isabel of Castile, wanted to install absolute monarchy throughout the Iberian Peninsula, but found he still could not defeat Catalan particularity, despite the impoverishment of Catalonia through its famines, plagues and wars since 1348.

There is a coda. On 7 December 1492, at about midday, Ferran was walking down the steps of the Plaça del Rei, Barcelona, when the 60-year-old Joan de Canyamars slipped through the guards and struck the king a blow with his machete from behind. Bleeding heavily, his collarbone broken, Ferran was lucky to survive, saved by his gold chain and thick clothing. His guards captured the assailant, but Ferran prevented their killing him because he wanted him interrogated to find out whether there was a conspiracy. Canyamars was officially considered a madman acting alone and was publicly tortured and executed. In recent years, it has emerged that he was not, in a legal sense, mad because he had been allowed to inherit from his father the year before and that he had been a *remença* peasant. It is speculation because this attempted regicide had no voice, but some historians believe he acted because of anger at the Sentence of Guadalupe.

The *remença* peasants tried the whole gamut of mobilisation: assembly and peaceful petition, payment of money, guerrilla warfare, negotiation, all-out war and, perhaps, terrorist attack. The most advanced and daring rebels were defeated, but their struggle led to widespread reform.

Beam and Splinter

The third class conflict of the fifteenth century was the revolt of the cities' middle classes, with the support of the poor, against the cities' rulers. There had been precedents, particularly in 1285, a year of poor harvest and increased prices, when an artisan Berenguer Oller led an uprising that took brief control of Barcelona. The revolt was put down and the unfortunate Berenguer Oller and seven others were tied to the tails of mules, dragged through the streets and hanged.

In the 1450s, an alternative power challenged the Barcelona ruling class of wealthy merchants and aristocrats for control of the city. The latter were known as the *Biga*, meaning 'beam' because they were the traditional upper class that, in their view, supported the edifice of the city. The lesser merchants, shopkeepers, 'artistes' (what we would call 'liberal professions') and artisans formed a party known as the *Busca* (the Splinter), which wanted currency devaluation to assist textile exports and protectionism to stop cheaper imports that were destroying their livelihoods. Just as he had supported the *remença* peasants, King Alfonso supported the *Busca* in order to squeeze money out of the nobles and wealthy merchants and weaken their power.

The *Consell de Cent* (Committee of One Hundred) that ran Barcelona had in fact 128 (not 100) members, drawn from 4 sectors of 32 members each: 'honourable citizens', merchants, 'artistes' and artisans. These latter were organised in guilds. This relatively democratic structure was undermined by the virtually absolute control exercised by the five 'honourable citizens' who led the Council. The wealth of these five councillors-in-chief derived from their agricultural estates and from the interest on loans to the king, City Council or *Generalitat*. Entrenched in their privilege, these ruling parasites resisted change, though a few 'honourable citizens' engaged in commerce did support the *Busca*.

Galceran de Requesens, formally representing the absent king, encouraged the *Busca* to organise themselves and demand of the king that the annual election of the councillors-in-chief should consist of only two 'honourable citizens', one merchant, one 'artista' and one artisan. Requesens intervened on the annual election day, 30 November 1453, to suspend the election and place five 'honourable citizens' of his own choice. These were some of the few who were favourable to the *Busca*'s demands. Alfonso then agreed to the *Busca*'s petition and, at the start of 1455, the *Busca* came to power in the city. Jaume Vicens Vives goes so far as to argue that 'in 1455 [Alfonso] imposed really democratic solutions to the aspirations of the people'.[8] The *Busca* coming to power occasioned a rupture between monarch and nobility that contributed to the Civil War of 1462–1472. The poor strongly supported the *Busca* who were those who provided work. The *Busca* was able to introduce protectionism against wool imports and reduce the tax burden on the poor, but Alfonso's death in 1458 led to their defeat. In these years of enormous tension, both *Biga* and *Busca* organised street gangs. Doctors called out at night requested the right to bear arms, so dangerous was the city. At the start of the Civil War, Requesens was imprisoned and several of the *Busca* were executed, as the king was no longer able to protect them. The 'democratic' interlude was over. The *Biga* returned to power.

Two salient points can be made about these years of struggle for municipal power in Barcelona. One is that, despite the defeat, a democratic advance was made. The citizens of Barcelona learned they could win reforms and gain more participation in city government. The other point is expressed concisely by Josep Fontana: 'One of the most dramatic paradoxes of our history [is] … the unnatural alliance between the Catalan social forces struggling for a democratizing programme and the Castilian sovereigns, whose political project was absolutism.'[9] The paradox is explained by the need of the Trastámara monarchs to use the *remença* peasants in the country and the *Busca* in Catalonia's main city to weaken the feudal nobility and wealthiest merchants, respectively. The Crown wanted to reduce the powers of the *Generalitat*.

The Spanish Empire

The civil war and the urban and rural class struggles, caused by the reduction in wealth and population through much of the fourteenth and all the fifteenth century, left Catalonia weak at just the moment when Castile was about to enter its most glorious period.

It is worth stepping back to look at the more powerful but more socially backward Castile, which from 1492 and then under the Hapsburgs from 1516 created the Spanish Empire that dominated

Europe for 150 years and the Americas for 300. Two basic factors define the divergence between Catalonia and Castile: the peninsula's geography and the conquest of Moorish territory. Most of the peninsula is covered by mountain ranges, natural barriers that isolate regions from each other. This led to an underlying tendency towards strong local pockets of power.

The second factor of divergence was how Moorish territory was 'reconquered'. Catalonia was relatively unaffected by Moorish culture. When the Moors were expelled from the areas south and west of Barcelona in the twelfth century, these lands in New Catalonia were in the main colonised rapidly by farmers from Old Catalonia. Castile, however, fought wars over several centuries to expel the Moorish rulers. Conquered Moorish lands usually became the property of successful military leaders or court lackeys (nobles) who formed large estates (*latifundios*) worked by landless labourers.

The 1469 marriage of Ferran who would become the king of the Crown of Aragon and Isabel of Castile formally united most of the Iberian Peninsula. 'Spain' was born. Ferran and Isabel are known to this day as the 'Catholic Monarchs', Ferdinand and Isabella in English.[10] The marriage united the peninsula in one state, which rapidly became the heart of a mighty empire; but, curiously and paradoxically, it signally failed to unite Spain.

The new two-headed state had extraordinary dynamism. The expulsion of the Moorish rulers was completed in 1492 with the capture of Granada. Navarre was absorbed. Naples was annexed. Spanish ships crossed the Atlantic ('In fourteen hundred and ninety-two/ Columbus sailed the ocean blue') and the invasion of America began. In the Alhambra Decree of 31 March 1492, the Jews were given four months to convert to Christianity or leave the country.

In the following century, the Spanish Empire ruled most of America and much of Europe under the new Hapsburg dynasty: Carlos (Charles) I (ruled 1516–1556) and Felipe (Philip) II (ruled 1556–1598). Yet, this state that presided over the greatest European empire since the Romans was a ramshackle association of fiefdoms in Iberia itself.

Its neighbour, the French absolutist state, had successfully crushed separatist aspirations, but the Spanish monarchy was unable to integrate its disparate parts. While it ruled lands from Peru to Flanders, it had no uniform state at home. In fact, the only organisations that bound the state together were its stable and long-lived monarchs and then the Inquisition, founded by Ferran and Isabel to detect falsely converted Jews and to make the Jews convenient scapegoats for popular resentment, illness and hunger. The Inquisition's introduction in 1487 into the Crown of Aragon was widely opposed, as it was a 'Castilian-based centralized judicial and police organ whose function was to control religious dissidence.'[11]

The Crown of Aragon's rejection of the Inquisition was fed by a tradition of giving refuge to persecuted Templars, Cathars and the 'Anti-Pope' Benedict XIII. This was not for any progressive reason, but because the Counts of Barcelona had often found it expedient to practise 'tolerance' of some religious differences, both because of interests (the Templars brought wealth) and because they ruled over a world that required complex balances (the Cathars were fleeing from enemy France).

In most of Spain, Carlos I (also Charles V of the Holy Roman Empire) was able to crush the towns' ancient liberties and privileges. At the first Spanish *Cortes* (parliament) after his arrival from Germany in 1516, he had to swear loyalty to Spain's laws before being acknowledged as king. 'You must know, Señor, that the King is but the paid servant of the nation,' he was told. 'With a very bad grace', in Karl Marx's words, Carlos took the oath. Within two decades, Carlos had dealt with this nonsense. He smashed the towns' *comunero* (commoner) rebellions in the 1520s and then turned on the nobles who had assisted him to crush the *comuneros*.

This new Spain had at the end of the fifteenth century a population of some 5–7 million people and the Crown of Aragon had only about 1 million.

> The political contrast between the two Kingdoms … was … striking. For in the Realm of Aragon, there was to be found perhaps the most sophisticated and entrenched Estates structure anywhere in Europe … *In toto*, this complex of medieval 'liberties' presented a singularly intractable prospect for the construction of a centralized Absolutism.[12]

Unlike post-Carlos I Castile, each of the three parts of the Crown of Aragon maintained their own *Corts*, with their permanent judicial and administrative bodies. The only open conflict of the sixteenth century came in 1591, when Felipe II's fugitive secretary, Antonio Pérez, took refuge in Aragon. An armed incursion attempted (and failed) to capture Pérez, but Felipe II did not take the opportunity to suppress the Kingdom of Aragon's particularity. The Hapsburgs ruled, in both Austria and Spain, through what was known as a composite monarchy.

Despite their success in doing away with Castile's ancient rights, both Carlos I and Felipe II preferred to install viceroys (in this aspect, the Crown of Aragon was treated as an overseas possession, no different from Milan, Flanders or Peru) and postpone the problem of the Crown of Aragon. Thus, there was no common currency, tax regulations or legal system in the new post-1492 Spanish state. There was no national division of labour and, partly in consequence, no administrative merger. Not even the massive flocks of sheep, which moved freely throughout Castile, from high to lowlands and from plains to mountains depending on the season (transhumance), were allowed to enter the Crown of Aragon's lands. Such huge flocks destroyed agricultural land. And when Carlos I was extorting money and troops for his overseas wars, he found that Catalonia flatly refused to contribute cash or men.

Nor did the economies of Catalonia and Castile coincide. The economy of Castile, 'the Australia of the Middle Ages', was wool-based. Sheep had replaced cereals, to the extent that Spain had to start importing the latter by the 1570s. While the Spanish state used northern ports, mainly Santander, to export wool to La Rochelle, Flanders and Germany and to import textiles and grain, and the southern ports of Cadiz and Seville for importing bullion from America and exporting to the growing markets there, the Crown of Aragon continued its multiple trading through its Mediterranean ports. The Mediterranean and Atlantic economies barely met. With gold and silver from Mexico and Peru, and especially after the discovery of the silver mountain of Potosí (in present-day Bolivia) in 1545, fabulous wealth was carried back in Spain's galleons to Seville and Castile. Castile's wealth resided in this extraction of minerals (accounting for some 25 per cent of all revenue), which made the need to develop manufacturing for trade less pressing. Absolutist states were 'machines built overwhelmingly for the battlefield'.[13] And war was near-constant throughout the sixteenth and seventeenth centuries. At the sixteenth-century peak of the Spanish Empire, about 80 per cent of state revenue was wasted on military expenditure. The Spanish Empire dominated the world for nearly two centuries, but its very wealth and

THREE GREAT CLASS STRUGGLES OF THE FIFTEENTH CENTURY

enormous military spending underdeveloped Castile itself. The Catalan writer Josep Pla explains the Hapsburg economy tartly in a reference that reminds us of the Spanish state's several bankruptcies:

> ...the wealth of America entered through the ports legally registered for trade with the other hemisphere and exited by way of frontiers in the north. This process was generally a way to pay back the finance lent to the Hapsburgs for their follies, usually by Genoese bankers. Those bankers were the discoverers of America.[14]

Karl Marx was conscious of the paradox of this powerful empire failing to unite its own country:

> Spanish liberty disappeared under the clash of arms, showers of gold, and the terrible illuminations of the auto-da-fé ... But how are we to account for the singular phenomenon that, after nearly three centuries of a Hapsburg dynasty, followed by a Bourbon dynasty – either of them quite sufficient to crush a people – the municipal liberties of Spain more or less survive? That in the very country where of all feudal states absolute monarchy first arose in its most unmitigated form, centralization has never succeeded in taking root.[15]

Marx is talking of more than the conflict between Catalonia and Castile, but the Crown of Aragon's different development is key to the centralising state's inability 'to crush a people'.

> Spain, like Turkey, remained an agglomeration of mismanaged republics with a nominal sovereign at their head ... despotic as was the government it did not prevent the provinces from subsisting with different laws and customs, different coins, military banners of different colors, and with their respective systems of taxation.[16]

Carlos I's suppression of the *comuneros'* revolt delayed the development of capitalism, which under other absolutist monarchies began to flourish in the towns as the power of the feudal nobles was reduced. Spain's economy was distorted by its marks of identity: war, sheep and bullion. In Pierre Vilar's words, its practice was 'the territorial and religious conception of expansion, rather than trading and economic ambition'.[17]

REBEL PORTRAIT: SOR ISABEL DE VILLENA

It may be pushing it a bit to see the daughter of a noble and ward of Queen Maria, the effective ruler of the Crown of Aragon in the absence of her husband Alfonso 'the Magnaminous', as a rebel. However, Isabel de Villena is one of the few women who speak from medieval times. If not quite a rebel, she has a distinct and independent voice.

Born Elionor in 1430 to a mother unknown to us and Enrique de Villena, a noble with family connections to the Crown of Aragon, she was taken into the court of her cousin the childless Queen Maria on her father's death when she was aged four. Close to the queen, she was educated in Valencia's wealthiest century in the cosmopolitan court of glitter and intrigue that was the model for the Byzantine court in Martorell's novel *Tirant lo Blanc*.

In 1445, Elionor entered the convent of Poor Clares founded by the queen (and still there in central Valencia, just across the dry river from the Parliament building) as Sor Isabel. She was elected Abbess in 1463, a post that she held for the rest of her life. Convents were where women who did not want to marry could take refuge from being dominated by a husband and the dangers of childbirth or where a woman had more chance of studying. Under Isabel as Abbess, the convent developed a large library and hosted something of a literary salon, attended by many writers of the time.

Vita Christi (*The Life of Christ*) is the only survivor of several books that Sor Isabel wrote to educate her nuns. It is an erudite text, showing her knowledge of Latin, theology and previous 'Lives of Christ'. It is written in an elegant Catalan. Its fame rests on its celebration of the women in Christ's life. It is often said to be a 'feminist' response to the misogynist *Lo espill* (*The Mirror*) of Jaume Roig, who as well as a famous poet was the doctor for the Poor Clares' convent. Roig's poem of 16,000 four-syllable lines is written as a warning to other men to keep away from women, because these are all evil and disgusting and mistreat men. Imagine Roig and Isabel's conversations!

Published in 1497 by the Abbess who succeeded Sor Isabel after her death from plague on 2 July 1490, *Vita Christi* was popular in the following decades. It opens and closes with the Virgin Mary's birth and death, but in general uses local rather than biblical stories. It challenges the common medieval dichotomy of unmarried women as a source of sin (whores) or to be revered on a pedestal (virgins). Sor Isabel reverses stereotypes: her women are clear and strong-minded, while the men are unreliable and tiresomely verbose. She has Jesus himself preferring women's minds. Women are honest creatures of God, not instruments of the devil. It is a *feminist* polemic against *misogyny*, even though these two words and the concepts they entail did not then exist. But feminist it is.

3

Revolution and Republic: 1641

Bon cop de falç!...
Strike hard with the sickle, defenders of our land...
Just as we cut the golden ears of wheat,
When the time is ripe we will cut our chains.[1]

Over-Reaching

The Crown of Aragon's trading prowess and imperial expansion into Provence and Valencia and across the Mediterranean was a brief glory. From the famine of 1333, the Black Death that reached Barcelona in 1348 and the class conflicts of the fifteenth century described in Chapter 2, Catalonia was in decline. This was no uniformly downhill straight line. In the fourteenth century, even while agriculture collapsed, trade dropped and masses of people were dying of plague or starvation, several great buildings were constructed in Catalonia's capital. Today, it is this collection of medieval buildings in Barcelona's Gothic quarter, alongside the *modernista* buildings of around 1900, that has made the city a beacon for cultural tourists – Gothic and art nouveau. That there is little baroque and few outstanding buildings between these two periods suggest strongly Catalonia's centuries of decline before its nineteenth-century renaissance.

The city's three great medieval churches date from the fourteenth century. The money spent on their construction is understandable, for they were started before the years of calamity and many people believed that completing these monuments to God would help avert hunger and plague. Most of Barcelona cathedral was built in the fourteenth century; Santa Maria del Pi was started in 1322; and the basilica of Santa Maria del Mar was started in 1329 and completed by 1383 – quick for a Gothic church, which reflects the city's wealth or the collective commitment of all classes to build it. This most beautiful, uncluttered building is known as the fishermen's or people's church, as it was built by the beach, in the quarter of artisans, traders, sailors and fishing families. It was paid for by the local guilds. It is not clear how much was voluntary labour and donation or how much was exacted by taxation.[2]

Outside Barcelona, Girona's cathedral, which boasts the broadest Gothic nave in Europe, dates from the same fourteenth century. In almost exactly the same period, the *Drassanes*, Barcelona's shipyard, was expanded and the new city walls were completed. The *Saló del Tinell*, the main hall in the Counts' palace in the Plaça del Rei, replaced an earlier building. In the fifteenth century, the main part of the *Palau de la Generalitat* was built. Robert Hughes comments:

> Barcelona's Barri Gòtic still contains the most concentrated array of thirteenth to fifteenth century buildings in Spain ... They are of every type: parish churches, town houses, government buildings, council halls, guild headquarters, industrial structures, and of course the Cathedral. The remarkable thing about this building boom was its manic quality. It flew, at least part of the time, in the face of economic reality.[3]

Nor did economic reality halt imperial expansion. Though the Crown of Aragon lost the Duchy of Athens in 1388 and the neighbouring Duchy of Neopatras in 1390, it gained Sardinia in 1409 and Naples in 1442. All this is to say that the death and impoverishment of swathes of the country's inhabitants did not halt Catalonia's rulers' expansionist ambitions and building programmes.

However, the diminished wealth of the country could not support such conquests. All commentators agree that a small country with a correspondingly small economy could not raise the taxation required to pay for these imperial ventures. Albert Balcells summarised the situation in Catalonia around 1500: 'Though Catalonia achieved some stability toward the end of the fifteenth century, when the Catalan civil war came to an end, economic stagnation, political immobility, and loss of cultural vitality ... affected the greater part of the population.'[4] Even so, after the Sentence of Guadalupe, 'the feudal class system had been undermined, allowing for a freer peasant society to develop'.[5]

Though the limitations of royal power in the *constitucions/furs/ fueros*[6] initially protected the Crown of Aragon from the over-taxation that Castile suffered, the Trastámara kings in the fifteenth century and the Hapsburgs in the sixteenth steadily eroded the independence and language of the area. More and more Castilian-speaking officials were sent to Catalonia. After 1492, Catalonia was entirely overshadowed by the strength and dynamism of the Spanish Empire. The Crown of Aragon disappeared as a political power in the Mediterranean. And it had no presence in the Atlantic: the Spanish Monarchs forbade Catalan and Valencian trade with America, which was reserved from 1518 to 1778 for Seville and Cadiz. The kings, no longer of course the Counts of Barcelona living in Catalonia but the monarchs of the Spanish Empire who lived in Madrid, convened the *Corts* of the three components of the Crown of Aragon less often. Under Carlos I, who reigned for 39 years, the Catalan *Corts* met eight times; under Felipe II, who reigned for 42 years, only twice. Political life stagnated. Without meetings of the *Corts*, the king received fixed payments from the *Generalitat* and the *Consell de Cent*.

Despite this 'economic stagnation' and 'political immobility', Catalonia's trading tradition was not snuffed out. Ships continued to cross the Mediterranean to buy, sell and exchange. Key to Barcelona's economy were the strong guilds. To learn and practise a trade you had to join a guild. They acted as closed shops, as insurance in case of injury or illness and were represented on the *Consell de Cent*. Guilds' rules were strict: clothing, food, length of service, members' religious obligations and the requirements of the craft were all stipulated. They had supported the *Busca* against the *Biga*. For six centuries, till nineteenth-century industrialisation, these craft guilds represented the hundreds of small workshops across the city. Workshops in the same trade tended to cluster together. To give an idea of the bustle and liveliness, it is worth quoting Robert Hughes on street names in the Old City of Barcelona:

Walking in the Barri Gòtic today, one comes across their names everywhere ...: Agullers (needle makers), Boters (cask makers), Brocaters (brocade makers), Corders (rope spinners), Cotoners (cotton weavers), Dagueria (knife grinders), Escudellers (shield makers), Espaseria (swordsmiths), Fusteria (carpenters), Mirallers (mirror makers), Semoleres (pasta makers) ... and many more.[7]

The workshop masters taught apprentices and employed skilled workers. Guilds' apprentices came from both the master's family and young men migrating from country to city.

Catalonia benefited from a system of inheritance that did not subdivide farms, which meant that farms did not become smaller and smaller and eventually unviable. If you were a younger son working on a farm, though, it meant that when the oldest son, the *hereu*, inherited the whole farm (under emphyteusis), you were often surplus to requirements or would spend your life in a permanently subordinate position. Many younger sons had to fend for themselves and could do so after the 1486 Sentence of Guadalupe when the *remença* payment was abolished. Those who did not become soldiers or priests swelled the ranks of the cities' guilds as apprentices.

Bandits

Others became bandits. Due to the inheritance system, to further intolerable squeezes as the Spanish monarchy's foreign wars led to over-taxation, and to a certain tradition of guerrilla war, as practised by *almogàvers* within Iberia against the Moors and overseas in Catalonia's conquests and later by *remença* peasants, bandits became common in the late sixteenth and early seventeenth centuries. This was not specific to Catalonia, but a phenomenon common throughout Europe, as the fetters of feudalism loosened. What was less common was that in Catalonia bandits were not just highwaymen or smugglers, but they also posed a challenge to the economic and political order. This was *social banditry*, in historian Eric Hobsbawm's term, that is, a primitive form of class struggle in pre-industrial societies. Hobsbawm argued that many outlaws in these decades of change were supported by the law-abiding peasantry. The bandits were seen as fighters against oppression.[8]

Towards the 1580s, two factions, based in different parts of the territory and with different interests, emerged. The *nyerros* defended the interests of feudal nobles and rich peasants and identified with Catalan rights against a monarchy that was sending Spanish-speaking viceroys to Catalonia and increasing the number of Spanish, that is, foreign in the *nyerros*' eyes, officials. Their territory of refuge was on both sides of the Pyrenees: Nyer that gave its name to the movement was a town in North Catalonia, now part of France. They were mountain people:

49

to some degree the conflict was between mountain dwellers and coastal and city people. The *almogàvers* had come from the Pyrenees; many *remença* guerrillas had found refuge there; later, in the nineteenth century, Carlists would, too. There is a long history of these mountain fighters, outside the king's law but not in general seen negatively by their neighbours, who understood that, if there was no work or if the work that there was kept people in servitude and/or poverty, theft from the rich was legitimate.

Against the *nyerros*, the *cadells* (pups) were groups organised by the urban merchants and bishops who supported the Spanish monarchy. The complexity of a mixed national and class struggle is seen. One might think that the defenders of Catalonia against the Castile-based Spanish state would not be supporters of feudal nobles; equally, that the rising urban bourgeoisie would not be allied to a foreign, absolutist monarchy. This complexity has given many arguments to those who inveigh against supporters of Catalan independence today. Catalan nationalism is based on backward-looking, feudal ideas, centralists are wont to argue, while the Spanish monarchy favoured trade, the coming bourgeoisie and modernisation. Reality is more complex: the revolution of 1640–1641 (see *Golden Ears of Wheat*) and the defeat of 1714 (see Chapter 4) would make the position of the Spanish state quite clear.

The *nyerros* have become, in legend, Robin Hood figures. They wore red hats, long cloaks and a badge of a suckling pig. They attacked the king's tax collectors and they ambushed the convoys transferring the cash collected to Madrid, which brought them enormous popularity. The *cadells* destroyed cattle and crops in retaliatory raids on *nyerro*-dominated areas. The *nyerros* defended peasants against these attacks: most of them were peasants. A low-scale, near-civil war rumbled on for decades.

The most famous *nyerro* leader was Pere Rocaguinarda, or *Perot lo lladre*, Pete the Thief, revered by the poor and hunted by the state. At times, his band had up to a thousand men and women: you needed a small army if you were going to assault carriages of coin escorted by the military. Rocaguinarda is a literary figure, too, the only real person to appear in Cervantes' *Don Quijote*. As Quijote and Sancho Panza travel at night, Sancho is terrified to bump into the legs of some 20 people hanging from trees. Quijote explains that these dead men in the forest are bandits, 'which makes me think I must be close to Barcelona'. As dawn breaks, the pair are surrounded by 40 live bandits. They quake in fear, but Roque Guinart, as Cervantes calls him, treats Quijote and Sancho with knightly hospitality. Cervantes has Quijote praise 'valiant Roque'. After three days and three nights with the knight and his squire as guests, Rocaguinarda escorts them to Barcelona's beach.

While Cervantes was idealising the outlaw in this second part of *Don Quijote*,[9] which did much to extend Rocaguinarda's fame and perhaps save his life, the real bandit had been captured in 1611. Given his popularity, the authorities did not find it expedient to hang him and he was released to fight in Naples in 1615. This most famous *nyerro*, who for years had ridden Catalonia's hills and roads robbing the king and harassing his officials, ended up serving the king in Italy. There is a romantic, anti-monarchical version of Rocaguinarda's end. He was popularly believed to have died in the 1640 Catalan Revolt fighting the king's troops. There is no evidence for this and historians usually assume that he died in Naples circa 1635.

Witch Panic

Outlaw women were less admired. This same period of social change saw widespread persecution of unorthodox women as witches. About 400 women were hanged for witchcraft in Catalonia from 1616 to 1622, the peak years of collective witch paranoia. Other than queens and abbesses, 'witches' are the first women named in Catalan history. Just some examples: the midwife Sança, accused in 1453 of killing a newborn, was acquitted thanks to neighbours' evidence in support. In 1471, Joana Call from Andorra 'confessed' under torture that she was a poisoner and with Catarina Tarrada and Esclarmonda Aymar had attended orgies with the devil. All three were hanged. In 1516, Margarida Guitarda of Llagunes 'confessed' to poisoning animals and people.

The Àneu valleys high in the Pyrenees saw the very first European law against witchcraft, composed in 1424.[10] Judicial killing of women in Catalonia lasted for over 300 years: the last recorded case was in 1767. In all, about 1,000 women were killed as witches in Catalonia. They were accused of consorting with the devil (sexual fascination was plentiful) in order to gain powers to destroy crops, make people ill or cause natural disasters. The accused were usually women who were foreign, outsiders or who lived alone, people who did not fit in. The (male) witch-finders who travelled the country were skilled at sniffing

Figure 3   Gargoyle of a witch, Girona Cathedral (Dámaso Martín)

out candidates for their accusations. Proof was the devil's paw-mark (he liked to appear in the guise of a goat) on a woman's back, even if no one but the witch-finder could see it. One of them, Joan Malet from Flix, made the mistake of accusing someone of 'good' family in 1549 and ended up burnt at the stake for false accusation, though not before he had extracted fees from numerous town councils and sent dozens of poor women to the gallows.[11] The 1619 memorandum of the Jesuit Pere Gil, a valiant priest who was threatened and assaulted for his opposition to witch-hunts, was raised to the king in Madrid and saw the beginning of the end of persecution.

Why did the outbreaks occur in these years? Though poverty was endemic, 1616–1620 were years of increased poverty and anxiety, caused by crop failures in a succession of cold years, and floods following torrential rains in 1617. Minorities, whether Jews or single women, are more sharply scapegoated at times of special fear and stress. The travelling expert, the witch-finder, was the catalyst.

The general background of misogyny is also important. For the dominant medieval church, women should be virgins or married, monogamous mothers; otherwise, they were sources of sin, as the poetry of Jaume Roig exemplifies (see Chapter 2). A more specific context was the gradual exclusion over many decades of women from their traditional trades as midwives and healers. Societies of apothecaries and doctors founded in the cities (educated men) were interested in taking over uneducated women's work. Midwives could easily be accused of witchcraft if a baby was stillborn or a mother died in childbirth. Wise women's skills as healers with herbal remedies could be translated into accusations that they were poisoners. And there was a factor specific to Catalonia, which meant that many more women were killed for witchcraft in Catalonia than in the rest of Spain: justice was not strongly centralised, but exercised by local nobles, who were more easily pressured by an impassioned population.

Golden Ears of Wheat

In 1621, Felipe IV inherited the Spanish throne. At once, he appointed the Count-Duke of Olivares as *privado*, king's favourite. Olivares was prime minister for 22 years, longer than anyone else in Spanish history. Olivares' increasing pressure against Catalonia brought into focus that members of a distant ruling class, rather than local women, were to blame for poverty, hunger and disorder. Awareness was growing among many sections of the population, nobles and merchants, peasants and town-dwellers, that Catalonia was steadily, and not so stealthily, being integrated into the designs of the Spanish state. Needless to say, there were also many sectors, much of the Church, rich traders, nobles fearful of their peasants and the growing number of officials around the Castilian viceroy, who saw their interests as coinciding with Madrid's. The frustrations of the Catalan peasantry, supported by much of the urban poor and the *Generalitat*, grew throughout the 1630s to erupt in the 1640–1641 revolution.

This revolution, or Revolt of the Reapers as it is generally known, was further complicated because it was part of the Europe-wide Thirty Years' War, which broke out in 1618. This was a war between the Catholic South and Protestant North; and also between the great powers jockeying for territory and influence. Olivares' principal aim was to unite in practice a state that was united only in theory, to turn the 'Spains' into one centralised Spain. With good reason, from his point of view, he saw that the defence of the Spanish Empire, under severe threat in Flanders and from a rising England, required a united country, with one currency, one tax system and one administration. To achieve this, he would have to suppress the Crown of Aragon's different political institutions and laws and obtain taxes and troops for foreign wars. Olivares' motto was *Multa regna, sed una lex*, – *Many Kingdoms, but One Law*. With enormous energy inspired by his understanding of the dire situation of a Spanish Empire near bankruptcy due to war on so many fronts, he worked unceasingly to put the idea into practice. As he wrote in his 1624 report (the secret *Gran Memorial*) to Felipe IV:

> the most important business of your monarchy [is] to become King of Spain: I mean, sir, that Your Majesty not be content with being king of Portugal, of Aragon, of Valencia, count of Barcelona, but that you work and think maturely and secretly to reduce these kingdoms that make up Spain to the style and laws of Castile, with no differences.[12]

In 1626, Olivares introduced the *Unión de armas*, the Union of Arms. This was an ambitious attempt to oblige all parts of the empire to contribute to a standing army to defend the state against the threat of French invasion. Catalonia was to supply (and pay for) 16,000 men. The king convened the *Corts* in Barcelona in 1626 to negotiate this, but his reluctance to stay long and listen to Catalan grievances in the first *Corts* in 27 years led to his failure to get Catalonia to agree to the 16,000. The nature of *Corts* proceedings made them intolerable to kings used to rapid obedience. The procedure was that, first, the arms (estates) discussed among themselves. Then they proposed new laws to the king, who had to negotiate and accept some proposals if he wanted to get his taxes paid. The entire process was lengthy and tiresome: pacting could take months.

In the following years, Olivares continued to press Catalonia. In 1632, the king travelled to Barcelona for another failed *Corts*. Olivares' plea for a united country was a century too late: the Catalans could see how Spanish over-spending on foreign wars had ruined its own backyard, Castile, plunging most of its inhabitants into poverty. Now Olivares wanted not only to do away with Catalonia's historic rights, but also to reduce it to the same condition as Castile. The *Corts* were adjourned *sine die*, to the frustration of both sides: Olivares did not get his cash and soldiers; the Catalans could not get any legislation approved. It was in this climate of tension that the bandit Serrallonga was executed (see *Rebel Portrait: Serrallonga*).

In 1635, France declared war on Spain, which Olivares used as the excuse to occupy Catalonia and to impose the *Unión de armas*. The 40,000-strong army that Olivares sent to the French frontier was billeted on towns and villages. As well as being a barely bearable economic burden, the army, like all armies in such a situation, committed abuses that led to numerous clashes. For example, in 1638, a military riot pillaged and burnt the coastal town of Palafrugell.

Robert Hughes quotes a senior Portuguese officer in Felipe IV's army, Francisco Maria de Melo, someone not guilty of especial sympathy for the Catalans, one supposes:

> There was no outrage they [Felipe IV's army] did not consider licit. They ranged freely around the country without treating it any differently from occupied territory, trampling its crops, stealing its livestock, oppressing its villages ... at times the mourning and unutterable sorrow bore witness to endless death and disaster.[13]

In 1639, Salses, in North Catalonia, was taken by the French. This frontier fortress was recovered in January 1640 at great cost. Catalan volunteers from Barcelona took part in the victory and felt much of the credit was due to them and not to Olivares' army.

Discontent with this army ripened like corn in a wet, warm summer. Violent incidents became more frequent. In May 1640, some towns refused to allow the army to enter. At Santa Coloma de Farners, an official sent to organise lodging for soldiers was killed. The military burnt the town on 14 May, a reprisal that led to protests throughout Catalonia. On 22 May, some 200 peasants burst into Barcelona to free the imprisoned Catalan *conseller* of the *Generalitat*, Francesc Tamarit. Hero of the recapture of Salses, Tamarit was in jail because he had objected to army abuses. Protests came to a head on Corpus Christi, 7 June 1640, the traditional day for starting the harvest, when some 400 or 500 reapers with their sickles gathered for hire on Barcelona's Rambles. A reaper was injured in a scuffle with soldiers. This led rapidly to clashes, to the cries of ¡*Visca la terra!* (*Long Live our Land!*) and *Death to the Traitors!* Reapers and the city poor began to sack houses of the wealthy, piling luxurious possessions on bonfires in the streets. Members of the City Council and

Generalitat attempted to calm the crowds. Josep Maçana, a city councillor, collapsed in the stress of the moment. Rumour ran that he had been killed by the king's soldiers. Enraged, the crowd raced down the Rambles to the Drassanes shipyard, where the viceroy, the Marquess of Santa Coloma, had taken refuge. Fleeing along the beach, Santa Coloma and his escorts were hacked down by the reapers before they could reach a boat. Judges, bishops and royal officials were then attacked all over the city. Rioting spread throughout Catalonia. Houses of the rich in Vic, Manresa and Tortosa were pillaged. Urban elites were seen as allied with the king, Olivares and the foreign troops billeted on the populace. The combined class and national character of the conflict was explosive.

The revolt of the reapers led to the composition of *Els segadors* (*The Reapers*), Catalonia's national anthem. This was not written at the time, but in the 1890s wave of nationalist sentiment. It is worth quoting because it shows the centrality of peasants in the Catalan imagination and because it is a surprisingly violent anthem:

> Triumphant Catalonia
> will again be rich and plentiful.
> Away with such conceited
> and disdainful people [i.e. the Castilian occupiers].
> *Chorus:* Bon cop de falç!
> Bon cop de falç, defensors de la terra!
> Bon cop de falç!
> (…Strike hard with the sickle, defenders of our land!…)
> Now is the time, reapers,
> now is the time to be alert.
> Let us sharpen our tools well
> for when another June comes.
> *Chorus*
> May the enemy tremble
> on seeing our flag.
> Just as we cut the golden ears of wheat,
> when the time is ripe we will cut our chains.

The Very First Republic

When the news of the killing of the viceroy reached Madrid, Olivares rent his garments. His policy had failed disastrously. He realised that immediate, direct repression was too risky in the context of the war with France. He sent another viceroy to pacify Catalonia, but the king's law was no longer respected. Fontana tells of a barber called Novis who was identified and arrested as one of the killers of Santa Coloma. Such a magnicide would normally lead to rapid execution. Popular pressure forced Novis' release. The only law now enforceable was Catalan law, invested in the President of the *Generalitat*, Pau Claris, a canon from Berga elected in 1638.

Conscious of the breach with the monarchy that the death of the viceroy meant and aware that Olivares was preparing an army of invasion, Pau Claris contacted the French Prime Minister Richelieu, who was only too happy, at first secretly, to promise protection to Catalonia. The *Generalitat* then broke explicitly with Felipe IV: it organised a new system of justice and a Catalan army and it took over the royal arsenal, stored in the Drassanes.

On 19 August 1640, Olivares attempted conciliation: the king convened a meeting of the Catalan *Corts*, but events were by now out of his control. The *Generalitat* assumed what was the king's prerogative and itself convened a new assembly. Based on the *Corts*, this was an amplified meeting of the 'arms'. On 10 September, 246 representatives met, including many more of the urban population, the 'royal arm' (remember that this was 'royal' only in the sense that the royal charter of the Counts of Barcelona had granted representation to this third estate). Shortly afterwards, this assembly swelled to 532 representatives, with 62 belonging to the clerical arm, 47 to the military and 323 to the royal arm. Popular pressure was so great that merchants and artisans held a decisive majority. The threat of Olivares' invasion united the poor peasantry and the popular classes in the cities, which had been on opposing sides 200 years previously in the Civil War and as recently as the times of *nyerros* and *cadells*.

In late October, Olivares' army of 24,000 men entered Catalonia from the south. The authorities at Tortosa and Tarragona surrendered to the invaders, swearing loyalty to the king. Their 'betrayal' of the Catalan cause was to no avail: the army killed hundreds suspected of loyalty to the *Generalitat*. This slaughter led to revenge killings in Barcelona of the last royal officials still in residence. Josep Fontana tells how Judge Antoni Gori, in his seventies and ill in bed, was tossed from his bedroom window to the street.[14]

Olivares' army hanged people in each town it took on its march north. At Cambrils, on the coast, between 600 and 800 Catalan soldiers laid down their arms: they were killed just the same. At Vilaseca, 200 were killed; at Salou, a similar number. The *Generalitat* organised resistance at Martorell, but lost several hundred men in a pitched battle. Olivares' soldiers were then given free rein to rob, rape, murder and burn their way through the town. Some 300 people were killed, with reports of children thrown to the rocks in the Llobregat river from the town's Roman Pont del diable (Devil's Bridge).[15] Figures may be exaggerated, but there is no doubt that Olivares and his commander the Marquess of Los Vélez pursued a deliberate policy of revenge and terror in their invasion.

On 16 January 1641, as Felipe IV's army approached Barcelona, Pau Claris declared Catalonia a Republic under the protection of France's Louis XIII. The Republic lasted only eight days, as Richelieu's representatives insisted that the French king had to be recognised as the Count of Barcelona if the *Generalitat* wanted French military help. The *Generalitat*, after the defeat at Martorell, saw no option but to accept.

In the Battle of Montjuïc, the coastal hill on the south side of Barcelona, on 26 January 1641, Catalan and French forces, though outnumbered, defeated Olivares' army. The defenders of the city – a mixed bunch of artisans, the urban poor, priests, women and Catalan soldiers – were more motivated than the attacking troops. They knew of the slaughter during the northward advance of Olivares' army. There was every reason to believe Barcelona would suffer the same fate. The *Coronela*, an unpaid voluntary defence force of some 4,000 men, organised by the guilds and sanctioned by the *Consell de Cent*, was key to the resistance. Proudly these volunteers wore blue uniforms, with both collar and ballooning cuffs in red.

This armed citizen militia was a revolutionary force. Its members took up arms to defend their city. Arms in hand, at the forefront of resistance, these lower-class people in struggle, like the *sometent* in the country (see Chapter 5), posed questions of class: Who really defended the city? Who really had the power? And who held the arms? These were questions that, in each subsequent major conflict with the Spanish state, whether in 1641, 1714 or 1843, worried the Catalan ruling class.

Olivares' defeated army retreated, another in a series of failures leading to his fall from power in January 1643. On the other side of the peninsula, Portugal took advantage of the Catalan war to seize independence. The French appointed their own viceroy, but showed little inclination to annex Catalonia. After Richelieu's death in December 1642 and Olivares' fall, Europe's Great Powers began negotiating a treaty to end the Thirty Years' War. The war left all sides exhausted.

In Catalonia, after the victory at Montjuïc, the revolutionary tide ebbed, assisted by President Pau Claris' sudden death on 27 February 1641 (rumoured to have been poisoned by Olivares' agents). Soon the French troops billeted on the populace became as irksome as the Spanish army before. The semi-independent republic under French protection that Pau Claris had negotiated was a pipe-dream. The French viceroys and governors rode roughshod over Catalan rights. French generals took over lands and titles of nobles absent in Madrid.

On 30 July 1644, Felipe IV's troops occupied Lleida and the king swore anew to respect the Catalan *constitucions*. Other towns near Lleida went over to his side. By early 1652, revolts were taking place against the French in favour of Felipe IV. The war rumbled on for several years more, with long periods of inactivity.

Finally, the Treaty of the Pyrenees was signed in 1659 and Catalonia – and the Spanish Empire – lost half of the Cerdanya, in the Pyrenees, and North Catalonia, the Roussillon from Salses to today's French–Spanish frontier. Olivares' great effort to unite the Iberian Peninsula under the laws of Castile had failed miserably. As a consequence of his policy, Catalonia was devastated and lost territory; Portugal was lost; and then Flanders was lost after the 'invincible' Spanish *tercios* (battalions) were defeated at Rocroi in 1643. As Perry Anderson summarised eloquently:

> In the cataclysm of the 1640s, as Spain went down to defeat in the Thirty Years' War, and bankruptcy, pestilence, depopulation and invasion followed, it was inevitable that the patchwork union of dynastic patrimonies should come apart: the secessionist revolts of Portugal, Catalonia and Naples were a judgment on the infirmity of Spanish Absolutism. It had expanded too fast too early, because of its overseas fortune, without ever having completed its metropolitan foundations.[16]

Catalonia lost a quarter of its population to war, hunger and plague during the 1640s. The Revolution of 1640–1641 that had built up steam throughout the 1630s ended in the January Republic lasting just eight days and the magnificent victory at Montjuïc over Felipe IV's army. It was a pyrrhic victory, for the *Generalitat* had exchanged Spanish for French tyranny. It is not easy to see what else the Pau Claris government could have done. Catalonia on its own was in no position to defeat the much larger army of Europe's dominant state.

In retrospect, if Claris and his people had hung onto their independent Republic, they might still have won the Battle of Montjuïc, where French forces were not decisive. The revolutionary movement, that is, the reapers, men and women from the guilds (the *Coronela*), priests in skirts with 'harquebuses in one hand and breviaries in the other' and the *miquelets* (rural militia), was decisive at Montjuïc.[17] Afterwards, though, it is difficult to see how they could have held off Felipe IV's armies indefinitely. Several historians point to how Pau Claris opted for Richelieu's protection in preference to mobilising the Crown of Aragon. It is not inconceivable that a concerted resistance by the three components of the Crown of Aragon could have kept Olivares at bay. This, though, is mere speculation. Aragon and Valencia were not interested in being drawn into the conflict. For all practical purposes, the Crown of Aragon no longer existed.

The English revolution and republic took place at much the same time, but outcomes were different. What happened in England is well known: Cromwell led an army based on the poor to overthrow the monarchy. Charles I lost his head in 1649. The Protectorate of the 1650s crushed the left of the revolution and installed a military dictatorship. The merchants of London, who were Cromwell's most fervent supporters, benefited from the overthrow of the old feudal order. Power passed to a new class: city merchants, represented by a bourgeois parliament that favoured capitalist development.

This did not happen in the Spanish state, which stagnated economically and politically in the eighteenth and nineteenth centuries: absolute monarchy and its associate feudal structures held back capitalist development in agriculture and industry. Merchant capitalism was developing in Catalonia, but in the 1640 Revolution it was not strong enough to throw off the dead weight of Spanish absolutism. In addition, Catalonia suffered from its geographical position, sandwiched between the absolutist French and Spanish states, unlike England, the dominant country on an island.

I have used the term 'revolution' to describe the events of 1640–1641. The gradual deterioration of relations between the monarchy and Catalonia took a qualitative turn in 1639 with Olivares' insistence on using Catalonia's terrain and resources for the war on France. This was the background to three decisive factors that, taken together, justify calling the events a revolution against the monarchy. The *Corts* was constituted in autumn 1640 by the *Generalitat*, which thus assumed the authority of the king, with a decisive majority of the lower classes represented in the royal arm. Then, the proclamation of the Republic in January 1641 by Pau Claris was a change of regime that derived its legitimacy from these *Corts*. And third, the key role of the citizen militia in the Battle of Montjuïc meant that this victory was radically democratic. In general, the revolution of 1640–1641 involved attempts to expand what we call today democratic rights: in the fights against excess taxation, the billeting of troops on the poor, and executions without trial. It was inspired by a Spanish war against France in which most Catalans felt more victims than partisans. The Catalan revolution failed, though it left deep resentment of monarchy and a tradition of armed resistance.

After 1652, the Spanish state was too weakened to defend Catalonia against France, but also too weak to destroy Catalan rights, though it re-occupied the country. For the rest of the century, Catalonia suffered a royal army billeted intolerably on the country and several incursions by the French. The one important change that Felipe IV achieved after 1652 was to change the rules of *insaculació*, the process by which potential Barcelona city councillors' names were drawn by lot from a bag. The king gained the right to vet all names before they were placed in the bag. This led in the conflicts later in the century to much greater support for the king from the *Consell de Cent*.

In 1687, what was known as the Revolt of the *barretines* (the floppy red cap, like the French cap of liberty, worn by peasants) started at Centelles. Its causes were all too familiar: billeting of Spanish troops, high taxes and – a new disaster – starvation following a plague of locusts. After a march on Barcelona with the cry *Long live the King! Death to the bad government! (Visca el rei i mori el mal govern!)* and various skirmishes, the monarchy was able to suppress this revolt in 1689, with the usual imprisonment, exile and executions, as fewer artisans and merchants of the coastal towns and city supported the revolt than in 1640. The king's policy of vetting the names of council candidates had changed the composition of the Barcelona City Council. Many of this new elite had made their money supplying the king's army; and, since Spain's loss of Flanders in the 1640s, new markets in Spain and Italy were opening up for Catalan textiles. John Elliott explains a telling anecdote:

> ...there was a growing colony of Catalan merchants in Seville and Cadiz, anxious to participate in trade with the Indies, to which they exported Catalan agrarian products, textiles, and metal and glassware. Significantly, when the Flemish consul in Cadiz, who had jurisdiction over foreign merchants, asserted that the Catalans, with a language of their own, fell within his remit, they protested that, as vassals of the Spanish crown, Catalans 'are, and are called, Spaniards, since Catalonia is indubitably Spain'.[18]

Rebel Portrait: Serrallonga

The other famous *nyerro* leader was less fortunate than Rocaguinarda. Joan Serrallonga (1594–1634) was a minor noble from the Pyrenees. He was active in the 1620s, the period when Olivares was beginning to enforce his aggressive policies towards Catalonia, so there was no chance of his being sent off to Italy to avoid the scaffold, as was the case with Rocaguinarda. The *nyerro* movement was crushed when Serrallonga was executed in January 1634.

Serrallonga's exploits have been celebrated in poems, plays and opera over the centuries and even in a Catalan television series in 2008. At the start of the twentieth century, Joan Maragall, one of Catalonia's finest poets, wrote *The End of Serrallonga*, which immortalised the bandit as a symbol of Catalan resistance. On the eve of execution, the bandit confesses his sins, yet he is boastful. Here he is, proud of being proud:

> The first of my sins is pride, Father:
> I have lodged a prince within my body;
> never could I suffer being governed by another:
> in commanding all others I relished no end.
> I detested for this reason the king of Spain
> and all alone waged war against him.
> He has put our land in strangers' hands...[19]

Each 'sin' is answered thus by the bandit, formally confessing yet in reality unbending. Towards the end of the long poem, the priest asks Serrallonga to confess his sin of loving his Joana. Like Ausiàs March, Maragall has Serrallonga refuse to accept that sex with the woman he loves is sinful.

One should be wary of these Robin Hood-like bandits, often romanticised for nationalist purposes and because everyone likes a good story. Many lived off the land, terrorising peasants, stealing in the name of Catalonia and justice while often robbing for their own consumption. Fiction captures the crude reality. Jaume Cabré, in his first novel *Galceran* (1978), describes the career of a famous bandit in the Second Carlist War of 1849, but the sad portrait he draws applies to bandits throughout the centuries. Galceran, a peasant schooled in violence by the abuses of the Spanish Queen Isabel's soldiers, is consumed by hatred and the desire for vengeance. Freedom fighter or criminal?

There is little romance. After several months in the hills, Galceran wants to give up the life of an outlaw, but he is a wanted killer and there is no going back to what he knows: his family and the tilling of his land. His life is short and bloody and ends in the dark horror of the scaffold. He becomes a myth, but in his day was feared more than loved. Another bandit tells him:

Villagers and peasants look at you each day with more fear. They keep quiet, they don't hate you, but panic can be seen in their eyes … it's your fault that groups of soldiers come and the people don't want anything to do with these scoundrels.[20]

4

Damn Them When You've Done:
1714

[Catalans are] so passionate about their patria *as to lose all sense of reason; and they speak only their native language.*

José Patiño, Felipe V's Governor of Catalonia in 1715[1]

In 1700, Carlos II died heirless in a ruined Spain:

> Between 1600 and 1700 the total population of Spain fell from 8,500,000 to 7,000,000 – the worst demographic setback in the West. The Hapsburg State was moribund by the end of the century: its demise in the person of its spectral ruler Charles II, *el Hechiʒado* [the Bewitched], was awaited in every chancellery abroad as the signal at which Spain would become the spoils of Europe.[2]

France's Louis XIV, the 'Sun King', grasped his opportunity and placed his grandson Philippe, Duke of Anjou, on the Spanish throne as Felipe V. At first, everything went well for Catalonia. At the *Corts* of 1702, the first to reach any firm agreements since 1599, the new king worked hard to overcome strong anti-French feeling. He stayed in Catalonia for four months and even honoured the country by marrying in Figueres the 13-year-old Maria Luisa of Savoy (Felipe was 18). He succeeded in obtaining support and moneys in exchange for a promise to uphold Catalan constitutions and for the offer of economic advantages to Catalonia. These included the rights to send two ships a year to America and to export wines and spirits without taxation. However, two key demands, that is, to quarter Spanish troops in barracks, not in people's homes, and to remove the king's control of *insaculació*, were not accepted.

When England and Holland backed a Hapsburg pretender against the Bourbons in 1701, another Europe-wide war broke out. The War of the Spanish Succession was a fight between the European powers over which of two absolute monarchies, the Hapsburgs or the Bourbons, should rule Spain and, more broadly, a struggle for European hegemony. The Hapsburg Archduke Charles (Carles in Catalan) and his allies saw in Catalonia, Aragon and Valencia, the former Crown of Aragon, the weak links in Bourbon control of Spain.

Despite Felipe V's concessions at the successful *Corts*, discontent with him re-emerged rapidly in parts of Catalan society, most immediately among the growing class of merchant capitalists. The war meant that Bourbon Spain and France cut off Catalonia's exports of textiles, wine and brandy to Holland and England. If there was no commerce, Felipe V's promise of exports without taxation was a hollow gesture.

Catalan merchants' prosperity had grown towards the end of the seventeenth century due to a new area of trade – no longer criss-crossing the Mediterranean, but looking to Lisbon, London and Amsterdam. Dutch and English liked to drink alcohol. The English company Heathcot & Crowe had set up a distillery in Reus in 1685. This was big business: from 1690 to 1696, Heathcot & Crowe exported through Reus's port Salou two and a half million litres of wine and brandy (*aiguardent*, literally 'firewater' – grapes were coarse, unsuited for fine wine, but could be turned into cheap brandy), mostly to England. Soap, wood and salt were other exports; the company's ships returned with tobacco, wheat and cod. The important contact between this English merchant class and Catalan traders brought wealth and also stimulated political thoughts: perhaps Catalonia could become a small trading nation, like Holland; and perhaps it could have a parliament that controlled the monarch, like England's after 1689.

Queen Anne of England acted energetically on reaching the throne in 1702. She summoned Mitford Crowe, a member of parliament and one half of Heathcot & Crowe, and urged him to return to Catalonia and foster his contacts there in favour of the Allies (Holland, England and Austria). She granted him plenipotentiary powers to negotiate on her behalf with Catalans discontent with Felipe V.

Crowe, nicknamed rather unimaginatively in his adopted homeland as *l'ocell*, the bird, was extraordinarily effective in winning support for the Allied cause. In May 1704, an Anglo-Dutch fleet blockaded

Barcelona, but the attack was premature. There was no uprising against Felipe V and the Allies failed to take the city. Catalonia's authorities were understandably ambivalent, sandwiched as they were between two powers. They replied to the commander of the Allied fleet, Prince Darmstadt of Hesse, formerly the popular Hapsburg viceroy sacked by Felipe V (see *Rebel Portrait: Joan Baptista Basset*), with an ambiguous: 'You well know to whom we owe allegiance'. However, the ensuing indiscriminate repression by Felipe V's paranoid viceroy Velasco against anyone even suspected of sympathies for the Archduke tipped the scales against Felipe V.

By spring 1705, the *vigatans* (people from Vic) had formed a para-military *miquelet*-style force and taken control of the inland Vic area. These rural proprietors had always backed Darmstadt and were now driven to action by Velasco's repression. It was not difficult to mobilise against the French Felipe V, as the French had invaded and occupied the land several times since the Revolt of the Reapers. The loss of North Catalonia in 1659 was remembered still and the French aggressions of 1689–1697 left an 'open wound ... The clergy were loud in their denunciations of French troops for profaning churches'.[3]

The Hapsburgs were accustomed to rule a composite state, both in Austria and Spain, that is, a state of several nations, whereas Felipe V's behaviour and his grandfather's long autocratic regime strongly suggested that, despite the *Corts* of 1702, the Bourbons were not planning to respect the *constitucions*. On 17 May 1705, an assembly of *vigatans* gave powers to two representatives to negotiate with the Allies. On 20 June, a secret pact was signed at Genoa between these two and Mitford Crowe, for the *Generalitat* itself was not yet prepared to break its oath of loyalty to Felipe V. *The bird* guaranteed in Queen Anne's name English troops and respect for all Catalan *constitucions*.

In autumn 1705, the Archduke's army took Catalonia when the *Generalitat* finally broke with Velasco and the *vigatans* led a rising to coincide with Darmstadt's Anglo-Dutch fleet attacking Barcelona once more. The Archduke himself arrived and was crowned King Carlos III of Spain in Barcelona in November 1705. *Corts* were held again and the Archduke became the third monarch in five years to swear loyalty to the Catalan *constitucions*. Archduke Carles (Carlos) included promises to restore North Catalonia and remove the monarch's right to oversee *insaculació*. Felipe V was so disgusted by the Archduke's concessions that he wrote: 'The Catalans have become more Republican than the English with their parliament.'[4]

The Hapsburgs briefly occupied Madrid in 1706, but it was a false triumph. The 1706 *Corts* were the last ever to be held. The war turned back in favour of the Bourbons. Felipe V's forces took Valencia after the Battle of Almansa in 1707, burning the city of Xàtiva, destroying the area's castles and eliminating the *furs*. Today, in powerful symbolism, the portrait of Felipe V in the Municipal Museum of Xàtiva hangs upside down. In October of the same year, Felipe V's army captured Lleida, capital of Catalonia's inland counties. The occupying army of about 40,000 overcame resistance lasting a month by the Archduke's 2,000 soldiers and the city's inhabitants. As in Barcelona in 1640–1641 and again, on a still greater scale six years later in 1714, workers and artisans played a key role in the defence of the city. After the siege, Lleida was sacked. Five neighbourhoods were razed. One thousand five hundred households were reduced to 600. The cathedral was turned into a prison. The city's economy was destroyed for generations.

The war then swung back in favour of the Hapsburgs, whose army occupied Madrid for a second time in 1710, but the death of the Archduke's elder brother in 1711 had disastrous consequences for Catalonia. Archduke Carles left Barcelona to occupy the throne in Vienna. England and Holland abandoned the Hapsburg cause to prevent the union of Austria and Spain, which was more unpalatable to them than the Bourbon alliance of France and Spain. In April 1713, the Treaty of Utrecht ended the war. Europe's main powers recognised Felipe V as King of Spain.

In the months after the signing of the Treaty of Utrecht, all Catalonia fell to Felipe V's armies, except for Barcelona and two small inland towns. As the Bourbon forces were harassed constantly by *miquelets*, Felipe V ordered instant execution of any captured *miquelet*, which led often to mass slaughter in villages, for the *miquelets* swam easily in the sea of Catalan peasantry.

The Siege

Felipe V was determined to settle the Catalan question once and for all. On 3 April 1713, he wrote with exaggerated belligerence to the Duke of Pópuli, the general in charge at the start of the siege of Barcelona:

'Although I do not consider that the blind stubbornness of the Catalans will reach the extreme of daring to resist, if they do not surrender within the term of two hours, they will all be put to the sword.'[5] Catalan stubbornness was not blind. They knew what had happened in Valencia after Almansa and in Lleida in 1707. In addition, the besieged still hoped that the Hapsburg pretender might intervene on their side.

Queen Anne of the newly United Kingdom (England and Scotland united in 1707) was known to be dying in 1713. Her heir designate was her cousin George, the Elector of Hanover. Catalan envoys succeeded in extracting a commitment from George to defend Catalonia. A British fleet deployed off Barcelona, as had occurred in 1705, would have broken the siege. Anne died on 1 August 1714, but Robert Harley and his Tory Government delayed George I's coronation until October 1714, when Barcelona had already fallen. The delay may simply have been due to the adverse winds cited as the reason that the new king could not sail to London from The Hague. Most believe, including the Whigs at the time, that the Tories deliberately delayed George's journey because he favoured the Whigs and so that Barcelona would fall before his arrival. Be this as it may, the United Kingdom had benefited greatly from the Treaty of Utrecht, gaining Menorca and Gibraltar and breaking Spain's monopoly of trade (in slaves and cotton) with Latin America. As Bolingbroke, the United Kingdom's Foreign Secretary, stated at Utrecht: 'It was not for the interest of England to preserve the Catalan liberties.'[6] Catalonia was hung out to dry by 'perfidious Albion', a state whose ruling class could not be trusted.

Widespread debate within Britain saw parliamentary motions and propaganda pamphlets by such famous writers as Jonathan Swift and Daniel Defoe. When he finally arrived, King George asked Felipe V to show mercy to the Catalans, but did little else. Whig consciences at the abandonment of Catalonia were uneasy; but British interests overcame any scruples. The 1714 pamphlet *The Case of the Catalans Considered* bore a quote from Congreve on its front cover that summed up the question with crude neatness: 'You gain your Ends, and Damn them when you've Done.'[7]

Catalonia was alone. A popular song expressed the reality: 'English went missing/ Portuguese signed/ Dutch will sign/ and then they'll hang us'.[8] The siege of Barcelona started on 25 July 1713. It was at first a blockade, rather than an aggressive siege. Catalonia was no longer a battleground fought over like a bone by the royal dogs of France and Spain. The French and Spanish armies were now united in their determination to crush Catalan resistance. On 2 April 1714, French-Spanish artillery began to shell Barcelona; and in July, the Duke of Berwick, the ruthless and able victor of Almansa, took over the command with orders to take the city quickly. He had access from the sea fully closed. He had zigzag trenches built to bring mortars closer to the walls. From July to September, it is said, some 30,000 shells were lobbed into the city. On 3 September, the outer wall was breached. On 11 September 1714, the walls were breached in several places and Felipe V's troops took the city.

There are a great many stories about this legendary siege, which has become the main trauma and historical impulse for Catalan nationalists. Known as the *Diada*, 11 September is today Catalonia's National Day, on which hundreds of thousands (recently, over a million) take to the streets. The day sees a number of patriotic ceremonies, in particular the moving homage at the Fossar de les Moreres (Mulberry Tree Grave – beside the basilica of Santa Maria del Mar) to those who died defending the city in 1714. The plaque on the monument reads:

No traitor is buried
in the Mulberry Tree Grave.
Even though we lose our flags,
it will be the urn of honour.

The defenders of the city against some 90,000 troops under Berwick consisted of about 5,000 soldiers: 3,500 members of the *Coronela*, commanded by Antonio de Villarroel, and several hundred regular soldiers of the Hapsburg army. There were also Valencian refugees, among them the charismatic Joan Baptista Basset and two companies of *maulets*, peasants in rebellion against Felipe V's restoration of nobles' possession of the land (see *Rebel Portrait: Joan Baptista Basset*). Basset became famous in the siege for his skill in mines and accurate artillery fire. The guilds that supplied their members to the *Coronela* were divided into six battalions, each defending a part of the wall. As in 1641, the *Coronela* was the heart of popular resistance: tailors, students, butchers, shoemakers, carpenters etc. formed its companies.

Berwick's sappers first breached the walls on 12 August, but resistance and Basset's mines meant his army was kept out. Barcelona's populace

Figure 4   Fossar de les Moreres. Mass grave and Memorial to the Dead in
1714 siege, Barcelona (Dámaso Martín)

was dying of hunger, dysentery and shells. The *miquelets* attacking
Felipe V's armies in the rear could draw troops away from the siege,
but not relieve it. On 3 September, Berwick offered terms of surrender
for a peaceful occupation with no pillage. Villarroel and the Chief
Councillor, Rafael Casanova, advised that victory was impossible and
further resistance would only bring more deaths, but a general refusal to
surrender forced the Defence Council to reject the ultimatum. Villarroel
resigned his command, but returned to the fray before the final assault,

which has led to his renown as someone who, despite disagreeing with the majority vote, accepted the majority decision, even though it meant putting his life on the line.

After several days of rain, Berwick's final assault started at 4.30 in the morning on 11 September. Twenty thousand troops poured in through seven breaches in the walls on the northern side of the city. The rains had dampened Basset's defensive mines, many of which failed to explode. Despite this, retreating from outer to inner walls and into the streets, the city's inhabitants, led by the *Coronela*, resisted. All the church bells rang above the explosions. All classes of citizens put up barricades and took up bayonets: old men and women, nuns, children, the wounded from the hospitals. The struggle ebbed and flowed through the mud, screams and clouds of gunpowder. The convent of Sant Pere was taken by the besiegers and retaken by the besieged. Berwick had to bring up reserves. By 11am, when there was a lull in the fighting, it is estimated that over 5,000 of Berwick's troops had fallen in conquering the first line of defence and 900 of the besieged had died.[9]

Casanova and the elderly Villarroel were wounded, the latter as he led a cavalry charge. He entered legend, or history, shouting as he lay on the ground, his horse dead and leg smashed: 'Keep advancing, no-one near me will retreat. Our task now is to die or win.'[10] That afternoon, negotiations for surrender were undertaken. Berwick refused to sign any guarantees. On the 13th, two members of the City Defence Council met Berwick to congratulate him on his victory and submit to the Bourbon king. Chillingly, Berwick answered that he knew of no Defence Council. The *miquelets* melted back into the peasantry. A week later, the castle of Cardona surrendered. The war was over. Many Catalans fled into exile.[11]

Running Sore

There are varying interpretations of these events. An official book from 1978 on the history of the Catalan *Generalitat*, depending on the nationalist historian Ferran Soldevila, glorifies the City Government for rejecting the offer of Berwick on 3 September by 26 votes to 4, despite Villarroel and Casanova's lucid support for accepting surrender without reprisals. What is missing in this book celebrating the return of the *Generalitat* after the Franco dictatorship is the mass of the city's inhabitants.

Despite the population's extreme physical and numerical weakness, they forced the City Government to resist. Mass bouts of religious fervour might suggest collective unreason, but it was also absolutely rational to believe, after Almansa and Lleida, that Berwick and the king could not be trusted to keep any guarantee of clemency and were hell-bent on crushing the Catalan *constitucions*.

Albert Sánchez Piñol's 2014 novel *Victus* inserts the city's poor and artisans into the argument. In this fast-moving fictional account of the siege (fiction, but it sticks to known facts), Sánchez Piñol is scathing about the politicians on both sides and highlights the courage of the city's defenders. He thinks very little of the vacillating Casanova and the rest of the City Government, though even less, to be clear, of Felipe V, Berwick and their lackeys. *Victus* is novel not history, but worth reading as a counter to conventional Catalan-nationalist history.

All sides recognised the courage of the besieged. Berwick himself wrote (though perhaps to justify his slowness in taking the city): 'Never before has greater determination been seen than that of the garrison and inhabitants of Barcelona.'[12] De Quincy, Berwick's general in charge of artillery, said: 'There is no other example of such a stubborn defence. If regular troops had done something similar, they would have conquered immortal glory.'[13]

Many Spanish centralists reject the Catalan nationalist story of a united people fighting for Catalan rights. These politicians and historians aver that Catalan nationalists romanticise 1714 for political ends. The centralist positions can be broken down into four main assertions. First, as this was the War of Spanish Succession, Catalonia was fighting not for its *constitucions*, but for who would be King of Spain. However, the two were not mutually exclusive, for whoever became King of Spain would decide what *constitucions* Catalonia would preserve.

The second argument is that the Catalans were divided and that the unity of Catalans against the foreign oppressor is a self-serving myth, as many wealthy merchants and nobles supported Felipe V. This is quite true: many left Barcelona before the siege tightened, settling particularly in the coastal town of Mataró, awaiting their opportunity and continuing to do business despite the war. This argument tends to confirm the class nature of this national struggle. The 'royal arm' (remember, poorer merchants, supported by artisans) was the backbone of the resistance, not the rich.

The third main argument is that the repression on the fall of the city is exaggerated: for instance, Rafael Casanova was allowed to retire to Sant Boi and lived to a ripe old age. As discussed below, the repression was thorough, but selective for good political reasons.

The fourth argument, or assertion without basis, is that the 1716 New Plan (*Nueva Planta*) decree abolishing Catalonia's independent institutions was not so oppressive as Catalan nationalists make out, since Barcelona enjoyed considerable prosperity in the following century. This argument is not convincing, as the account above of Heathcot & Crowe's business suggests. John Elliott states that in the late seventeenth century the 'Catalan monetary system was stable, and this stability had laid the foundations for economic growth'.[14] Merchants were prospering from exports from the rural economy: wine, brandy and textiles. Thus, the suppression of Catalonia's *constitucions* under the New Plan did not open the way to economic development. Rather, the war halted an economic resurgence that was already under way.

Felipe V's instructions to Berwick were clear as crystal: 'As to the form of government to be given to the City, you will arrange it and place it at once on the same basis as Castile's, without the slightest difference or variation at all.'[15] Martial law was implemented. Basset was imprisoned in Ondarrabia. Villarroel was imprisoned in Alacant. The *vigatà* Josep Moragues, who had led the *miquelets* and other forces based in the fortress of Cardona in harrying Felipe V's armies, was dragged by galloping horses through the cobbled streets of Barcelona. His head was placed in a cage and exhibited at the city's Sea Gate until 1727.

Yet, Felipe V was wise enough to institute a reign of only partial terror and selective slaughter. Moragues' head was a clear warning to anyone thinking about rebellion. Meanwhile, nobles and merchants returned from Mataró. They and the king coincided in their desire to get the economy of Spain's once-wealthiest city running again as quickly as possible.

The occupation of Catalonia led to the New Plan of January 1716, whose 59 clauses codified that the king would be above the law. Felipe V could dispense justice, order events and raise taxes just as he wished. There was no longer any need for tiresome negotiations with recalci-trant *Corts*. City councillors were no longer chosen through *insaculació*, but directly nominated (for life sometimes) by the monarch. Catalonia entered fully into French-style absolutism: one king, one law, one language. Justice was to be administered in Spanish; schoolchildren taught in Spanish; preaching (important when many were illiterate and most believed in God) had to be in Spanish, too (though this propaganda measure probably backfired, as many peasants did not understand Spanish). Barcelona University was closed and a new one opened in distant inland Cervera, to reward the town for its support of the Bourbons in the war and, more importantly, to keep ideas away from the dangerous capital. Citadels were built to dominate Lleida and Barcelona. Neighbourhoods in Lleida had already been destroyed; in Barcelona, the Ribera, a quarter of some 900 houses on the north side of the city, badly damaged by mortar fire and on 11 September, was demolished and the citadel built in what is now the Parc de la Ciutadella (Citadel·Park). This troublesome city was now hugged in a deadly embrace by the cannons of the fortress on the hill of Montjuïc and of the new citadel. Catalonia's great nineteenth-century poet Jacint Verdaguer wrote that 'the hateful citadel [was] like a running sore/ on a beautiful face'.

All of Catalonia's political institutions and foral laws mentioned in this book so far were abolished by the New Plan: the *Generalitat*, the *Consell de Cent*, the *Corts*, the 'arms' and local municipal bodies. The Spanish state finally achieved what Olivares had aspired to.

On 1 April 1716, a new tax was introduced: the *cadastre*, basically a property and salary tax (nobles, military officers, the clergy and government officials were, naturally enough, exempt). The *cadastre* became a permanent source of conflict. Despite military occupation, as little as 40 per cent of the *cadastre* was collected in the 1720s. As John Elliott puts it: 'The sums to be levied moved upwards over the course of the century, leaving the mass of the Catalan population with a fiscal burden that has been calculated as double that which fell on Castilian taxpayers.'[16]

The only major area that survived the counter-revolution was Catalan civil law. The conquerors recognised that it would be too chaotic and damaging to business to change these laws of property and commercial contract. Inheritance of the land continued to be for the eldest son, which meant that, as land was not subdivided on the owner's death, a relatively wealthy peasantry developed.

One Chained Knife

Catalonia lost the last vestiges of independence in the War of the Spanish Succession. The possibility (or fantasy) of its developing into a small trading state, like Holland, was eliminated. Catalan nationalist historians like Ferran Soldevila see 1714 as the end of the Catalan nation. Even Josep Fontana, from a Marxist rather than a nationalist tradition, poses the question in a chapter heading of whether it was the 'End of the Catalan Nation?'[17] As discussed earlier, the concept of 'nation' or 'nationalism' was little used until the nineteenth century, but it is a useful anachronism to describe the identity with a territory and community that most Catalans felt, especially against Spanish centralism. The common cry of 1640 and 1714, ¡*Visca la terra!*, still used today, expresses loyalty to a place, a language, laws and rights.[18] In reality, Catalonia's medieval independence as the leading area, or state, of the Crown of Aragon had finished in 1412 or 1492 (one can bicker over the date). Under the Hapsburgs, its national rights were steadily eroded.

National consciousness meant that, when Catalonia as an entity fought against centralist absolutism, there was a certain unity between classes. In other periods, such as the fifteenth-century conflicts, the peasantry and/or city artisans fought the rich landowners and/or city merchants. And always, as the account of 1714 has shown, there was a layer of the upper class within Catalonia who sided with the absolutist monarchy. These became known at this time as *botiflers*, an insult still used today to describe Catalans who support Spanish nationalism. Josep Borrell, the EU's Foreign Minister, is a prime example.

For the poor, 1714 did not mean an end to the hunger, disease and killing of the war years. The post-war period was even hungrier. Grain was confiscated to feed the army of occupation, who were again billeted on the population. Sporadic revolts were suppressed with customary ferocity. Peasants were forbidden to carry arms, which meant that wolves proliferated. According to Simon Harris, all Catalans were humiliatingly restricted to 'one single knife per family attached by a chain to the kitchen table'.[19]

Many fled to the hills and the centuries-old tradition of 'social banditry' was renewed. Smuggling, theft, murder and executions all increased throughout the eighteenth century. The Bourbon authorities did not mind too much an insecure country where the poor were forced to live from crime. They did not mind that the country was not peaceful, as long as it remained pacified. Catalonia's governor José Patiño wrote to the king in 1715 that the Catalans, 'passionate for their fatherland ..., respect the orders of Your Majesty and justice not out of affection and love, but because of the superiority of your arms'.[20] The Bourbons were realistic.

Paradoxically, at the moment of the greatest defeat for Catalan political aspirations, the Catalan economy boomed. As argued above, this growth had started before the War of the Spanish Succession. After the war, it was assisted by military occupation, which brought social stability in the towns and low wages in the workshops. Rosi Song and Anna Riera, in their exciting book on the history of Catalan food, point to the 1720s craze for chocolate, seen in the new luxurious shops and hot-chocolate establishments and a rapid increase in chocolate imports, a clear indication of surplus income to spend on consumption.[21] Vilar commented sardonically that the Catalans avenged their political defeat economically. Catalonia's external boundaries also enjoyed peace. The constant wars of the seventeenth century between France and Spain, often fought in Catalonia, ceased from 1714 (with the exception of a brief conflict concerning Sicily in 1719–1720), as France and Spain were both ruled by the same Bourbon family. This 'peace' lasted till 1789 when the French branch ran into serious trouble.

Agriculture was still the basis of the economy. Vines, rising up sparsely soiled hillsides, were extensive in southern Catalonia and *aiguardent* and wine were again exported. Surplus capital from agriculture was invested in textile manufacture, an early sign of Catalonia's coming industrial revolution. To compensate for the Spanish Empire's loss of textile production in Flanders and Italy, Catalonia began to supply an internal market in Spain. By 1760, Spain's coastal areas had exceeded Castile in population, resources and standard of living, which have lasted up until the present. Spain is still a state dominated politically from the centre, but more prosperous round the edges.

The eighteenth century was also Spain's great century of exploitation of America. Previously it had ransacked America for its silver and gold. As this mineral extraction declined, economic exploitation of the colonies grew. Africans were seized to work sugar, cotton and tobacco plantations as slaves in Santo Domingo, Cuba and Peru. A prosperous class of white and creole exploiters developed in the Americas: trade to and from this new market replaced the galleons of bullion. In 1778, the monopoly of Seville and Cadiz on American trade was lifted. Catalan business took advantage.

REBEL PORTRAIT: JOAN BAPTISTA BASSET

Visca Basset abans que Carles III!

Joan Baptista Basset was the most radical of the leaders in the War of the Spanish Succession, as well as the greatest expert in artillery and explosives. He was born in 1654 in Alboraia, a town just north of Valencia city, to an artisan family.[22] Unlike all other leaders in the war, he was no privileged child of the upper classes. He spoke the language of Valencia's artisans and peasants. Little is known of his early years, except that in 1670 he killed a man. He enrolled in the army, a common way of evading prison or the scaffold, and for the next 35 years fought all over Europe. In the late 1680s, he was befriended by Prince Darmstadt (born 1669) of Hesse, despite their differences of age and class. Darmstadt financed Basset's studies of military engineering and technology, particularly explosives. In 1697, Darmstadt, employed to command the Hapsburg army and with Basset alongside him, successfully evicted the French invaders from Catalonia. At the *Generalitat*'s request, this popular aristocrat was appointed viceroy of Catalonia in 1698, but was sacked in 1701 by the new Bourbon king.

In 1704, Darmstadt and Basset, sailing from Lisbon, captured Gibraltar from Felipe V.[23] After a year as Governor of the Rock, Darmstadt took the fleet to besiege Barcelona, where he was killed by a bullet in the successful assault on Montjuïc in August 1705. Earlier that month, Basset landed at Altea and marched on the city of Valencia. Felipe V's forces melted away before a general uprising in favour of Basset. By December, the carpenter's son Basset was the Hapsburg viceroy in Valencia city. At the same time, Lleida fell to the *miquelets* and Archduke Carles entered Barcelona.

At this moment of triumph for the Hapsburg pretender, Basset took two decisive measures to reverse the injustices suffered by the Valencian peasantry. He abolished the tithes that the peasants paid to the nobles and sanctioned occupations of nobles' estates. This direct-action land reform made him a hero for the ages and leader at the time of the *maulets*, the poor peasantry in revolt.

The *maulets* were the Christians brought to work the land after the expulsion of all Moors from Valencia in 1609. Throughout the second part of the century, they rebelled against their conditions, culminating in a general uprising and sharp defeat in 1693. They aspired to ownership of the land under the conditions laid down by Jaume I 'the Conqueror' in the thirteenth century. Basset backed the *maulets'* demands.

Aware that his small army that had disembarked at Altea and the *maulets* were not going to be sufficient to defeat a Bourbon attack, Basset called on the Archduke to send reinforcements. These arrived under Lord Peterborough, but the new army altered the balance of forces. Peterborough's political agenda was quite different. Logically enough, he and Archduke Carles wanted former property relations restored. Peterborough proceeded to evict *maulets* who had occupied nobles' lands and had Basset deposed and arrested. Many *maulets* took to the hills in revolt, with the cry *Long Live Basset before Carles III! Visca Basset abans que Carles III!*

After Berwick's victory at Almansa in 1707, Basset was released to organise resistance. Although Peterborough detested his social measures, he recognised his popularity and military skills. It was too late. Basset and the *maulets* continued to fight as guerrillas before he and a reduced following escaped to Catalonia in 1708. When in early 1713 the now-Empress Isabel, the Archduke's wife, abandoned Catalonia and all the Hapsburg generals went with her, Basset refused to leave. He led guerrilla groups that harassed the Bourbon armies. Then, as Felipe V's forces closed on final victory, Basset entered Barcelona with two companies of *maulets* and was appointed Head of Artillery. The presence of this legendary soldier from another part of the Catalan lands, a believer in social justice for the peasantry and expert in mines and artillery fire, raised the morale of the besieged.

Captured on the fall of Barcelona, Basset was imprisoned in Alacant, then taken on foot and in chains the 700 kilometres to Ondarrabia, in the Basque Country. He must have been tough, for at the age of 60 he survived the journey. There are two versions of his death. One is that on a brief French incursion in 1719 he was evacuated from Ondarrabia to Segovia, where he was only released a few months before his death in total poverty in January 1728. The other version (less likely, alas) is that the French incursion released the elderly Basset and he found his way to Vienna, where he was honoured by the Archduke to whom he had been so loyal and who had so mistreated him.

The *maulets'* uprising combined defence of Valencia's ancient national rights and a social rebellion against the nobles' possession of the land. National consciousness gave an impulse to class demands. Basset was their undisputed leader.

5

The Inanimate Corpse

The Catalan, placed between two fires, and alternatively the dupe and victim of Spain and France, has no reason to love his neighbours, although willing to side with either, whenever ... it suits his private and local interests. This has always been a marked, and perhaps necessary policy on the Pyrenean frontier, and is the result of position.

Richard Ford[1]

Catalonia is a *terra de pas*, a thoroughfare or strategic crossroads. The area was both buffer and contact between the Carolingian Empire and Al-Andalus when it was the Hispanic March. In later centuries, it became a battleground between the Spanish and French states. There were no fewer than seven French invasions of Catalonia from 1638 to the last, in 1823. In addition, its long coast was open to pirates, which is why, as protection against pillage, many coastal villages have two neighbourhoods: one built a couple of kilometres inland and one with fishing families' shacks (hotels, now) on the beach. A *terra de pas*: it has been ravaged by war. And this means, generation after generation of slaughter, famine, rape, livelihoods destroyed.

The suffering of the seventeenth and eighteenth centuries was followed by yet another war at the start of the nineteenth century. In the name of the liberties won in the French Revolution, Napoleon sought to extend his European empire to Iberia (Invasion Six). Bonaparte calculated badly. The military genius failed to grasp the politics of Spain. As much as the retreat from Moscow, his eventual defeat in Spain led to his downfall. Karl Marx revelled in Napoleon's discomfiture:

Thus it happened that Napoleon, who, like all his contemporaries, considered Spain as an inanimate corpse, was fatally surprised at the discovery that when the Spanish State was dead, Spanish society was full of life, and every part of it overflowing with powers of resistance.[2]

Napoleon also miscalculated Catalonia's desire for independence. Several times during the years of French occupation (1808–1814), he reminded Catalans that Charlemagne had defended them from the Moors and he would now defend them from the Spaniards and English. His army occupied Barcelona on 29 February 1808. This was achieved by bloodless trickery: with permission from Madrid to march across Spain in order to invade Portugal, General Duhesme's army, when apparently resting outside Barcelona, seized Montjuïc and the Citadel by surprise. In 1810, the French set up a puppet Catalan Government, with Catalan its official language. The newspaper *Diari de Barcelona* was published in French and Catalan. From 1812 to 1814, Catalonia was actually annexed to the French Empire as four *départements*.

Earlier, in 1793, the revolutionary Republic had occupied Barcelona (Invasion Five) with a view to Catalonia becoming an 'independent Republic under French protection' (the formula of Pau Claris in 1641). However, Robespierre was strongly opposed to exporting revolution. He believed revolutions had to be based on the conditions within each country and favoured strengthening France's borders over any foreign adventures. He 'urged the need to respect existing treaties, and the rights of small nations and neutrals'.[3] In 1794, the French withdrew.

Napoleon did not heed the 'Incorruptible' and his appeal to Catalonia's anti-Castilian spirit failed. Catalonia's merchants were now comfortable with Bourbon rule, which had given them access to Spain's internal market and, from 1778, the right to trade with Spain's American colonies. Nor were these prosperous traders keen on Bonaparte's declared desire to open the Spanish market to French textile manufacturers. Allison Peers concluded that: 'Catalonia had at last, so it seemed, become an integral part of the Castile-ruled Spain of the Bourbons.'[4] More plausibly, Napoleon's failure to win over Catalonia was just another example of how liberty cannot be exported on the points of bayonets. Robespierre was right.

Together, Yet in Profound Contradiction

Despite profound internal differences, all sectors of Spanish society were hostile to Napoleon's invasion. The Spanish monarchy, nobility and clergy were terrified of losing their heads to the Revolution they saw incarnate in Napoleon. The reforming liberals – a minority that had increased in influence in the eighteenth century as trade and towns expanded and Enlightenment ideas filtered into the country – were not averse to French ideas, but were hostile to French invasion.

The popular classes of the cities entered Spanish politics decisively on 17 March 1808, when a rising at Aranjuez forced the abdication of the weak Carlos IV in favour of his son Fernando and the ousting of the corrupt Chief Minister Godoy, even as all three were preparing flight before the advance of Napoleon's general Murat. Aranjuez was followed by the insurrection of 2 May 1808, against Murat's occupation of Madrid. The rising, put down in blood, occupies a quintessential position in Spanish history. Today, Madrid celebrates the heroic revolt with a bank holiday and jingoistic excess. The politicians of the conservative Partido Popular (PP) who make the patriotic speeches do not blush, even though they are the heirs of the upper class that fled the French and not of the nameless fighters.

The 2 May insurrection is famed too because of Goya's ferocious paintings, *The Charge of the Mamelukes* and *The 3rd of May in Madrid*, which shows the summary executions; the former shows battlefield cavalry trample civilian revolt. Goya had plenty of time to study more horrors during the long war against French occupation, producing his black-and-white series of drawings, *The Disasters of War*. Whereas Velázquez 150 years earlier had painted handsome nobles on caparisoned horses and in feathered helmets when the Spanish Empire still (just about) dominated Europe; Goya, enraged by Napoleon's corruption of the French Revolution's Enlightenment ideals, drew the dirty degradation of war. While bankrupt, absolutist Spain collapsed in 1808 and a new, modern state struggled to emerge and failed to do so, Goya's painting and drawing were already in the vanguard of modernity.

Napoleon invited royal father and son to a conference at Bayonne, where they and the nobility were so scared that they accepted Bonaparte's brother Joseph as king. Bonaparte then imprisoned both Carlos and Fernando. The Spanish ruling class no longer ruled. As Marx commented: 'All the constituted authorities, military, ecclesiastic, judicial and administrative, as well as the aristocracy, exhorted the people to submit to the foreign intruder.'[5]

The cowardly attitude of the state's inept ruling class had one very positive consequence: the popular classes were free of their king and government! All over the state, local administrations were disbanded and governors, senior officials, judges etc. were attacked, sometimes killed. This did not mean that the May insurrection in Madrid and following revolts throughout the state were revolutionary in content: workers, artisans and peasantry were physically free of their ruling class, but not ideologically. Fighters covered with religious medals fought the atheist French. They were for the imprisoned Fernando VII, God and independence and against both French invasion and the French Revolution. Pierre Vilar summarised this complex situation:

> The movement is not just anti-foreigner, but prolongs the uprising of Aranjuez, expressing *internal* discontent … For some, the eighteenth century's work has to be undertaken again and France should be imitated at the same time as it is resisted. For others, the patriarchal absolutism of Fernando is the guarantee of tradition: the *fueros*, medieval economic individualism, the intimate union of religion and politics, this is what needs to be defended. In a word, 'liberal' Spain *versus* 'Carlist' Spain, 'red' Spain *versus* 'black' Spain, these now exist, together against the enemy, yet in profound contradiction.[6]

Spain's central *junta* (council) of resistance, formed in September 1808 in a buzz of manoeuvre and intrigue, was incompetent and reactionary. It put as much effort into suppressing democratic local *juntas*, reviving the Inquisition and muzzling the press, as into organising proper resistance to the invader. After the disastrous defeat of a Spanish army by the French at Ocaña on 19 November 1809, the central *junta* risked no more frontal battles. The following years saw British armies under Wellington combine with constant popular resistance and guerrilla war to defeat Bonaparte by 1814. The state's cantonal nature was reflected in ineffective central coordination: without the monarchy to hold the state together, each area organised on its own.

The French were amazed that the centre of resistance 'was nowhere and everywhere'.[7] With the failure of coordinated, statewide resistance, only the popular movement combated the invader. And resistance was principally through guerrilla warfare, organised by local *juntas* to intercept supplies and harry the French, who might have been magnificently organised, but found that: 'Thousands of enemies were on the spot, though not one could be discovered'.[8] The very word *guerrilla* that we use in English is Spanish. It means, literally, 'a little war'. Guerrilla warfare was a part of Catalan culture from the times of the *almogàvers* and then Verntallat and Pere Joan Sala in the great peasant revolts of the late fifteenth century. Guerrilla warfare was to continue in the Carlist wars later in the nineteenth century, and even after the Spanish Civil War when, in the 1940s, the *maquis* fought Franco's Civil Guard (see Chapter 11). This guerrilla tradition has often been romanticised as intrinsic to Spaniards' anarchistic, individualistic spirit. Rather, it responds to the peninsula's mountainous geography and to uneven development, that is, the failure of the state to integrate all its component areas.

I have sketched above some of the all-Iberia situation (Napoleon's invasion embraced Portugal, too), both as background and because Catalonia's resistance followed a similar pattern. To the chagrin of many Catalan nationalists today, the long struggle against Napoleon was not in the name of a free Catalonia, but to defend the Bourbon, Spain's imprisoned King Fernando VII, known as 'the Desired' and a beacon for freedom fighters in Catalonia, all across Spain and in the Americas.

The Drummer Boy

Catalonia's war was particularly tough. The French armies lived off the land as much as they could, as did the Spanish armies that came and went. From 1808 to 1814, mortality was 50 per cent higher than in the preceding five-year period. In 1809, the hardest year of the war, Catalonia saw the fewest births and the most deaths of any year from 1800 to 1817. As usual, death was due more to disease and famine than to wounds. Occupying forces regularly raided villages for food, forcing inhabitants to flee and sleep rough in the hills.[9] Ronald Fraser estimated that Catalonia lost about 75,000 lives during the war.[10] He reached this figure by adding the increased deaths during the years of the war to the startling drop in births. The total population in 1805 was about 1 million.

The rising against the invaders in Catalonia did not start in occupied Barcelona, but in smaller towns. In May and June 1808, as news came of the revolt in Madrid, local rebellions in Vilafranca, Manresa and Tortosa expelled the authorities who had accepted French occupation in order to cling onto their posts. Local mayors learned rapidly and, to avoid being kicked out or killed, placed themselves at the head of the movement.

Saragossa (capital of Aragon) had risen against the French on 24 May 1808. Four days later, the news inflamed Lleida, which revolted and sent delegates all round Catalonia. Duhesme answered this summons to rebellion by announcing that any Catalan carrying arms would be shot out of hand and that any French blood shed would result in the town where this occurred being burned to the ground. This knee-jerk reaction was reinforced by arrant over-confidence. By 1808, Napoleon seemed invincible. Invasion of Spain would easily add another second-rate country to his European empire.

The very first victory in Spain against the invader took place in Catalonia, at the Bruc pass near Igualada. As at Aranjuez, the urban poor initiated events. In Manresa, the textile industry had collapsed, due to the suspension of trade with the Americas after the destruction of the Spanish fleet at the 1805 Battle of Trafalgar and the subsequent British blockade, leaving as many as two thousand of the town's eight thousand inhabitants unemployed. In enraged response to Duhesme's ultimatum, this 'idle' populace publicly burnt all official French paper and seals. To avert further disturbance, local notables deposed the French-appointed mayor and council and set up a defence *junta*. Astutely they involved the craft guilds, representing skilled workers. It is worth citing the guilds' joint statement, to grasp the ideology of the resistance: '[to] defend the town, the Principality and the whole Kingdom [Spain] from the hostilities and violence which the Emperor may attempt to carry out. The guilds' will [is] solely to defend Religion, King [Fernando] and Country [Spain].'[11] The *sometent* (the local volunteer militia) at Manresa and Igualada, where on 4 June a similar rising in a similar context of mass unemployment took place, was placed on alert.

On 5 June, 4,000 Neapolitan conscripts under the Austrian General Schwartz and the French flag marched out of Barcelona. The *sometents* of Igualada and Manresa, in their white breeches and red bonnets, assembled at the Bruc pass with an array of alarmingly deficient ancient arms: muskets, hunting guns and wide-mouthed blunderbusses, scythes and knives. They were artisans and shopkeepers, some peasants and many unemployed textile workers, men and women, highly unsuited to fighting Europe's dominant army. Fortunately, they were led by several experienced military officers. In a confused battle, the troops of 'the ever unlucky bungler Schwartz' were at first surprised, then rallied and finally had to retreat.[12] Even against such a motley amateur force as the *sometent*, it was hard to take a pass when attacking uphill. Facing a second 'punishment' mission a week later, the *sometent* also held the Bruc pass.

The news raced round Catalonia. Resistance redoubled. On 18 June 1808, a Council of Resistance (*Junta Superior*) was formed at Lleida, supported by ten local councils. The Bishop of Lleida led this Council. As there was no organised alternative to the rotten old ruling class that the insurrectionists had removed, they had, alas!, to accept the authority of other leading members of this rotten old ruling class. The French, meanwhile, failed to take Girona: 'pursued by Cadalgues, [Duhesme] ... lost his cannon, baggage, and reputation'.[13] These Catalan successes made the previously undefeated French fear for their supply lines and withdraw to defend them.

This brief account (Ronald Fraser's is so much richer in the detail that brings history to life) shows the reactionary ideology (for God and King) of the uprisings, ideology that foreshadows the Carlism of the 1830s.[14] However, the *sometents* were also centres of agitation against the remains of feudal tithes, of antagonism towards both Spanish and Catalan authorities and of clamour to relieve hunger with work. I mentioned above that nationalist historians have been uneasy with the ideology of the resistance to Bonaparte. Scratch a bit deeper, though, and one perceives that the *sometents* were defending their land and their livelihood against a hated invader: similar, indeed, to what their fore-runners had done in 1640 and 1714, only that in 1808 the invader was the hated Bonaparte, not the hated Hapsburg or hated Bourbon.

Though there were few outbreaks of explicit Catalanism during the war, the Spanish army was generally disliked for its failure to raise sieges and for living off the land. Duhesme himself reported: 'The Catalans in general are zealous supporters of independence: their haughty character makes them see the king of Spain as a despot.'[15] Many Catalans deserted the Spanish army to join the *sometents*. Nevertheless, resistance was conducted in the name of the 'desired' Bourbon king. It was later that the story of the *Timbaler de Bruc* (*Drummer Boy of Bruc*), which every Catalan schoolchild today has had drummed into him or her, grafted Catalanist legend onto history. This local lad from Santpedor (Pep Guardiola's home village), Isidre Llussà, supposedly beat his drum with such constant ferocity throughout the defence of the Bruc pass that the sound bouncing off the surrounding mountains, including the holy mountain of Montserrat, frightened Schwartz's army into believing that the *sometents* were much more numerous than they really were.

French Sheep

As in the rest of the Spanish state, reforming liberals (usually the bour-geoisie, intellectuals and some artisans of the cities) and traditionalists (clergy, landowners and the peasants who most directly suffered the occupying army) were at loggerheads despite being allies in the same struggle. This was the moment when a group of far-sighted Catalan liberals sought to play a key role in the reconstruction of the Spanish state. They took part in the 1810 parliament in Cadiz, a trading city second in Spain only to Barcelona. This famous parliament did not represent the population as a whole, as there was no democratic franchise, but the ideas of a layer of liberal intellectuals. Their debates crystallised in the influential constitution of 1812, inspired by the French revolutionary constitution of 1791 and the North American one of 1787–1789. The Cadiz constitution included the end of absolute monarchy (though not the end of monarchy), abolition of remaining feudal privileges, division of powers, adult male suffrage, dissolution of the monasteries (though not the removal of Catholicism as the 'national' religion), annual meeting of parliament etc.: in short, the classic ideas of a bourgeois revolution. These liberals, actually and symbolically confined to Cadiz bay's *Isla (Island) de León* by the war raging throughout the peninsula, depended for protection on the British fleet. They had, in Marx's famous and disdainful phrase, 'ideas without deeds', whereas in the rest of Spain, the people at war performed 'deeds without ideas'.[16] Marx's rhetoric was exaggerated. Although the 1812 Constitution could not be implemented, it was a momentous document calling for parliamentary democracy against absolutist monarchy. Abhorred by reactionaries, it inspired liberals throughout the nineteenth century.

The Catalan bourgeoisie and its enlightened intellectuals saw an opportunity to take part in building a modern Spanish state that would support their interests. The president of the Cadiz *Cortes* was the Catalan jurist Ramon Dou. The most prominent of the Catalan deputies was the elderly economic historian Antoni de Capmany, who had supported and promoted the progressive reforms of Spain's 'enlightened despot' Carlos III in the 1770s. As member of the Commission drafting the new constitution, Capmany found himself in a fateful contradiction. The Cadiz constitution aimed to unite the state, which meant that the historic Catalan *constitucions* removed in 1714 would not be restored.

Significantly, the document did not start 'We, the people...' like the US Constitution, but preferred the French centralist formulation: 'We, the nation.' Capmany had warned early in the war:

> We must fear that the despotic plan, ... which astute Bonaparte is spreading throughout Europe, will reach Spain ... In France everyone's just French, i.e. sheep ... This unity and indivisibility, which suited the despotic rule of the Directory, then suited the still more despotic Bonaparte. What would the Spanish be, if there weren't Aragonese, Valencians, Murcians, Andalusians, Galicians, Extremadurans, Catalans, Castilians etc.? Each of these names arouses pride; from these small nations is made the mass of the great Nation.[17]

The Cadiz constitution followed the centralising model that Capmany feared, yet it would also be a modernising constitution that would abolish absolutism and foster both trade and the Industrial Revolution, whose first signs were being seen in mechanisation in Catalonia's textile industry. It would open the door to removing the dead weight on Catalan business of a state with a more backward economy. For this reason, with caution, Capmany and his fellow deputies from Catalonia were prepared to vote for the new Spanish Constitution. This was what historians have called a sort of 'dual patriotism', defending the Catalan *pàtria* (fatherland) while constructing the Spanish nation. In slightly different forms, the assertion of Catalonia as a nation within the Spanish nation would be repeated several times, notably in Prat de la Riba's proposals in 1906 and Maragall's Statute of 2006. As with later attempts, Capmany's effort would founder on not unjustified Spanish suspicion of Catalan motives: *these wealthy Catalans want to run our country*! In immediate, practical terms, the Cadiz parliament failed when Fernando VII, released from captivity, reverted to an absolutist regime in May 1814.

The Siege of Girona

The French besieged several Catalan cities during the Napoleonic invasion. They held Barcelona, but no other major Catalan town. Girona, as it dominated the supply line from France, was besieged briefly twice in 1808, Lleida and Tortosa suffered long sieges in 1810 and Tarragona succumbed after a 55-day siege ending in particularly cruel slaughter in 1811. The most famous of these was the third siege of Girona, which lasted seven months, from May to December 1809. Some accounts put the deaths of Girona's 8,000 citizens at 50 per cent, though Fraser calculates 20 per cent. In addition to the 8,000, there was a military garrison of about 9,000 soldiers.

Girona today is one of the wealthiest cities in the Spanish state but, at that time, it was a small agricultural town, much less developed than Barcelona, Reus, Manresa, Sabadell or Terrassa where industry was being born. It possessed, though, an enormous Gothic cathedral, a disproportionate number of priests (one in twelve of the population) and a huge fortress. The French army decided not to attack the city from the plain of the River Ter, its weakest point, as experience had made the French wary of fighting the Spanish in city streets (see the account of the siege of Saragossa below). General Verdier sought to subdue the fortress, called Montjuïc like the castle overlooking Barcelona, with artillery bombardment. An attempt to then take it through a breach in the walls failed, costing the French a thousand dead. Finally, the fortress fell in August after three months of shelling. This was not the end of the siege but only the end of the prologue. The garrison retreated to the town.

The head of Girona's defence, Mariano Álvarez de Castro, was a stubborn martinet and able organiser. Scornful of Barcelona's gentle capitulation at the start of the war, he was determined to write himself and his 'heroic' city into history by resisting at all costs. And this he did, at the eventual cost of countless lives, including his own. The citizens were organised into companies of 100: one of friars, one of priests, one of students, several of members of guilds, each commanded by an experienced military captain. The Santa Bárbara company consisted of '120 "young, robust and male-spirited women, without distinction of classes", as Álvarez's founding order put it'.[18] Widespread medical precautions were taken, too: in a siege, disease was more lethal than shells.

The siege continued for four months after the fall of the fortress. The French could afford to bombard and wait, as long as no Spanish army arrived to relieve the town. General Blake was tied down in Aragon and it was not till 1 September that a daring attempt to deliver food and reinforcements succeeded. Blake organised a feint attack on one side of the city. The French general St. Cyr moved his troops, led to believe that the Spanish army was attacking frontally. In torrential rain, 4,000 troops and 1,500 loaded mules then entered the city through the gap created in St. Cyr's lines. Morale in the town was boosted, though the 3,000 soldiers who stayed to reinforce the garrison ended up consuming most of the food they had brought with them. This was the only relief during the siege, apart from individuals, often relatives, slipping through the French lines from the countryside. The French stopped this by releasing guard dogs and placing string attached to bells all along the heights. On 1 November, Blake attempted to relieve the siege again, but failed and lost several hundred soldiers.

The people's valour and Álvarez's determination were shown on 19 September, when the French assaulted the town through three breaches in the walls. They were repulsed in hand-to-hand fighting, leaving some 250 of the besieged dead, but 600 besiegers. 'Behind the breaches, the defenders had prepared a second line of defence, cutting wide pits, constructing barricades and opening loopholes in houses.'[19] The intransigent resistance is, inevitably, reminiscent of Barcelona's in 1714. During the two hours of fighting that day, a witness wrote that everyone in the city remained calm, offering the little drink and food that was available to the defenders and escorting the wounded to hospital.

The end was terrible. Everyone was starving. Physical weakness affected judgement. Houses were rubble. Corpses were unburied. The streets stank of rotting bodies and excrement. The end came on 11 December. Álvarez was delirious and, against his wishes, the town and garrison agreed to capitulate. Some 3,400 ragged soldiers, out of the 9,000 of the original and reinforced garrison, were able to march out and lay down their arms. A thousand soldiers had died. Civilian casualties were higher. The night before the capitulation, several hundred people, fearful of reprisals after surrender, tried to cross the River Ter to break out of the city. Some drowned, some were shot down, some did escape. Ford says the French lost 15,000 men in the siege.[20]

Spain Lacked a Cromwell

When the war ended with Napoleon's fall in 1814, Catalonia was as devastated as it had been a hundred years earlier, after 1714. Released from captivity, Fernando VII re-entered Spain through Catalonia to a hero's welcome. Feeling strong in popular support and British backing, once in Valencia in 'grotesque and literally sickening procrastination' of the modernisation of the state,[21] Fernando decreed that the 1812 Constitution of Cadiz and its laws were null and void, 'as if such events had never occurred and were removed from time'.[22]

Napoleon's armies swept away the last vestiges of feudalism and spread the values of the bourgeois revolution throughout Europe – with the exception of Spain. It was a cruel twist of history that the very Fernando VII who, when imprisoned by Bonaparte, had been the 'desired one' of the peasants and townspeople fighting the invader was now the oppressor. He had, of course, no interest in alleviating the wretched poverty that assailed Spain after years of war, aggravated by the 1816 crop failure and terror caused by ash from the volcanic eruption in Indonesia that blotted out the sun.

It was not his subjects' hunger, but international politics that rocked Fernando VII's regime. On 1 January 1820, Colonel Rafael del Riego refused to set sail to put down the independence fighters in Spanish America and demanded that the king swear the 1812 Constitution.[23] As well as assisting the victories of Bolívar and San Martín in America that shattered Spain's transatlantic empire, the rebellion brought to power a liberal government in Spain from 1820 to 1823. In Barcelona, a huge demonstration in March 1820, supported even by workshop and factory owners, ushered in the liberal regime. These were the years when the new capitalist class and the new working class found common ground against absolutism. Pressed by mass mobilisations throughout the state, Fernando VII found it expedient to sign the Constitution.

Showing suicidal respect for Fernando VII, Riego and the liberals failed to depose, exile or execute him when they had the chance, a mistake that proved fatal for their revolution. As Shelley cried in his *Ode to Liberty*, inspired by Riego's revolt:

Oh, that the free would stamp the impious name
Of KING into the dust!

'Spain lacked a Cromwell', Joaquín Maurín summarised drily.[24]

The Holy Alliance of Russia, France, Prussia and Austria was established at the 1814–1815 Congress of Vienna immediately after the fall of Napoleon, in order to restore conservative regimes throughout Europe. This ruling class feared the Spanish liberal constitution that the French and American Revolutions had spawned. In 1823, on behalf of the Holy Alliance, France sent the army known extravagantly as the 'Hundred Thousand Sons of Saint Louis' (Invasion Seven) to assist Fernando VII. Repression and exile followed the overthrow of the liberal regime. Fernando died in 1833. The last word on Spain's last absolutist monarch can go to Karl Marx: 'Ferdinand VII, a despotic coward, a tiger with the heart of a hare, a man as greedy of authority as unfit to exercise it...'[25]

REBEL PORTRAIT: AGUSTINA OF ARAGON

Agustina Saragossa i Domènech was born in 1786, probably in Reus. Catalan though she was, she became the symbol of heroic Spanish resistance to Napoleon. Legend has it that, obsessed with military matters, she hung around barracks from a young age. In 1803, she married an artillery soldier Joan Roca. When Barcelona was captured by Napoleon's army in 1808, she fled with her son to Saragossa, while Joan was mobilised (he fought in the second defence of the Bruc pass).

When French forces reached Saragossa on 15 June 1808, they saw a city with poor defences and thought it would be easy to take. Overcoming resistance at two gates, they entered the city, only to be trapped in the deserted streets by armed volunteers suddenly stepping from every doorway to shoot them down. An elite Polish cavalry detachment galloped deep into the city but, on trying to withdraw, they were pulled from their horses near the Portillo gate by a group of women led by Casta Álvarez. Chastened, the French regrouped and started to bombard the city in a conventional siege. Agustina, along with numerous other women, supported the soldiers on the ramparts by supplying water, food and encouragement.

On 2 July, the French heavy guns breached the defences at the Portillo gate. A grenade killed various Spanish artillerymen and the French saw their advance clear. Agustina then seized a taper from a dead defender, applied it to the cannons and kept the French at bay until reinforcements arrived. The French eventually abandoned the siege on 13 August.

Agustina at once became famous for her courage and decisive action. The city's defending general Palafox saw the propaganda value of Agustina's feat: her surname was changed from Saragossa to the Spanish name for the city, Zaragoza. The woman from Catalonia turned into 'Agustina de Aragón'. She joined the army and she became

Figure 5 Monument at Fulleda (Lleida) to Agustina of
Aragon (Elena Sagristà)

the first woman soldier recorded in Spanish history, rising to become a
Lieutenant of Artillery.

She participated in the failed defence of the city against the second
French siege, in 1809, and was taken captive. She refused to swear loyalty
to the conquerors and, on the way to captivity in France, escaped. Her
son, who was with her, died of typhus. Agustina reached Seville and
was reincorporated into the army. She took part in numerous military
operations, was for a time a *guerrillera* and fought at the Battle of Vitoria
in 1813, the decisive defeat of the French in Spain.

Legends swirled around her. She became the Spanish 'Joan of Arc'.
Goya drew her as *La Artillera*, the Artillery Woman, the only named

person in his *Disasters of War* series. She is said to have met the Duke of Wellington, inventor of the boot and victor of the Peninsular War, who rewarded her with two jewel-encrusted pistols.

Byron was so impressed by her story that he vaingloriously implied he had known her in 'softer hours' and romanticised in *Child Harolde* the 'Maid of Saragossa':

> Ye who shall marvel when
> you hear her tale,
> Oh! Had you known her
> Softer hours!
> Her lover sinks – she sheds no
> ill-timed tear;
> Her chief is slain – she fills
> his fatal post;
> Her fellows flee – she checks
> their base career;
> The foe retires – she heads
> the sallying host.

Her legend and individual fame have obscured her real representativity. Agustina was not the only woman to fight the French: in Saragossa, Girona, Tarragona and numerous other sieges, women took part in the typical 'support' activities, supplying food, water and ammunition and nursing the wounded. They also took up arms like Agustina. In Saragossa itself, Casta Álvarez's squadron had slaughtered the French army's cavalry. It is here in 1808 that women – apart from queens, witches and abbesses – are first recorded in Spanish history. Agustina, daughter of peasants from Fulleda near Lleida, lit a cannon's fuse and fired her way into history.

Unlike most epic stories of military heroism, Agustina's had a happy ending. She was reunited after the war with her husband, received a military pension (though it was paid irregularly) and had another child, Carlota, who spread her mother's fame with a hagiographic biography. Agustina died in 1857 at the age of 71.

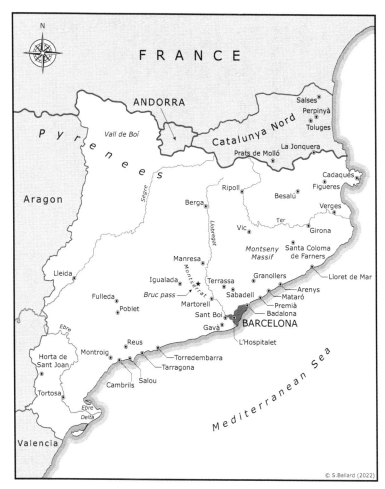

Map 2   Catalonia (map by Sebastian Ballard)

PART II

The Working Class Moves Centre Stage

Figure 6   La nena obrera (The Working Child). Painting by Joan Planella i Rodríguez (1885). Courtesy of the Museu d'Història de Catalunya (Barcelona)

6

Rose of Fire

Barcelona has taken the lead in all insurrections, against every established authority...: the low populace ... being always ready to raise the banner of revolt. A difficult language, rude manners, a distrust of strangers, and proneness to revolution, make this a disagreeable city.

Richard Ford, 1845[1]

God, King, Fatherland

Fernando VII's only child Isabel was three years old in 1833. His widow and fourth wife María Cristina became Regent. His brother Carlos refused to accept the new queen and the First Carlist War (1833–1840) broke out, another stage in the long struggle between the new and old orders. Indeed, from 1820 to 1875, there were five civil wars fought on Catalan soil, as constitutional democracy and the bourgeois revolution struggled against reaction.

The First Carlist War was occurring at the same time as the Industrial Revolution was beginning to transform Catalonia. Carlism was a mass movement based on a small peasantry that owned the land outright or through semi-permanent leasehold and had nothing obvious to gain from the liberal reforms that benefited city merchants and manufacturers. Inland and in the Pyrenees, they rallied to the pretender Carlos' banner of restored rights and traditional values. Priests dominated these rural villages, often isolated in mountain valleys. This was the same peasantry (remember, still *most* people before the rise of an industrial proletariat) that had fought Napoleon 25 years earlier with religious imagery pinned to their blouses. The POUM leader Joaquín Maurín theorised a century later that: 'The Carlist wars ... are at bottom nothing other than separatist movements deformed by the leftovers of feudalism ... Their main centres were Catalonia and the Basque Country, which are where the national question was alive.'[2]

Maurín's formulation is important because one of the lines of attack of Spanish nationalists today is that the separatist movements in the Basque Country and Catalonia are the heirs of Carlism as they are based in the same rural areas, and thus are retrograde. Maurín's formulation points to the reverse: Carlism was a 'deformed' expression of the national question, which preceded Carlism.

Just as Bonnie Prince Charlie and the Jacobite revolts in Scotland have been romanticised, so, the Carlists. Both movements wanted to turn back the clock to a mythical golden age of prosperity and peace, rejecting the bloody birth throes of capitalism. There are dozens of films and books about the Carlists (at least 20 novels, including several by Pérez Galdós, Spain's best-known nineteenth-century writer). If you read Joseph Conrad's *The Arrow of Gold* (1919), you can breathe some of this world of Carlist conspiracy. Conrad shared the romance in the ultra-conservative values of God, Fatherland and King.

In sharp juxtaposition, at the same time and sometimes barely a few dozen kilometres away from the war being waged between the believers in the divine right of kings and María Cristina's Spanish army, a proletariat was being moulded in the new factories in Barcelona and nearby cities such as coastal Mataró, inland Terrassa and Sabadell and up the Llobregat and Ter rivers, with their water-driven textile plants. The coincidence in time of Carlist Wars in the country and large factories and a proletariat forming in the cities is a particularly vivid example of the compression of history, what Trotsky would later call combined and uneven development.

A new economic model was developing in Catalonia: internally, Castilian grain and wool were exchanged for Catalan textiles, while externally the continuing export of rough brandy financed the purchase of raw cotton. The 1,424 tonnes of raw cotton imported in 1820 rose to 3,395 in 1834.[3] Bottle and cork manufacture flourished alongside the wine cellars and *aiguardent* distilleries. This rapid expansion of Catalan industry was also based on the success of Catalonia's entrepreneurs, who enriched themselves in Cuba, Puerto Rico and Santo Domingo (the Spanish colonies in the Americas that had not won independence) with slave plantations growing cotton, tobacco and sugar cane. Cotton was king: 'Whoever says industrial revolution says cotton.'[4]

Terrible Earthquakes

From 1835–1843, Catalonia's cities saw *bullangues*, tumults or riots, year after year, as capitalism was born in blood and fire. Events in the first *bullanga* in summer 1835 show some of the complexity of María Cristina's convulsive regency. Right-wing liberals, grouped in the 'Moderate' party, held the state government, but state authorities in Catalonia were fearful of revolution led by the 'Progressive' party of liberals (the industrial bourgeoisie) who wanted the implementation of the 1812 Constitution or a version of it. The insecure and impoverished mass of unemployed – drawn off the land by the prospect of factory jobs and/or driven off the land by war – were volatile. The constant possibility of revolt from below led the state authorities to often turn blind eyes to Carlist attacks on progressive liberals, seen as potential leaders of these revolts.

In July 1835, five liberal militia members were captured and tortured by a Carlist gang that included priests. This sparked off on 22 July attacks on monasteries in Reus, then the second city of Catalonia. On 25–26 July, the anti-clerical rebellion spread: sixteen priests were killed and several monasteries were set on fire in Barcelona. Such acts of mass rage were not so much about rejection of religious belief as about the oppressive role of the Church, which was not just the ideological arm of the ruling class but also the country's main landowner.

The wave of anti-clericalism extended beyond the cities. Abbot Oliba's Ripoll monastery, the Benedictine monastery at Sant Cugat and Cistercian Poblet, the largest monastic complex in Catalonia, were sacked and the tombs of the eight Counts of Barcelona buried at Poblet were vandalised. The royalist tourist Augustus Hare wrote of Poblet in 1871, 36 years later: 'An abomination of desolation ... the most utterly ruined ruin that can exist. Violence and vengeance are written on very Stone ... as if the shock of a terrible earthquake had passed over them.'[5]

August 5 saw a new focus of popular rage. General Bassa, sent by the state government to repress the anti-clerical/anti-Carlist revolts, was thrown from his official mansion's balcony in Barcelona. His corpse was then dragged through the streets and burnt alongside a statue of Fernando VII that had been smashed off its pedestal. That very night, the main tax office, police headquarters and the first mechanised factory in Barcelona, the Bonaplata works, were set on fire. This was a bitter blow to the rising bourgeoisie who wanted only peace to make money, but were squeezed between a distant and ineffective government in Madrid, a Carlist war rampaging through the countryside and a city proletariat flexing its muscles. In this sequence of events, the Carlist war linked, through this act of Luddism against the unemployment caused by war and mechanisation, with the first episodes in a proletarian class struggle against capitalism.

In response to fury at the power of the Church, not just in Catalonia but throughout the state, the monasteries were formally disentailed in 1836–1837, under the only Jewish prime minister to have governed Spain, the liberal economist Mendizábal. The outstanding Spanish politician of his times (not too difficult, perhaps: most prime ministers were generals), Mendizábal had spent his years of exile after the 1823 overthrow of the liberal triennium in England studying Adam Smith. To carry through the liberal revolution and defeat Carlism, Mendizábal saw that the Church's power had to be reduced. The dissolution of many (not all) monasteries and convents opened up an enormous amount of space in the cities. Sale of the land brought cash into the coffers of an impoverished state and benefited the wealthy who could buy the land: in Barcelona, many of the new factories in the Raval in the 1830s and 1840s were built on expropriated monastery land.[6] The famous Boqueria market and the original Liceu opera house, both on the Rambles, were constructed on Church land. Three-quarters of all Church land in Catalonia was sold from 1837 to 1845, nearly all to the rising urban bourgeoisie. In addition, to compensate the Church for lost revenue, the state agreed to pay for church schools, priests and buildings, an agreement highly beneficial to the Church that persists to this day.

Imagine the shock of the deeply religious followers of the pretender Don Carlos in the countryside. A girl child on the throne, a woman as Regent, a liberal Jew leading the government, Poblet and Ripoll desecrated, priests killed, monasteries burnt, the Church deprived of land and privileges! The known world was tottering.

Proneness to Revolution

From 1835, the new working class moves centre stage. From the burning of the Bonaplata factory until 1843, the city of Barcelona and its neighbouring industrial towns were in constant ferment. Barcelona became known as the *rosa de foc*, the rose of fire. In these stressful years of the *bullangues*, an urban proletariat was forming in overcrowded, diseased tenements and overexploited workshops and factories. Vicens Vives divided the members of this new proletariat into *operaris* and *miserables*, workers and the wretched. We can rename these as workers with jobs in the workshops and textile factories and a huge reserve army of labour, which kept wages low. There was no security: workers could in a flash tumble out of a job into indigence. Almost certainly, those who burnt Bonaplata's factory were *miserables*, while its workers stood alongside their boss to defend it.

These *miserables* were the shock troops of extremism during the decade of the liberal Revolution in Catalonia ... the semi-beggars raised the flag of disorder. They didn't know what they wanted, but there were a lot of them and they were driven by hatred for a society that rejected them.[7]

Not all urban revolts, *bullangues*, were down to the *miserables*: *operaris* took part in the *patuleia* militia and the Jamància revolt (see *Shelling the City*) alongside *miserables*. Needless to say, for the military from Madrid trying to keep law and order in this troublesome Catalonia, everyone was the *hez del pueblo* (dregs or excrement), in a notorious phrase of the late 1830s Army Head de Meer, or, as the Carlist Count de España put it: 'scoundrels ... a crowd of suspects who, pretending to beg, wander through Barcelona with blankets over their shoulders, dressed in rags'.[8]

Though all readers will recognise the dire conditions of the Industrial Revolution, it is worth concretising certain specifics of Catalonia. In 1852, a doctor Joaquim Font reported that men, women and children worked 12 or 13 hours a day in premises contaminated by dyes and without ventilation. Infected water caused four major cholera epidemics in Catalonia: in 1833, 1854, 1865 and 1885. Alcohol was a cheap, but harmful substitute for water. Living conditions were atrocious: one toilet for a whole block, entire families in one room, common illnesses such as glaucoma, typhoid and tuberculosis and outbreaks of bubonic plague. Ildefons Cerdà, the utopian socialist who planned Barcelona's city expansion – once the hated walls designed to keep inhabitants in as much as to keep enemies out came down in the 1850s – published in 1856 a study of the city's working class. A couple both working with two children could survive in poverty. Others went hungry even though they worked. Cerdà collected data on 54,272 workers in various industries (32,223 men and 22,049 women) and found they earned 8.55 rals a day on average. This figure is meaningless without Cerdà's explanation that this amount only allowed a single person to pay for food (daily: bread, sardines, some vegetables; cod on some Saturdays, rarely meat), lodging and clothes. Children meant a deficit. Unemployment meant destitution: overnight you became a *miserable* in rags. Outside Barcelona, the situation was worse. The average wage for 1,200 textile workers surveyed in Vic and Berga was 20 rals a week – less than half the Barcelona wage.

At this time, the density of population in Barcelona's old city was about 1,000 persons per hectare, one of the highest in Europe (very high density is still the case in the Raval and in the neighbouring city of L'Hospitalet). Life expectancy averaged 36 years for the rich and 23 years for the poor, if figures for children who died before the age of six are included. One in two children of the poor died before this age; one in three, of the rich. If children dying before the age of six are excluded, life expectancy was around 50.[9]

There is nothing original in these figures: they were similar throughout Europe in the Industrial Revolution. What was original were two things: the explosive relationship between Madrid and Catalonia, with the fault-lines between political centre and economic periphery starkly clear. And second, how class struggle was sharpened by particularly long hours, unhealthy conditions and low wages, more than in most of Europe as Catalan textile magnates struggled to compete with a stronger Holland and England. There is a smattering of truth in the pleading of Catalan industrialists that they *could* not increase wages. Their costs were higher than in Holland and England; their profit margins, tighter.

The new bourgeoisie had contradictory concerns. Fearing the also new power of the working class, it relied on the military authorities, controlled from Madrid, to keep the 'mob' under control. At the same time, it did not trust the military to deal with the Carlists. Though the latter had fewer than 10,000 armed fighters in Catalonia, the Spanish army of 30,000 was incapable of defeating them.

In January 1836, news that the Carlists had killed 33 liberal prisoners in the village of Sant Llorenç de Morunys inflamed workers and bourgeoisie alike. The news was false (fake news wasn't invented yesterday), but led to an assault on the Ciutadella, the hated citadel built to oversee Barcelona after 1714, and the slaughter of about 100 Carlist prisoners held there. Radical liberals, the 'petit bourgeoisie', that is, small proprietors, artisans, shopkeepers, took advantage of the protests to press for the 1812 Constitution. Manufacturers, the bourgeoisie, supported the protests at first, for they abhorred reactionary Carlism; but when riot and slaughter went shockingly too far, they switched sides and supported the military authorities in restoring order.

'Order' reached its maximum expression under the Baron de Meer, appointed Captain-General (Head) of the Spanish Army in Catalonia in 1837. All demonstrations were banned. The baron had a Republican journalist shot in Barcelona's Rambles, had a number of radicals deported, suspended City Councils and disarmed civilians. Vicens summarised: 'The Catalan bourgeoisie urged on the first local military dictator in order to re-establish order in the city and at its factories.'[10]

While the bourgeoisie and their dictator de Meer were more concerned with repressing workers, the Carlists succeeded towards the end of the 1830s in organising a parallel administration in northern Catalonia, with its own coins, postal service and, according to Fontana, university.[11] The Carlist mini-regime ended in disaster with more progressive youth confronting the obscurantist clergy. Don Carlos sent the notorious Count de España, responsible for the repression in 1820s Catalonia on behalf of Fernando VII, to Carlist-occupied Berga to heal divisions, but the elderly Count was murdered and his body thrown into the River Segre. By July 1840, the defeated, demoralised surviving Carlists had crossed into France.

Shelling the City

General Espartero met with the Queen-Regent in Barcelona and used his victory over the Carlists to oust her. From 1840 to 1843, he was the Regent. The end of the war with the ultra-rightists did not mean that class war diminished. The bourgeoisie continued to waver. Against Carlist absolutism, it was a revolutionary class. Against the workers, it welcomed de Meer's local dictatorship. In 1842, it at first sided with the workers against Espartero, before again changing sides.

The *bullanga* of 1842 was against military service, the state's refusal to allow the demolition of the city walls and Espartero's abuse of the liberal constitution. The bourgeoisie supported the protests because it was outraged at the announcement of a free-trade agreement with Britain that would damage the Catalan textile industry. By 1842, feudalism was a fading memory, but a medieval tax on produce brought from the country into Barcelona still existed and was the catalyst for the insurrection. On the afternoon of Sunday 13 November 1842, a group of workers refused to pay the tax at the Porta de l'Àngel on returning from an outing. In the argument, one of them was arrested. An immediate demonstration in the Plaça Sant Jaume demanded his release. Attacked by the army, the demonstration turned into a full-scale *bullanga*. Cobbles were torn up for barricades. A delegation requesting the release of those arrested was itself arrested. Crowds started their own demolition of the walls at the hated Citadel. Army patrols were attacked all over the city. In classic fashion, stones and furniture were hurled onto soldiers from windows and the flat rooftops. Church bells rang out all over.

The Army Head Antonio van Halen was forced to withdraw with his army to the Montjuïc fortress: memory of the deaths on the beach of Santa Coloma in 1640 and in the street of Bassa in 1835 recommended prudence to Madrid-imposed authorities. Some 165 soldiers were injured and 42 were killed in the days of rioting. This should not be seen as merely the revolt of the *hez del pueblo*, as it involved a serious attempt by the liberal authorities of Barcelona to force the central government to adopt the 1837 liberal constitution, a watered-down version of the 1812 one. In the absence of the Madrid authorities, the merchants of Barcelona and the militia formed a *junta* to run the city.

Enraged at the riots, the ejection of the army and the cries for republicanism and Catalan independence, Espartero came in person to Barcelona and threatened to shell the city from the castle of Montjuïc. Republican views were common in Spain among liberals inspired by the French Revolution. The short-lived newspaper *El Republicano* published in these days a 'Revolutionary Manifesto' calling for armed struggle, written by a pioneer of Catalan Republicanism Abdó Terrades.

Terrades was elected mayor of Figueres in 1842, Spain's very first Republican mayor, but was not permitted to take up the post, as he refused to swear loyalty to the monarchy, and was jailed. Terrades was a novelist and dramatist, and organiser of secret societies to fight for the Republic, like the *Carbonari* in Italy. Not just an intellectual, he was involved in most of the *bullangues*.

Republicanism was alive, but the threat of independence was not so explicit. Yet, it was always implicit in any refusal to follow the Madrid government's policy. A battalion engaged in knocking down the Citadel during the 1842 *bullanga* affirmed their right to recover land that had been seized 'by the force and caprice of a tyrant' in clear reference to 1714 and asserted that their action was 'because we are free, we are Catalans'.[12] The Barcelona *junta*'s 17 November declaration uttered the dreaded word: 'Independence of Catalonia from the Court until a just government is restored and Spanish industry is fairly protected.'

The *junta* running the city took fright at Espartero's threat to shell Barcelona. Various dignitaries, such as the industrialist Salvador Bonaplata (the same whose factory had been burnt in 1835), the bishop and the later-famous French consul Ferdinand de Lesseps, interceded with the Regent. On this climbdown by the respectable rebels, the *miserables* and workers then formed their own radical militia, called the *patuleia* (the gang) with its red and black banners. When the bourgeois *junta*, in order to appease Espartero, disarmed the *patuleia*, the latter with dark humour formed a *Junta de los desesperados* ('Council of those without hope'). City militias had a long tradition. What was different with the *patuleia* militia was its independence of the city authorities – quite unlike the *Coronela* of previous centuries.

Incredibly, the furious Espartero rejected all petitions. The French socialist Étienne Cabet, later founder alongside many Catalans of utopian colonies in Louisiana, witnessed the day-long shelling on 3 December 1842: 'Over three hundred buildings are in ruins. The entire quarter around the City Hall has been razed and the front wall of the City Hall has been burnt.'[13]

Repression followed the shells. The city militia was disbanded, 17 members of the *patuleia* (those without hope) were shot, all newspapers except the conservative *Diario de Barcelona* were closed, the newly legalised cotton-workers union was banned. A huge fine was imposed on the city (though this was never paid). Espartero had drowned the revolt, but he lost the popular support he had gained by defeating the Carlists. Few in Catalonia lamented his fall the following year.

Joan de Déu Prats summarised: 'Spain moved at different speeds and Barcelona was the laboratory where the country experimented with its social changes. This is why a recurring comment among certain politicians in Madrid is that Barcelona should be shelled every fifty years.'[14]

The 1843 *Jamància* revolt was the last *bullanga*, the longest lasting and a precursor of the Europe-wide rebellions of 1848. The *Jamància* lasted from September 1843 to mid-1844. In a sign of the persistent sharpness of historical memory in an oppressed nation, a revolutionary collective *En Lluita* (*In Struggle*) named its premises *La Jamància* – opened in Gràcia, in 2008.

The revolt spread throughout Catalonia and seriously worried the government that it could inspire a statewide revolution. Again, the 'progressive' liberals who wanted the implementation of María Cristina's 1837 constitution and sectors of the bourgeoisie formed alliance with their workers and the *miserables* against the army of Madrid. The Barcelona *bullanga* was finally suppressed by another general, the Catalan Joan Prim, shelling the city on various days in October and November 1843. No need to wait fifty years. Gas street lighting had been installed in Barcelona in 1842, the first city in Spain to light up its night – to see all the better its own government shelling the city two years running. Catalans could be forgiven for believing that the Spanish government thought that Catalonia was already a foreign country.

Prim was a 'moderate' liberal, now shelling the radical liberals. The defeat of the movement in Barcelona in early November 1843 did not mean the end of the *Jamància*: Prim had to reduce Sabadell, Terrassa and his native Reus one by one in the following months. Girona and Republican Figueres were still in revolt in early 1844. The *bullanga*'s defeat was the defeat of the radical liberals for a generation – until 1868 when Prim (now a 'progressive' liberal) overthrew Queen Isabel.

After the *Jamància*, the last *bullanga* of a leaderless, restless urban proletariat in formation, it was the workers' organisations that began to structure the movements of rebellion. Mutual Aid societies had been legalised in 1839, allowing the cotton-weavers union to form in 1840. Other unions followed quickly.

The disdainful Tory Richard Ford's magnificent guidebook, first published in 1845, already defined Barcelona as 'the Manchester of Catalonia, which is the Lancashire of the Peninsula'.[15] However, he thought in his usual rambunctious language that it would soon cease: 'to be a really manufacturing commercial town … [because] … sieges damage the buildings, impoverish the citizens, and encourage the worst tendencies of the savage *populacho*'.[16]

Slave Money

Ford was wrong. Despite the savage *populacho* and Madrid's hostility, commerce and industry thrived. From 1843 to 1868, the Spanish state had 28 governments. This chronic instability was due to the conflicts of the 'progressive' and 'moderate' parties, in short, the fight to impose a liberal constitution and the moderates' rejection of the limited parliamentary democracy proposed. The highly immoderate moderates were favoured by the queen and the progressives often came to power through a military intervention, a *pronunciamiento*. This contradicts any instinctive preconception of the army: in mid-nineteenth-century Spain, the army was the country's main disciplined and coherent organisation. Thus, it tended to defend constitutional rule against the caprices and corruption of Queen Isabel and the oligarchy. Prim and Espartero supported the 'progressive' part of the ruling class – despite their notorious bombardments of Catalonia. The progressive alliances of military officers, a small urban middle class and working-class democrats (this third group did the dangerous, dirty work of throwing up barricades) was inherently unstable and, on each occasion, soon disintegrated.

Despite these impediments, Catalan industry developed strongly – not only in agriculture-based products and textiles, but also in engineering. The interests of the Catalan ruling class, who wanted government controls on imports to protect their lean profit margins, inclined them to support the progressive party in Madrid, though their interests diverged sharply with those of all governments in Madrid. One can understand this divergence through the figures: Catalonia in 1868 contributed 22 per cent of the Spanish state's industry, while Madrid's contribution accounted for just 3 per cent. Spanish governments were based on the owners of large rural estates, a government bureaucracy and a military elite.

The sources of capital for the Catalan industrial revolution were internal, arising from an agricultural surplus then invested in capitalist concerns, and external, both from trade with Spanish America, where the expanding *criollo* class in the cities formed a market for Catalan products, and from slave plantations. Slavery was essential to the development of European capitalism, as Marx summarised:

Without slavery there would be no cotton, without cotton there would be no modern industry. It is slavery that has given value to the colonies, it is the colonies that have created world trade, and world trade is the necessary condition for large scale machine industry.[17]

Catalonia's capitalists benefited directly from Spain's occupation of Caribbean islands. A significant anecdote is that the first railway in the Spanish Empire was not the one usually cited, that is, the one running along the coast between Mataró and Barcelona, opened in 1848, which was the first in peninsular Spain, but the line between Güines and Havana in Cuba, opened in 1837 to carry coffee and molasses from inland plantations to the port. Both these lines were privately financed. The State did not start to finance railways till the 1850s and these all ran to and from Madrid, the spider at the heart of its web.

Palm trees, apart from a squat one called the *margalló*, are not indigenous to Catalonia. Yet you can still see, scattered throughout the land, large houses with one or a few slim, high, elegant palms. These were the sign of the successful *indià*, not Indian in the sense of Native American, but someone who had left for the Indies and returned rich. The names of several of these entrepreneurs are well known throughout Catalonia and even internationally – Gaudí's patron Eusebi Güell was the rich and cultured son of an *indià*, Joan Güell (1800–1872). The historian Montserrat Llorens wrote: 'The life of [Joan] Güell is the life of Catalan industry in the nineteenth century, the struggle for survival of an industry that many theorists had condemned to death shortly after its birth.'[18]

Many other *indians* returned to invest in the Industrial Revolution. The most well-known name is surely Facund Bacardí (1814–1886) from Sitges, founder of the white rum company. The wealthiest of all was Josep Xifré (1777–1856), who was born in Arenys, a coastal town 25 miles north of Barcelona. His father owned four trading ships, but went bust a few years after Josep's birth. Aged 20, Josep set off for Cuba and made his fortune in the tanning business. He and his brother, who had emigrated to Buenos Aires, paid off their father's debts. Josep gained a monopoly on the hides slaughtered in Havana. Restricted from trade with Europe by the Napoleonic Wars, he exported to North America not just leather, but also sugar, coffee and tobacco. He moved to New York, invested in construction (building entire streets on Manhattan Island) and married his agent's daughter, Judith Downing, in 1819.

When Xifré returned to Catalonia in the 1830s, he bought land and constructed, most famously, the *Cases d'En Xifré* (Xifré's Houses) on Barcelona's harbourside, home today to the *Set portes* restaurant. The neoclassical 'houses' are a single rectangular building occupying an entire city block with sculptures of mythical figures, famous explorers and the sources of his wealth. No modesty was desired or required of the rich *indià*: there was no shame in flaunting his success, despite its origins in slave plantations.

Not untypically, the slave-owner became a philanthropist. Xifré built a hospital in Arenys, paid for the new Barcelona fire brigade and financed numerous charities. Unlike Joan Güell and other *indians*, Xifré did not invest his money directly in industry, but in property. His father's ruin, caused by pirates capturing one ship and the English sinking another, made him cautious in business. Thus, Xifré avoided the fate of several *indians*, like Bonaplata, who had their factories attacked in the *bullangues*.[19]

Joan Güell, despite all the problems of Catalonia's industrial development (political instability, economic adversity, workers' struggle), succeeded in running a successful textiles factory and founding Spain's largest engineering plant, La Maquinista. He, Bacardí and Xifré are prime examples of dynamic, uneducated, highly intelligent entrepreneurs overcoming multiple obstacles. Of course, it did help that the money they gained in Cuba was through the export of produce from plantations worked by slaves; and that Güell's factories in Barcelona paid such low wages that he had to go into exile to avoid the fate of Sol i Padrís, the managing director of his textiles factory, killed in the 1855 General Strike.

In reality, few returned rich from the 'Indies'. Unlike Joan Güell or Josep Xifré, most Catalans who left for the Americas are not recorded in the history books. They died there of tropical fevers or returned in rags, broken in spirit and health. Lloret de Mar, port for a large hinterland, has Catalonia's main museum on the *indians* and a number of their houses. It also has a moving plaque on the waterfront to the many from Lloret who 'emigrated to America to make their fortune and had no luck'.

Unions or Death

Class struggle in Catalonia came to a head again in 1854–1855. A severe cholera epidemic assailed Catalonia in July 1854. Factories, shops, businesses closed. Those who could, fled to the countryside. To combat the microbe, wrongly believed to travel by air, bonfires fed with tar were lit at every crossroads, covering the cities with foul smoke. Workers, whether *operaris* or *miserables*, were starving. The Madrid government was, finally, persuaded to authorise, on 12 August, the demolition of Barcelona's hated walls, which relieved hunger by employing 7,000 workers. Some 6,500 people died in the epidemic in Barcelona out of a population of about 150,000. The government also ceded to workers' agitation by halting the introduction of automatised looms, the *selfactines* (a Catalanism derived from the English 'self-acting') that would destroy still more jobs than the earlier mule jennies had.

The following year, 1855, saw Spain's first General Strike, whose main slogans were for the ten-hour day and a stark *Unions or Death*. The strike was centred on Barcelona, but spread to Igualada and other Catalan towns. The catalyst was a new governor, Zapatero, who at once lifted the ban on *selfactines* and on 6 June executed union leader Josep Barceló, outrageously framed for taking part in a murder by Carlists. The only evidence against Barceló was given by a prisoner involved in the murder, who was granted immunity in exchange for his statements. To allege that trades unionists were allied with ultra-rightist Carlists sounds bizarre, but was a common feature of ruling-class propaganda at the time.

It was on the first day of the strike, 2 July, that Josep Sol i Padrís was shot dead in revenge for Barceló's legal murder. Things got even more serious for the ruling class when Zapatero ordered the city militia to fire on a workers' demonstration and the militia refused. The central government sent warships and so many troops that these had to sleep in the bullring. Repression and detentions broke the strike in nine days. Workers were imprisoned, some shot, many deported to Cuba. The same old story? No, something basic had changed. No longer were workers disorganised, rising furiously in a *bullanga* alongside the *miserables*, their impetus channelled by the liberals into support for a democratic constitution. There was still state terrorism and workers' violent responses, there was still destruction of machinery. Ideology was not socialist: the 1855 strikers still appealed to Espartero who had returned to power in Madrid as a 'progressive liberal'. Espartero! The very same regent-dictator who had shelled Barcelona in 1842. There was a change, though: 1855 was a workers' general strike. For the first time, the working class breathed the strength of collective mass action for its own demands.

Rebirth

In addition to the impoverished and threatened peasants who followed Don Carlos and to a developing industrial proletariat, a third movement comes into play in the 1830s, the Catalan *renaixença*, *rebirth* or *resurgence*, gazing back like Carlism to a romanticised past, but looking forward unlike Carlism to a modern future.

There is polemic about the birth and basis of modern Catalan nationalism. Many avow that Catalan nationalism was born in the nineteenth century in the interests of the industrial bourgeoisie. This is still echoed today by a Jacobinist left that defends the unity of Spain, at its best believing that a centralised state is most likely to introduce progressive reforms and, at its worst, suffering from unacknowledged anti-Catalan racism. Others argue that Catalan language and culture are rooted in the peasant and working classes. Though political Catalan nationalism was first given organisational form in the late nineteenth century by the industrial bourgeoisie, it was workers and peasants who, despite the repression post-1714 and its acceptance in practice by the prosperous classes (as long as property law remained untouched), had never stopped talking in Catalan.

The *renaixença* is often dated to 1833 when a Catalan clerk Aribau in Madrid wrote an ode of sentimental homesickness in Catalan. Bonaventura Aribau himself was a centralist who wrote mainly in Castilian and distinguished himself by supporting Prim's shelling of the '*tontos maleïts*', evil fools, of Barcelona's *Jamància* revolt. Nevertheless, Aribau's patriotic poem was the catalyst for a movement to recover Catalan identity. Recovering language was central to the *renaixença*: at that time, nearly all Catalans who wrote or conducted business did so in Castilian. The movement was also one of 'historical memory': to celebrate the forgotten glories of medieval Catalonia. In 1859, the medieval recitals of poetry and song known as the *Jocs florals*, Floral Games, were relaunched. Jacint Verdaguer (1845–1902) won these in 1865, causing a sensation as he arrived in traditional peasant dress and *barretina* to receive the prize. Verdaguer, who became Catalonia's national poet, combined accessible language and sophisticated literary verse. With powerful feelings for wild Pyrenean nature, he evoked the country's glorious past and its abject current state. In the 4,000-line *Canigó*, he calls on Catalans to rebuild their country. It is a romantic vision of an idealised past – feelings often mocked by Spanish nationalists. Yet, however mythologised and idealised, that past of medieval power and artistic grandeur was real.

Nationalist ideology was rife throughout Europe at this time of the construction and consolidation of nation-states. Catalan nationalists were inspired by the liberation of Spanish America in the 1820s, by the Greek independence struggle, by the developing national movement in Italy. Nationalism did not flourish only in oppressed nations. In the early nineteenth century, Spanish historians also began to rewrite their history, in this case of the *Reconquista*, the name given to the centuries-long wars to drive the Moors out of the Iberian Peninsula – from the Battle of Covadonga in Asturias in 722 to the expulsion of Boabdil from Granada in 1492. The nineteenth-century idea of the *Reconquista* became a founding myth of the creation of a united Christian Spain that expelled alien Moorish invaders and their religion.

Though secession from the Spanish state was a minority current in *renaixença* cultural circles, some fascinating quotes from the employers' organisation as early as 1836 suggest that independence was an idea expressed by participants in the *bullangues*: 'If there were independence, the capitalists would flee Catalonia with their fortunes' and 'the government's first measure would be to prohibit the sale of our manufactured goods in all the other provinces of the kingdom'.[20]

The context changes; the content remains. These two threats, of disinvestment and boycott of markets, are exactly the same as those that the Spanish ruling class wielded during the run-up to the 2017 independence referendum. The significance of the quotes is that if the employers felt the need to warn publicly against independence in the 1830s, it meant there was a significant movement from below in its favour. The conclusion is that the modern Catalan nationalist movement was born in all classes of society at a similar time. Nationalism's roots lay in growing bourgeois awareness that the state government would not prioritise the interests of Catalan industry. And its roots also lay in the understanding among intellectuals, workers and peasants alike that Madrid and its army were responsible for their oppression.

REBEL PORTRAIT: BLACK CARLOTA

Espartero, Prim and their like did not only slaughter Catalans. The Spanish army was also occupying Cuba, which had not won independence along with the rest of Latin America in the 1820s. A principal reason was that its local *criollo* ruling class feared what had happened in the neighbouring island of Santo Domingo, where slaves had overthrown the French plantation owners and founded Haiti, the first black republic in America. The Cuban plantation economy, based on slavery until 1886, was to bring enormous riches to Catalan business till Cuba's independence from Spain in 1898.

Slave resistance was constant. It took several forms: suicide, infanticide and abortion in a refusal to bring slaves into the world, risky escape by boat to Haiti and, most spectacularly and positively, direct action, which involved burning crops and the slave-owner's mansion or killing the slavers. In that same 1843 that Prim bombarded Barcelona, the most famous Cuban slave uprising of the century took place. It was led by *la negra Carlota*, Black Carlota.

On 5 November 1974, the Cuban government decided to send troops to support the MPLA (Popular Movement for the Liberation of Angola) in its fight against the South African army invading Angola before its independence from Portugal, scheduled for 11 November. The Cuban intervention was decisive in stopping Washington and Pretoria's plans to halt the decolonisation of southern Africa. Gabriel García Márquez wrote:

> On another such November 5, in 1843, a slave called Black Carlota, working on the Triunvirato plantation in the Matanzas region, had taken up her machete at the head of a slave rebellion ... It was in homage to her that the solidarity action in Angola bore her name: Operation Carlota.[21]

Of Yoruba origin, kidnapped from Africa as a child, the adult Carlota lived at the Triunvirato sugar mill. From August 1843, she and her companions were preparing a revolt. To be successful, a revolt, they knew from the bitter experience of failed attempts, had to be well organised: first, the slaves themselves had to be persuaded; and then, when the day came, everyone had to know exactly what to do against overseers with no scruples and many firearms. They contacted, mainly through drums, slaves on nearby plantations. The slave-owners thought that drumming was a religious pastime and did not realise that a skilled drummer could send messages. On 3 November, Carlota and her comrades freed a dozen slaves in a raid on the neighbouring Acana plantation, including their leader Fermina, who had been in shackles since an abortive uprising in August. At 8pm on 5 November, Carlota and her rebels managed to kill the Triunvirato plantation manager and his overseers with machetes, seize their guns and torch the main house. The uprising spread throughout Matanzas province, freeing slaves from at least five other sugar plantations, as well as coffee and cattle estates.

The rebellion was so dangerous to property relations that the USA sent a corvette to Havana in support of the island's military commander, General O'Donnell. Despite their skills in communications and guerrilla tactics, the Africans were finally defeated by the better-armed Spanish. After a year's resistance, Carlota was captured in November 1844. She was tied to horses that were whipped in opposite directions and was torn apart. Cuban history knows 1844 as the 'Year of the Whip' because of the repression. Though Carlota, Fermina and their comrades lost their lives, their courage inspired widespread slave resistance throughout the rest of the century – and the defeat of the white supremacists in Angola.

7

Free Men and Women

Neither women workers exploited in the factories nor slaves at home and in the family! For a communist and libertarian society without bosses or gentlemen, with free men and women!

Teresa Claramunt[1]

Republic

In September 1868, yet another *pronunciamiento* of General Prim forced Queen Isabel into exile. A six-year period of upheaval that climaxed in the First Spanish Republic of 1873–1874 opened. Trade unions were legalised. Strikes won wage rises. Freedom of worship was permitted. Male suffrage was extended. Barcelona's citadel was finally knocked down. Mass demonstrations protested recruitment to fight the Cuban independence movement and called for a Republic. The Federal Democratic Republican Party was legalised and became hegemonic in Catalonia: in the 1869 state election, 28 of the 37 Catalan deputies were Republicans.

Prim manoeuvred and browbeat the Spanish parliament into electing a new monarch, Amadeo from Savoy (is he the only *elected* king in history?). Amadeo arrived in January 1871, days after the assassination in Madrid snow of Prim, his main supporter. After this ill-starred start, political agitation did not let up and Amadeo resigned 25 months later, finding it impossible 'to govern so profoundly disturbed a country'. That same day, 11 February 1873, the Spanish *Cortes* proclaimed the First Republic. As Amadeo sailed back to Italy, a huge workers' demonstration on 13 February outside the Barcelona Regional Council demanded arms, social measures and a federal republic.

Language at this time often sounded pro-independence. Intransigent Republicans called for an *Estat català*, Catalan state, but in fact they were calling for a federation of states within a Spanish state. The historian

Pere Anguera explained: 'What most citizens were demanding was not independence, though some were, but political autonomy, or to put it in other words, they wanted to be Spanish without having to become Castilianized.'[2]

The early months of the Republic were electric: demonstrations and declarations pushed for a confederation of Iberian peoples, including Portugal and Gibraltar. None of these ideas were new: they had been swirling round radical debating circles for decades. The more moderate Republicans were not keen to declare the Catalan state unilaterally. They argued that they should wait for the Spanish state elections due in May 1873 and the new constitution that would follow. When these elections gave a Republican victory, popular pressure for declaring the Catalan state within a federal republic increased. Soldiers rose in Reus on 6 June. On 10 July, in the anarchist stronghold of industrial Alcoi, in the southern Catalan-speaking lands, a Committee of Public Safety, in effect a workers' government, took power. Police had fired on a demonstration during a general strike for a 20 per cent wage rise. Furious strikers burnt the houses of the factory owners and killed the Republican mayor. This sharp peak of class struggle lasted three days before government troops suppressed it. If the Paris Commune had been crushed in 1870, even less likely was the success of a workers' government isolated in a small city like Alcoi.

In Murcia, in south-east Spain, the federal state was declared in the same month of July 1873. Unlike the Catalan republicans, they did not wait for prior statewide agreement. Engels wrote a polemic on the lack of solidarity from Catalonia with the Murcia rebellion, which he blamed on Bakunin's anti-political ideas.[3] The Spanish Republic collapsed because of these divisions: each area, each 'canton', was so intent on its own rebellion that different areas of the state failed to unite in a common struggle against a centralised army.

The main tasks of the democratic revolution posed by the Spanish state's federal republicans consisted in destruction of the monarchy, a land reform to break the semi-feudal power of the landowners in Andalusia and Extremadura, implementation of a federal structure and separation of Church and State. Though the Catalans Figueras and Pi i Margall were briefly Spanish prime ministers, the Catalan Republicans did not push through this democratic revolution. The radical petit bourgeoisie is a class without the ability to follow an independent line.

Dependent in coming to power on the working-class movement, it ended by attacking its base and losing power to the monarchists, representing the army and big landowners. A strong statewide lead could have obviated the diffusion of revolutionary strength into the various cantons and the suppression of the noble but doomed Alcoi revolution and Cartagena canton.

In January 1874, General Pavia (popularly but falsely believed to have ridden his horse into parliament) overthrew the Republican government. That same month the Murcia rebellion, which had succeeded in organising its own armed forces, coinage and tax collection, was crushed with the taking of Cartagena.[4] The revolution was defeated with Pavia's coup and the fall of Cartagena. The Republic fell in December 1874 with Isabel's son Alfonso XII placed on the throne. It was the Bourbon Restoration. Unions were banned again. A new centralist constitution was approved in 1876.

Bakunin

In the expectations and chaos after the fall of the monarchy, in November 1868, a 40-year-old black-bearded Italian called Giuseppe Fanelli stepped off the train from France in Barcelona. Fanelli, who spoke little Spanish and less Catalan, was Bakunin's emissary and he is always cited as bringing anarchism to the Spanish state. The reality is less legendary: no one person carries a new ideology in his suitcase as if he/she were selling soap. The General Strike of 1855, the militancy of the Catalan urban rebellions and labour movement, the ferment of Republican, federalist ideas and prior contact with the First International since it was founded in 1864 – all these factors meant that Fanelli was casting seed on fertilised ground.

Whether due to Fanelli or not, it was anarchism rather than Marxism that became Catalonia's main revolutionary ideology. Bakunin's ideas connected with an underlying popular political culture, particularly strong in Andalusia, Valencia and Catalonia. The *bullangues* with barricades, the occupation of the streets and direct attacks on ruling-class figures, the lack of confidence in political organisations (the 28 Spanish governments from 1843 to 1868, with two squabbling ruling-class parties hostile to workers' demands, inspired no confidence in the efficacy of politics) and distrust of a central state known mainly for military repression were all more conducive to anarchism than Marxism. We should note that social-democratic gradualism held even fewer attractions than Marxism for the Catalan working class, given the brutality of the central government and the behaviour of capitalists with narrow profit margins who had often been educated on slave plantations in how best to treat workers.

In June 1870, 89 delegates met in Barcelona to found the Spanish Federation of the First International. The theses of Bakunin rather than Marx were adopted: direct action to overthrow and abolish the state and abstention from all political action, meaning no parties and no voting in elections. As Engels wrote in October 1872: 'In Spain, the International has been from the moment of its foundation a pure appendix to Bakunin's secret society.'[5]

Anarchism had little impact on the Catalonia of the 1873–1874 Republic, dominated by republican federalism, as explained above. The anarchists' apoliticism meant they did not grasp the moment: the 1873 Republic was an opportunity to finally attain the bourgeois revolution. To dream of smashing the state was an idle fantasy. The petit bourgeois Republicans were incapable of defeating the great landowners. Consolidation of the Republic needed a working class fighting for clearly defined democratic demands. Decades later, Lenin summed up:

> This was a struggle for the Republic, a democratic revolution not a socialist one ... However, the Bakuninists rejected political activity, participation in elections etc. And then they were against participating in a revolution that did not have as its aim the total emancipation of the working class.[6]

Successive attempts to form trade unions, defeated by waves of repression, date from 1840. A number of important, short-lived unions rose and fell from 1868 to 1874. One example was *Les Tres Classes del Vapor*, Three Kinds of Factory, founded in 1869 in the textile industry: it had 8,500 members and was one of 38 unions in Catalonia at the time. It was able to feed some 2,300 people for 15 weeks during a strike in the coastal town of Vilanova i la Geltrú. It succeeded, jointly with other unions, in winning the eleven-hour day in the Barcelona area. Victories were possible, but the going was tough. The workers' movement was fragmented and bosses' and state violence was fierce. At Centelles, beside the Montseny massif, two members were shot dead in a strike, as was the son of one of the factory bosses. The defeat of the revolutionary period with Pavia's coup in January 1874 and the subsequent restoration of the Bourbons led to the collapse or ghostly clandestinity of these small unions.[7]

Although its political strategy was lacking, the greatness of the anarchist movement was seen in its magnificent education of the working class, drowned by the state and employers in abysmal ignorance as well as poverty. In the late nineteenth century, in every *barri* of every Catalan town and city, *ateneus*, athenaeums, were opened, teaching literacy and everything under the sun: politics, literature, history, sciences ... This feat was recognised by the ruling class, which, whenever it could, shut down these educational centres. Schools, where they existed, were Church-dominated. The clogging repressive role of the Church, backed up by both a state and three Carlist wars, produced generations of anarchists with a visceral hatred of Catholicism. They called their children Llibertat (Freedom) or Vida (Life – name of Frederica Montseny's daughter) rather than Maria (the Virgin), Dolors (Pains) or Montserrat (Catalonia's sacred mountain). Anarchism, slandered as unthinking, bomb-throwing culture, became Catalonia's principal educational tool for the new proletariat.

Political Nationalism

The defeat of the Republic and the 1874 Restoration of the Bourbons brought years of quiescence in the workers' movement. The late 1870s saw the capitalist boom, known as Gold Fever, *La febre d'or*, also title of a famous novel by Narcís Oller, the first major novelist in Catalan since Joanot Martorell. The realist Oller pinpointed the rise of a new breed of vulgar speculators who revered money and social position.[8] Much of the Gold Fever boom was due to the phylloxera fly, which had appeared in France in 1863 and quickly destroyed its vines. Catalan wine producers danced ecstatically as their prices soared. The Madrid government imposed a 15-mile cordon along the Pyrenees where vines were to be eliminated to stop the flies' advance, but, in Robert Hughes' phrase, 'Catalan growers, stubborn and myopically provincial, ... would rather have cut off their own toes' than cut down their vines.[9] Their refusal was understandable, as *rabassaires*' rights to their land depended on the survival of their vines. In 1879, the aphid crossed the Pyrenees: a million acres of Catalan vineyards were destroyed by 1890. The wine boom was over.

The *Eixample*, Expansion, of Barcelona was distinguished by the ostentation of the wealthy's new mansions as they poured out of the confines of the Old City once the walls were knocked down in the 1850s. Frustrated by lack of political power, the Catalan magnates, like Joan Güell's son Eusebi the patron of Gaudí, poured their money into spectacular *modernista* buildings. They also began to adopt nationalist ideas. The bourgeoisie's attempt to lead Spain, seen in Capmany's commitment to the Cadiz parliament, had failed.

In 1879, the first daily paper in Catalan, *El diari català*, was founded by Valentí Almirall, theorist who pushed the bourgeoisie from regional Catalanism towards explicit nationalism. The *renaixença* had been a cultural revival, but by the end of the century was spilling over into political organisation. 1887 saw the *Lliga* (League) *de Catalunya* founded as a conservative nationalist political party and in 1889, at the Barcelona World Fair, the Catalan ruling class showed off its wealth to Spain and the world.

A founding document of nationalism, the *Bases de Manresa*, was promulgated in 1892. This draft constitution called for Catalan autonomy, a return to Catalonia's traditional counties instead of the four provinces it had been divided into in 1833 (and still is today), Catalan as the only official language and no Spanish political parties. Despite its relative mildness (no mention of independence), the document caused outrage in Madrid. The greater tension with Madrid led to such absurdities as a prohibition on talking in Catalan on the new-fangled telephone.

It was in these last years of the nineteenth century that a wave of nationalist pride led to the adoption of the *senyera* as a national flag and the composition of the national anthem *Els segadors*, quoted in Chapter 3. The bourgeoisie looked to the glorious medieval past and, simultaneously, opened itself to every international fashion and invention. The increasing confidence in Catalan identity led to wider use of the Catalan language.

Propaganda by Deed

The anarchists made themselves heard first by bombs, not mass struggle. The Catalan ruling class's showy wealth (what's the point of being rich if you can't show off?) inspired Santiago Salvador to hurl two Orsini bombs from the *galliner* (literally, hen-coop), the 'gods', the fifth floor of Barcelona's Liceu opera house, into the stalls on 7 November 1893. Twenty people were killed. Asked before his execution if he repented, Salvador replied that he was sorry that only one of the two bombs had exploded. Such was the passion and belief of a conspiratory current within anarchism who believed they could destroy the ruling class through 'propaganda by deed'. The idea was that 'direct action' (such as assassination or bombs) focused attention on injustice and inequality, ignited a spirit of revolt among workers and sowed terror among the bourgeoisie that would cause retaliatory violence climaxing in revolution.

There were 21 anarchist terror attacks in Catalonia in 1892–1893 in a spiral of attack, repression and new attack in vengeance (the same was occurring in neighbouring France). In 1893, Martínez Campos, Army Head in Catalonia, was victim of a bomb. He was only lightly injured, but his beloved horse died. A turning point came in June 1896, when a bomb hurled into Barcelona's Corpus Christi procession killed twelve workers and children. The bombing may well have been a police operation to discredit anarchists, as working-class outrage was widespread and the police then used the attack to close down anarchist *ateneus* and round up some 400 activists. Many of those arrested were avowed enemies of terrorism, like Josep Llunas who before his detention had criticised the bomb-throwers in his weekly paper *La Tramontana*:

> Authors of ... repugnant acts who try to cover up their madness or evil nature under the cloak of ideas they neither understand or practise, neither know or study, let them understand that the honourable defenders of these ideas spit in their face.[10]

Couldn't be clearer. Llunas was one of the leading anarchists of the time. He had joined the movement aged 20 in 1872. Organiser and theorist of 'the Idea', as anarchism was known, Llunas co-founded a short-lived Spanish Workers' Federation in 1881. In his view the terror caused by anarchist violence undermined attempts to build anarchist unions. This division between those who believed in propaganda by deed and those who believed in building mass unions was clear from the very start, though the dividing line between the two currents was never rigid.

Llunas was worker, anarchist republican and freethinker. He was a Catalan who actively defended his right to talk in Catalan. *La Tramontana* was a journal written in Catalan. In it, for example, Llunas featured the case of the feminist anarchist Teresa Claramunt, accused of shouting violent slogans. The policeman giving evidence at her trial had to admit he had not understood what she was shouting. Acquitted, Claramunt criticised the state for sending police to Catalonia who did not understand the language. Llunas reported on his own case in 1895 when a government representative at a public meeting demanded he speak in Spanish and he refused, to general acclaim. Llunas took advantage of the incident to attack the middle-class nationalists of the *renaixença* who had not defended him. 'Rather than Catalanists who love Catalonia, they are sectarians with a reactionary idea wanting to take Catalans back to the Middle Ages.'[11] Llunas believed with considerable reason that the bourgeois nationalists of the *Lliga* wanted to control Catalonia to maintain wage slavery in a country dominated by the Church. He defended a freethinking, internationalist workers' Catalonia.

Stories like those of Llunas and Claramunt are important because the Catalan ruling class has often preached that anarchists were not *real* Catalans, but Andalusians or Murcians who had migrated to Catalonia. This belief is in part due to bourgeois fear and racist prejudice; and, in part, to consciously misleading propaganda. It is true that several famous anarchists were indeed immigrants, such as the Liceu bomber Santiago Salvador, or later in the 1920s Durruti and Ascaso. Until the last years of the nineteenth century, however, immigration to Catalonia's factories was predominantly from the Catalan countryside and from neighbouring Valencia and Aragon. It was only in the early twentieth century that the rural impoverished began to flee the hunger of southern Spain.

There is also a view that, even if anarchists were Catalans, they were not interested in defending Catalan culture and language. For sure, anarchists like Llunas and Claramunt placed the class struggle before the national struggle, but their rejection of the bourgeois nationalism of Almirall, the *Bases de Manresa* and of the *Lliga* did not mean that they ignored national rights. The working class and peasantry had always spoken in Catalan, even if schooling and newspapers were in Spanish. For such as Josep Llunas, speaking in Catalan was absolutely normal. And it was also part of hacking off the shackles of the state.

The authorities did not wish to be subtle in differentiating between different currents of anarchism and Llunas and the other prisoners were subjected to months of torture in the Montjuïc fortress after the Corpus Christi bombing. The ruling class took advantage to undermine democratic rights with still more draconian anti-terrorism legislation. To some extent, the state attack on an entire movement backfired. Though the 400 prisoners were held incommunicado, Ferran Tarrida, one of the few prominent anarchists to be released early, reached Paris and began to publish accounts of torture that were taken up by the international press. An anecdote illustrates the success of Tarrida's campaign. In May 1897, he was invited to address a workers' rally in London's Trafalgar Square. Knowing no English, his intervention consisted in taking off his clothes. The public was horrified at his scars of torture. Questions were asked in the House of Commons. A 'Spanish Atrocities Committee' was set up in London, precursor of the massive international solidarity movements of 1936–1938 and 1975. There was such widespread protest at the 28 capital charges and confessions extracted by torture that 63 of the 87 defendants in the Montjuïc show-trial were acquitted, including Llunas and Claramunt. Eight people were condemned to death and five were executed.[12]

A few months later, on 8 August 1897, Prime Minister Cánovas, founder of the Conservative Party and architect of the 1874 Bourbon Restoration, was shot dead while on holiday at a spa by the Italian anarchist Michele Angliolillo in vengeance for these executions and for his policy of repression in Cuba. Propaganda by deed declined after the Corpus Christi bomb, but did not cease. Spanish Prime Ministers Canalejas and Eduardo Dato were assassinated in 1912 and 1921, respectively, and in 1906 Alfonso XIII and his English bride Victoria Eugenia were spattered with blood by a bomb in a bouquet of flowers tossed gently by Mateo Morral from a balcony onto their Madrid wedding procession. It killed 23 guards and spectators.

Syndicalism

Terrorism by the few shook the state as it was intended to, but most anarchists like Llunas and Claramunt were involved in educational and trade union work. It was anarcho-syndicalism that was growing during these years. This was the movement to build anarchist unions organising workers independently of any bureaucracy. The aim was a revolutionary general strike that would remove the bosses and introduce workers' management of the economy. The recession of 1898–1899 following the victory of the Cuban independence movement led to the General Strike of February 1902, demanding a nine-hour working day. The strike, the biggest yet in the Spanish state, was solid for a week throughout Catalonia. 'Violent clashes with the Civil Guard and the army, with five hundred arrested, left a hundred dead ... and the anarchist movement knocked out.'[13] The strike failed, but showed the strength of the labour movement, whose sectoral unions would come together in the CNT in 1910.

The growth of anarchism, immigration from southern Spain and the recession post-1898 led to a strange phenomenon, the rise of Alejandro Lerroux's Radical Party and his 'Young Barbarians', thugs who propagated Lerroux's ideas with knuckledusters and knobkerries. Lerroux was an incendiary orator with an anti-clerical, Republican and anti-Catalanist content. 'The working masses must attack the convents and raise nuns to the rank of mothers', was his most famous contribution to culture.[14] He could sound highly revolutionary but was lowly reactionary. His function was to distance Catalan workers from both Catalanist positions and anarchism. Known ironically as the Emperor of the Paral·lel (Barcelona's great avenue of working-class cafés and music halls, opened in 1894), Lerroux was probably financed by the state. He fled Catalonia for his native Cordoba in 1914, pursued by charges of corruption. His later career saw him Conservative prime minister from 1933–1935 and a supporter of Franco after 1936. His name has entered the Catalan language to describe any political operation to encourage Spanish nationalism in the Catalan working class.

Despite anarchism and despite Lerroux, Catalan nationalism consolidated itself with the massive election victory (44 out of 47 seats) of *Solidaritat catalana* in April 1907. This was a one-off united front of Catalan nationalist organisations formed after the military in November 1905 had trashed the offices of *Cu-cut*, a satirical magazine that had mocked the army in a cartoon. The assault was not punished. Rather, the king himself praised the military action and a law was passed that any libel against the fatherland or army would be judged by military tribunals. Catalan indignation – it was clear that the law was aimed at Catalan nationalists – led to unprecedented unity. *Solidaritat*'s programme was based on the *Bases de Manresa*, updated by Enric Prat de la Riba, the main nationalist political figure of these years, who published *La nacionalitat catalana* in 1906. This book theorised a distinction between *pàtria* (fatherland) and *estat* (the state). Prat de la Riba suggested a formula for how the state's most prosperous area could fit into that state.

Mobilisation was massive after the *Cu-cut* attack: for instance, on 20 May 1906, 100,000–200,000 people marched in Barcelona against the new law.[15] Despite the great electoral victory of *Solidaritat catalana*, success was short-lived. Dominated by the bourgeoisie, organised around the financier-politician Francesc Cambó in the *Lliga*, the coalition was wrecked by the *Setmana tràgica* (Tragic Week) of 1909. The *Cu-cut* events showed that the army would be the self-appointed guarantor of the unity of Spain and scourge of Basque and Catalan nationalism, a role it fulfilled for the rest of the century. No more nonsense of 'liberal' *pronunciamientos*.

REBEL PORTRAIT: TERESA CLARAMUNT

In her life of revolutionary struggle, Teresa Claramunt (1862–1931) defended Catalan rights against state oppression, organised workers in the textile factories and founded feminist collectives. Born in Aragon, she started work in a Sabadell factory at the age of 16. Aged 20, she was one of the leaders of the seven-week strike in Sabadell that won the ten-hour day.

In 1884, she took part in founding an anarcho-syndicalist union in Sabadell, now agitating for the eight-hour day. She then spent some years in Portugal with her first husband, escaping police persecution for her union and political militancy. Back in Catalonia, in 1889 she and other women founded the Autonomous Working Women's Association (*Societat Autònoma de Treballadores*). The Association lasted only till 1892, victim of the repression of all anarchist organisations during this decade of terror, but its brief life was of enormous importance. On its several premises, it organised free lectures and evening classes for women. It offered practical support to moneyless women. It published pamphlets and books on women's oppression and liberation. Claramunt and her companions were working-class women, fighting against double exploitation: for equal pay and conditions in the workplace, and also convinced that women had to organise independently of men, to gain the confidence to throw off the burden of religion and stop being 'slaves of male slaves', that is, domestic servants of their wage-slave husbands. In March 1896, a play of hers, *The World that is Dying and the World being Born*, was put on. The theatre was completely surrounded by the Civil Guard, fearful of the protests such a play might inspire.[16]

Regular arrest was a way of life for Claramunt. She was so badly beaten after anarchists were rounded up following the Corpus Christi bomb of 1896 that she suffered health problems for the rest of her life. Despite not being found guilty of anything in the Montjuïc trial, she was deported from the Spanish state and lived for a time in both London and Paris.

In 1898, she returned to Catalonia and became prominent as a writer as well as orator, with *La Tramuntana* and the journal of Frederica Montseny's parents, *La Revista Blanca*. She founded *El productor* in 1901 and edited *El rebelde* in 1907. As well as writing, she continued to be a front-line agitator and organiser. In the February 1902 General Strike in Sabadell, in an advanced state of pregnancy, she harangued male workers who were doubting whether to strike, striking her belly melodramatically and shouting: 'This son of mine will not be a coward like you!' She went on a speaking tour round Andalusia with her second husband in 1903, but was arrested in Ronda and sent back to Barcelona. That same year saw the publication of her influential pamphlet arguing that women's liberation had to be the work of women themselves and that lack of education was the main cause of women's dependency.

Claramunt was arrested again after the *Setmana tràgica* and expelled from Catalonia to Saragossa, where she lived until the early 1920s. She participated in the founding of the CNT in 1910, even though her health had deteriorated. She was imprisoned again for CNT agitation in the general strike of 1911. The police continued to harass her, ransacking her home after the assassination of the Cardinal of Saragossa in 1923. Despite being partly paralysed, the 'Spanish Louise Michel' could still speak on occasion and, when she did, drew huge crowds. She died on 11 April 1931 and was buried on 14 April, the very day mass demonstrations were rejoicing at the declaration of the Second Spanish Republic.

Claramunt is a shining example of anarchist culture. She was educated through collectives that fostered skills in organisation, writing and public speaking. The anarchists, though devoted to learning in the *ateneus*, were not strong on women's liberation. It was women who ran anarchist homes and, when activists, gave moral and material support to men rather than stand as equals.

Teresa Claramunt's life of struggle showed that it was perfectly possible and absolutely logical to be feminist, trades unionist, anarchist and Catalanist Republican, all at once. Her example was an inspiration to *Mujeres Libres* (Free Women), the mass anarchist women's liberation organisation of the Civil War.

8

The Mass Strike – Europe Burning

I've got a feeling we're going to catch up with the Russians. That would be beautiful, Europe burning at both ends!
Dario in Victor Serge, Birth of our Power[1]

Tragic Week

One of the most famous uprisings in Catalan history was the 1909 *Setmana tràgica* (Tragic Week), which like all explosions against oppression cast light into society's concealed contradictions.[2] In 1906, at the Conference of Algeciras, the imperial powers ceded to Spain control of northern Morocco, about one-tenth of the previously independent country, while France governed the rest. Spanish Morocco was a buffer zone to prevent France, already in control of Algeria, dominating the Mediterranean's southern coast. This was a 'gift' to the Spanish ruling class as there were valuable iron ore and phosphates to be exploited, but a poisoned gift as the country was dragged into a colonial war to defend mining interests that lasted twenty years.

> The experience did more than anything to dehumanise and brutalise the Spanish soldiers known as the Army of Africa and contribute to its messianic belief in its role as saviour of the Motherland ... this would have a murderous effect in 1936 as the Africanista officers played the central role in the coup. As Franco ... put it: 'Without Africa, I can scarcely explain myself.'[3]

Rif independence fighters attacked soldiers building a railway from mines to Melilla on 9 July 1909. Reserve troops were called up. A particular incident on 18 July highlighted class tensions. As conscripts were boarding ships in Barcelona, a number of wealthy ladies began to hand out religious medals and cigarettes. There was a riot as mothers and wives of the conscripts drove off the parasites. The men threw the medals into the sea. The women chanted 'Throw away your arms ... ¡*Que es vagin els rics!* Send the rich to Africa! ... The priests to Africa!'

Rejection of conscription was a class question, for young men with money could purchase freedom from conscription; and it was a national question, for Catalans did not see why they should fight wars on behalf of the Madrid government. The loss of life of conscripts fighting against Cuban independence forces in 1898 was still fresh in people's minds.

Tension built. A natural leader María Monje emerged to arouse the crowds. The women (Teresa Claramunt among them) forced workers, men and women, into not just a general stoppage against conscription on 26 July, but also into an insurrection, a *bullanga* as extensive as any of those of the 1830s and 1840s. *Solidaritat obrera*, the federation of anarchist unions formed in 1907 as a response to *Solidaritat catalana*, did not at first support it. Lerroux, whose speeches had contributed to extreme anti-clericalism, did not support it at all. Although central government propaganda alleged it was a separatist movement, the Catalan nationalists not only did not support the revolt, but they also called on the central government to quash it.

On 27 July, a strike committee was formed by anarchists and socialists in uneasy alliance, but rapidly events overtook this rather scant leadership. Workers decided to take over the factories, but the factory-owners anticipated them with a lockout, leaving the workers in the streets. Anarchists stormed a police station to release arrested comrades and burn police files. The government declared a state of war, which meant the army was shooting to kill, but, in a serious development for the ruling class, army recruits refused to open fire. Barricades went up (76 in Gràcia alone), trams were overturned, railway lines into Barcelona were torn up. The protests spread rapidly throughout Catalonia. In Sabadell, Granollers, Mataró and Premià, revolutionary committees proclaimed the Republic.

On 28 July, churches and monasteries were set on fire. One demented participant, inspired by Lerroux's morbid oratory, danced with the mummified corpse of a nun, inspiring even greater horror in the prosperous half of Barcelona. A military barracks was taken. More police stations were attacked. Crowds were fired on from monasteries, which led to the burning of more religious institutions.

Though the state looked for leaders among followers of Lerroux and anarchists, it was largely a leaderless uprising. The anarchist Anselmo Lorenzo wrote proudly: 'A social revolution has broken out in Barcelona and it has been started by the people. No one instigated it. No one has led it.'[4] Spontaneity and lack of leadership were no virtues, though. The revolt collapsed after a week, as troops were drafted in by ship. Some political focus had been provided by the town council of Gràcia, incorporated into Barcelona in 1897, declaring for the Republic. The cry was taken up and demonstrators packed Barcelona's Plaça Sant Jaume to urge the City Council to proclaim the Republic. The councillors did not dare to do so. Without working-class leadership that could push towards revolution, the revolt petered out, though the ruling class was so shaken by events that it paid the week's wages to its workers. Just as the *Cu-cut* incident had shown the abyss between the Spanish army and Catalan nationalists, so the *Setmana tràgica* drove a wedge between the city's working class and nationalists. It showed the true colours of Prat de la Riba and Cambó, who called on Spanish Prime Minister Maura to crush the revolt with utmost severity. To his credit, the great nationalist poet Joan Maragall pleaded with the authorities to cease repression and address the poverty, injustice and exploitation that underlay the uprising. Maragall's friend the ultra-Catholic architect Gaudí fell into depression on seeing so many churches burnt and, after several weeks prostrated in bed, redoubled his efforts to build the Sagrada Família basilica, whose *raison d'être* was to expiate the excesses of democracy and the sins of anarchism.

Anarchist commentators reject the idea that the insurrection was defeated for lack of leadership, 'myths about the limits of popular spontaneity', as Bookchin wrote.[5] They argue that the main problem was lack of support in the rest of the state. The UGT (Socialist trade union) dragged its feet and only convened a General Strike for 2 August, two days *after* the end of the insurrection. Catalonia was isolated.

When after a week apparent peace returned, some 100–150 civilians and eight policemen or soldiers had been killed and about 80 religious institutions (churches, schools, monasteries) had gone up in flames; and 1,725 people were then tried for 'armed rebellion'. Five scapegoats were executed, including the anarchist founder of progressive schools and theorist of education Francesc Ferrer i Guàrdia. Ferrer i Guàrdia was executed for his ideas and what he may have wanted to do – not for what he did.

Ferrer i Guàrdia had founded the *Escola moderna*, Modern Schools, in 1901. By 1906, the movement had 50 schools in Barcelona province and others scattered throughout the Spanish state. They were co-educational. They valued science and reason, exalted nature, included play and excluded religion. Punishments and prizes were forbidden. Ferrer also published pamphlets and books on education. Ferrer and the schools were a threat to Church monopoly of education. Instead of religious indoctrination, children were learning to think critically. It was no coincidence that the state executed this most dangerous pedagogue: after all, educating children to be critical of capitalism is more radical than burning down a church. It did not help Ferrer i Guàrdia's case that Mateo Morral, who had dropped the bomb on Alfonso XIII's wedding procession, was a former librarian at the main office of the *Escola moderna*. With Ferrer's execution, his schools were closed, though his legacy has lived on in both 1930s anarchist schools and traditional Catalan education (*l'escola catalana*), with their emphases on science, nature, no religion and no punishment.

Revolutionary Mass Strikes

The *Setmana tràgica* led to the founding of the *Confederació Nacional de Treball* (National Labour Federation – the CNT) at the end of October 1910. From its founding conference in Barcelona to its defeat in May 1937, the CNT, led by anarcho-syndicalists, was the main organisation of labour in Catalonia, Aragon, Valencia and Andalusia and was strong in the rest of the state.

The need for statewide coordination had been argued for many years. Sectoral unions often rose, only to be crushed by repression. To defeat capitalism, organisation on a wider level was essential: there was little point in winning majority support in Catalonia when troops, conditioned to treat Catalonia with suspicion, could be sent from Madrid to put down a strike or revolt.

The founding of the CNT opens a period lasting three decades when Barcelona was the centre of class struggle in Western Europe. The Spanish state, the Catalan bourgeoisie, Catalan nationalists and the working class led by the CNT struggled with each other for control of the city. It was a long, *armed* conflict, with the bosses resorting to hired gunmen, military dictatorship and, finally, full-scale civil war.

The CNT rejected both 'propaganda by deed' and parliamentary politics. Its weapon was the mass, revolutionary strike. It was extremely decentralised, both geographically and in different branches of industry. It grew rapidly, destroying the Young Barbarians' influence. Spain was neutral in the First World War, which brought big profits for exporters of both military equipment and basic goods. The prices of the latter rose, reducing working-class standards of living, as wages stagnated.

From late 1916, both the Socialist union the UGT and the CNT were thinking along the lines of a general strike to defend the standard of living. It was just about the only period that the two main union federations worked effectively together. The two unions organised a successful 24-hour stoppage on 18 December 1916, supported by wide sections of the population. This was preparatory for the indefinite general strike planned for August 1917. The international context was favourable: revolution had broken out in Russia.

The one-day strike of 18 December showed how the unions acting together could draw middle sectors of the population behind them. Just as *Solidaritat catalana* had united Catalan nationalists a decade earlier, so the two unions working in concert strengthened working-class unity in action. It was not to last: familiar divergences arose. The UGT was calling its strike 'revolutionary' because it wanted to change the government; the CNT, because it wanted to destroy capitalism. Nevertheless, the CNT and UGT both convened the August 1917 strike, of extraordinary violence even for Catalonia. For instance, in Sabadell the army used artillery to destroy the union offices coordinating the strike. After a week's street fighting, by 18 August, the government had restored 'order', leaving 71 dead and thousands arrested throughout the state.

The war boom collapsed in 1918 and factories laid off workers. A new wave of strikes hit Catalonia. Socialist revolution was a reality in Russia and was breaking out in Hungary and Germany. Lenin was one of several who saw parallels between the Spanish and Russian states. Both countries had a proletariat that was small but strategically powerful, in a predominantly agricultural country with a ruling class in permanent crisis. The native bourgeoisie was weak and foreign investment was high. Both capitalisms were geographically and economically peripheral to Europe's main economies, France, Britain and Germany. These parallels led Lenin to think that Spain was the country most likely to see Europe's second socialist revolution. Barcelona was Petrograd in waiting. Victor Serge, working in a Barcelona sweat-shop setting type in 1917, thought so too. The first fifteen chapters of *Birth of our Power* explain concretely and lyrically the build-up to a major strike, the oratory, the doubts, the preparations. The news from Russia inspires the workers. Serge draws vivid individuals, weathered in countless defeats, who 'have this tempered courage, this burning hatred, this exaltation that makes fighters of them in the pain of their daily existence', coming together into a revolutionary mass.[6] Serge, activist before writer, had the gift of showing the rank-and-file with all their potential and limitations. He takes his readers inside the revolutionary movement. There is a tragic edge, because these people full of doubt and hope are up against tough odds and know they will most likely go down to defeat. It was in Barcelona that Victor Kibalchich first signed an article Victor Serge; it was in Barcelona that the individualist anarchist of the Bonnot gang became the anarcho-Bolshevik that believed in collective struggle.

After 1917, the anarcho-syndicalists led by Salvador Seguí and Ángel Pestaña pressed hard to turn the CNT into a federation of industrial unions instead of craft and sector unions. This was the *sindicat únic*, single union, approved at the July 1918 CNT Congress in Sants. This advance, Pestaña wrote, turned 'clothing workers, laborers, [and] carpenters' into a 'phalanx of producers conscious of their rights and ready to defend them at any moment'.[7] It meant that everyone working in a workplace would be in the same union, instead of, say, the carpenters being in one and unskilled workers in another. This contributed strongly to the victory at the Canadenca power plant, where the rest of the workforce came out in solidarity with sacked office workers.

The Canadian Energy Company

The most profound strike of this period was at the Canadenca, then the biggest energy company in Europe (its three chimneys now adorn a park on the site, at the harbour end of Barcelona's Paral·lel). The spark was the dismissal of eight workers in the billing department for joining the CNT after suffering a wage cut. On 5 February 1919, the whole billing department came out – 140 people. These 140 were then sacked. The CNT called for a general strike in the sector. This started on 21 February. The strikers occupied the plant. The spark flared into a six-week stoppage. The strike covered all basic services: electricity, gas and water, all of which were owned or part-owned by the Canadian company. Barcelona was left in midwinter darkness and cold. Trams couldn't run. Factories had to close. No newspapers were printed. CNT General Secretary Salvador Seguí wrote of ruling-class terror:

> The partial power-cuts which were inconvenient at first soon became almost total ... The dark and silent nights, accompanied by violent episodes and the disturbing presence of resentful and unoccupied workers, unleashed panic in the affluent classes. Many saw signs of the insurrection that Petrograd had lived through or were reminded of the fear they had felt during what they called the *Setmana tràgica*.[8]

Army Head Milans del Bosch tried a new tactic: he recruited all the Canadenca workers into the army and ordered them back to work on 6 March. Those who refused would be dismissed and tried by military courts. Milans had serious problems with his tactic: the graphic arts union, practising 'red censorship', refused to publish his decree.

Few scabbed. Milans had 3,000 Canadenca workers arrested, which led the CNT to call a general strike throughout Catalonia. The demands had soared as the stakes were raised: freedom without charges for all those arrested, the eight-hour working day and the legalisation of all sectoral unions banned by the government. The 1885 Chicago Haymarket slogan of 'eight hours work, eight hours rest and eight hours study' became popular (no time, though, for cooking, sex or childcare). By March, 70 per cent of all Catalan workers were on strike. It is known in the history books as a 'peaceful' strike: in its 44 days just one bomb exploded and four people died, unlike the dozens of dead in 1902, 1909 or 1917. This can be attributed to workers' collective power that kept the direct-action groups in the CNT quiet and forced the government and its hooligans to rein in.

Salvador Seguí, known as *el noi del sucre* 'Sugar Boy', had risen to prominence in the 1917 strike.[9] Now he negotiated with representatives sent by the central government. Seguí didn't have it easy: many in the CNT were outraged that he should sit down to barter with the bosses and government at a time when the army had occupied the city and were tearing up any CNT card they found. In addition, he'd been let out of jail to negotiate, which increased suspicion. But Seguí prevailed. At a meeting in Les Arenes bullring, at the other end of the Paral·lel from the Canadenca power station, Seguí's prestige and oratory got the deal accepted by an assembly of 25,000 workers on 19 March. The importance of the Canadenca is that the strike was won: all arrested workers were released; the companies would readmit strikers without reprisals; the CNT was recognised; wages were raised; and strikers would be paid half the days they were out. On 3 April, the government decreed the eight-hour day.

The years 1918–1919 were also the time of the Spanish flu.[10] This pandemic, the most serious of the twentieth century, created little religious fervour in Catalonia, unlike the Black Death in the fourteenth century, though in other parts of the Spanish state religious processions calling on God to intervene contributed to mass infection. The CNT, even though the flu was particularly virulent among young workers, paid little attention to it.

The CNT's newspaper, *Solidaridad Obrera*, mentioned the flu only in passing. In one case, an account of a labor dispute in the coffin-making industry concluded that it was absurd for employers to refuse salary increases while they were doing such terrific business.[11]

Workers were used to disease and sudden death. Nevertheless, it is reasonable to think that the fear and insecurity of a pandemic contributed, in a climate of mass struggle, to militancy.

The Canadenca victory swelled the CNT to some 700,000 members, becoming in Chris Ealham's term 'the lodestar of the dispossessed'. Yet, victory quickly turned sour, for the bosses refused to implement the agreement. The Canadenca strike settled the eight-hour day in law, but not in reality. On 31 March, the murder of a local CNT secretary, Miguel Burgos, opened the period known as *pistolerisme*, gun law. The bosses' organisations, terrified of CNT power, supported the foundation of the *Sindicats Lliures* (Free Unions). This was a union of conservative workers led by a bunch of armed thugs, often coming from Carlism, who began to kill strikers and CNT leaders. In addition, the *llei de fugues* became common, whereby the police and army could shoot to kill and be exonerated because the victim was 'killed while trying to escape'. The *sometent*, the historic volunteer self-defence force, was now mobilised, not to defend Catalans as it had at the Bruc pass in 1808, but as a paramilitary force to beat up workers. The CNT responded by organising its own armed self-defence squads. The years from the end of the Canadenca strike to Primo de Rivera's coup in September 1923 made Barcelona as notorious as Al Capone's Chicago for street violence.

Murder Squads

Three main currents could be defined within the CNT. Coming out of the Canadenca strike, the anarcho-syndicalists were in the ascendancy. They had won a huge struggle and masses of workers had joined the union. The strategy of building towards a revolutionary general strike was well consolidated. However, the extreme reaction of the Catalan bourgeoisie, who accused the central government of capitulation and organised the *Sindicats Lliures*, reduced the possibilities of collective protest in street or workplace. In addition, several leading anarcho-syndicalists were killed by the bosses' gunmen. This swung the initiative within the CNT towards the second current, the purer anarchists, many of whom took up arms, not only in revenge killings against the bosses' gunmen, but also to act as bodyguards to leading militants, to guard union offices and to collect union dues. These action groups of urban guerrillas were fighting the police, army and *sometent* for control of the streets. They gave themselves some good names: *Los Desheredados* (The Disinherited), *Los Indomables* (The Uncontrollables) and *Els Fills de Puta* (The Sons of Bitches). They also resorted to bank and payroll robberies, as the repression strained CNT funds, habitually used to support families of jailed and unemployed members. It should not be assumed, though, that all 'pure' anarchists were gunmen: many were entirely peaceful and utopian, forming groups dedicated to education, Esperanto, vegetarianism or nudity.

The third group were the pro-communists, who supported the Bolshevik revolution. The CNT affiliated to the Third International in 1919. The affiliation lasted only until 1922, as it had more to do with general sympathy for revolution than any ideological agreement, but during these first years of the Russian Revolution, victorious Bolshevism was an inspiration to all revolutionary parts of the workers' movement: 'Who in Spain, even being an anarchist, was too proud to call himself a Bolshevik?' wrote CNT militant Manuel Buenacasa.[12] The

CNT's affiliation took Joaquín Maurín and Andreu Nin, later founders and leaders of the revolutionary Marxist POUM, and others to Moscow as delegates to the third Congress of the Third International in 1921.

The harassment of the CNT was extreme after the Canadenca. The *Sometent* hunted down and beat up CNT members daily. In November 1919, the bosses locked all known CNT members out of the workplaces for three months. From 1919 to 1923, there were 424 politically motivated killings in Barcelona, 40 of them bosses, 30 police and 250 union activists (mostly CNT). The *Sindicats Lliures* claimed that it lost 53 of its members to CNT murder squads (Vidal Aragonés says 42).[13] On 27 November 1920, Andreu Nin survived an attack by flinging himself to the ground in a bar while Josep Canela, with whom he was talking, was shot dead. The revolutionary lawyer Francesc Layret and Seguí himself were other prominent victims.

The murder squads killed with impunity, with the connivance of the Civil Governor Martínez Anido and his police, the central government and the bosses' organisations. The case of Bravo Portillo illustrates government policy. He was a police inspector who operated as a German spy in the First World War. He was jailed for killing an anti-German industrialist, then at once pardoned by Milans del Bosch to be put in charge of a murder squad recruited from Barcelona's police informers and crooks. They gave themselves the name *La banda negra*, the Black Band, and Bravo Portillo was nicknamed the *Angel of Death*.

Here's an example, to indicate the fear, danger and courage of trying to organise a trade union in these terrible years. On 16 July 1919, two men knocked on the door of Pau Sabater, president of the CNT's powerful textile dyers union, and asked him to step outside. Next day he turned up dead with three bullets in the Collserola hills. A man arrested for the crime said he was an informer, reporting directly to Bravo Portillo. The police investigation went no further. In September 1919, a CNT action group shot dead the *Angel of Death*.

Nationalist histories of Catalonia covering the first two decades of the twentieth century tend to focus on the struggles of conservative Catalan nationalism, closely linked to big business, to build on the *Bases de Manresa*. In the acute class struggle of these years, this nation-alism strongly supported the Spanish state in its attempts to eradicate anarchism. The Catalan nationalists' support for state governments after the *Setmana tràgica* gave them a certain space to lobby in Madrid for limited devolution in Catalonia. They took advantage, too, of the deep divisions in both the liberal and conservative parties, to persuade Madrid to permit the founding in 1914 of the *Mancomunitat de Catalunya*, Commonwealth, the first time since 1714 that there was an all-Catalonia representative body. Firmly committed to being autonomous *within* the Spanish state and with little money or powers, the *Lliga*-led *Mancomunitat* concentrated on important cultural reforms, such as consolidating the Institute for Catalan Studies, encouraging use of Catalan in the press and literature, standardising the language under the linguist Pompeu Fabra and founding institutions such as a Catalan meteorological service. The *Mancomunitat*, presided by Prat de la Riba till his early death in 1917 and then by the architect Josep Puig i Cadafalch, committed itself to giving every village a school, a road and a telephone service. Dozens of Romanesque churches, including the magnificent murals in the Pyrenean Vall de Boí, seen as evidence of Catalonia's medieval greatness, were also catalogued and protected at this time.

In 1923, Spain's Restoration system of two alternating parties in government, set up by Cánovas in 1874, finally collapsed. The Army Head in Catalonia Primo de Rivera took power in a coup with the support of Cambó's *Lliga*. By 1925, he had not only illegalised an exhausted CNT to Cambó's delight, but dissolved the *Mancomunitat* supported by Cambó. Nin summed up: 'The industrial bourgeoisie of Catalonia, despite their aspirations to devolution, shut their eyes to the Spanish-centralist, anti-Catalan character of the new government, because they saw in it a strong force capable of destroying workers' organisations and halting terrorism.'[14] Cambó – and most capitalists – would repeat this later when backing Franco. In both cases, fear of revolution was greater than any desire for national rights.

REBEL PORTRAIT: FRANCESC LAYRET

The *Sindicats Lliures*' most distinguished victim was Francesc Layret (1880–1920), a man who always walked with crutches because of a childhood illness, probably polio. He, like Josep Lluna and Teresa Claramunt a generation earlier, is an example of how there was no Chinese wall between radical Catalanist republicans and anarchists. In Layret the national and class questions intertwined in sophisticated revolutionary politics. From a comfortable family, he became a lawyer

Figure 7   Plaque at Balmes, 26, Barcelona. It reads:
Here Lived and was Murdered
FRANCESC LAYRET
Defender of the Oppressed
1880–1920
(Dámaso Martín)

for the CNT and was prominent in both the 1917 general strike and
the Canadenca victory. Despite Seguí's insistence, Layret refused
payment for his work for the CNT. He was a fierce critic of conservative
Catalanism, ardent propagandist in favour of the Bolshevik Revolution,
strong supporter of unity in action between the UGT and CNT and
co-founder in 1916 of the *Partit Republicà Català* (Catalan Republican
Party) and its paper *La lucha* (*The Struggle*), which quoted him in April

1918: 'Catalonia needs a Catalan workers' party. If it existed, I'd join it, but that party cannot be created by politicians, it has to be done by the workers themselves ... intellectuals can only join it.'[15]

Layret represents the red thread in Catalanism, running on into the BOC and POUM in the 1930s, the PSAN in the 1970s and to the CUP today. He opposed both the CNT's abstention from political action and Catalan nationalism's submission to the state government. In June 1919, he won election to the Spanish parliament in the constituency of Sabadell, defeating two right-wing candidates. He wrote:

> We will go there [to Madrid] in a spirit of unrelenting opposition. Openly revolutionary, undertaking the work of agitation that the continuing suspension of civil rights and state of war prevent us doing in the press or at meetings. That's how we will build confidence among the mass of people who have put their trust in us.[16]

On 29 November 1920, Martínez Anido ordered the mass detention of CNT activists and their deportation to Menorca. As Layret was leaving his home the next day to defend those arrested, he was shot in the face seven times by gunmen. Mercè Micó, wife of Lluís Companys, Layret's close friend from their schooldays and one of those deported, had come to fetch Layret in a car and witnessed his murder. A general strike, in rage at Layret's murder, closed down Sabadell and Barcelona the following day. Class struggle did not stop at Layret's funeral, where the huge procession was attacked by Civil Guards whose sabres even marked the coffin.

Companys won the by-election in Sabadell, replacing Layret as workers' representative. Lawyer and CUP leader Vidal Aragonés summed up the importance of the revolutionary republican Layret: '... one of the first to see national and social liberation as inseparable'.[17]

9

The Giant Awakes

*The basic concern of the [new Republican] government is to leave intact the
foundations on which the monarchy rested and to avoid being outflanked by
the masses, who naturally enough demand that the democratic revolution
is fully carried out.*

Andreu Nin[1]

When the dictatorship of Primo de Rivera fell in January 1930, the
Spanish working class was, in the words of Joaquín Maurín, 'a sleeping
giant'. The giant stretched awake during the following 15 months, with
frequent strikes to recover ground lost under the dictatorship. Most of
the ruling class saw that the monarchy, so closely aligned as it had been
with Primo, was doomed. They organised elections for 12 April 1931.

The Republic ran out of the ruling class's control from the start. Victory
in the municipal elections for Republican parties was so overwhelming
that it led to massive, joyous demonstrations throughout Spain. On 14
April, King Alfonso XIII caught the train for exile. No Marxist, yet he
grasped the situation: 'We are out of fashion,' he complained. He was
following a family tradition: his father Alfonso XII had left for exile with
his grandmother Isabel in 1868; his great-grandfather Fernando VII and
great-great grandfather Carlos IV had been exiled by Napoleon. You
had to go back to Carlos III who died in 1788 to find a Spanish monarch
who had not spent part of his life in exile. The tradition has continued:
Don Juan, Alfonso XIII's son, lived most of his life outside the Spanish
state; and his grandson Juan Carlos, king from 1975 to 2015, was born
in exile in 1938 and was forced to leave the country again in August
2020. We await the definitive moment, when Felipe VI packs his and his
daughters' bags and the whole sorry family ceases to live as parasites on
the Spanish people, to defraud the Exchequer and to steal through its
'business' operations.

The instability of the Spanish monarchy is not just anecdotal, but also reflects the weakness of the Spanish state. In 1931, it was a backward capitalist country: 45 per cent of the employed population was in agriculture; 26.5 per cent was in industry; and 28 per cent was in services. Industry was concentrated in textiles, engineering, construction and mining in and around Barcelona, Bilbao, Valencia and Asturias. In Catalonia, textiles were still the main industry, with about 150,000 workers, half of them women.

A capitalist mode of production had still not broken up the huge unproductive estates in southern Spain. The starving peasants of Las Hurdes in Extremadura, seen in Luis Buñuel's searing 1933 film *Tierra sin pan* (*Land Without Bread*), were only an extreme example of an impoverished, illiterate peasantry and landless labourers in Extremadura and Andalusia.

The relative weakness of the Spanish bourgeoisie was mirrored in the economic and ideological clout of the Church and in the Army tradition of intervening in politics. Spain was a capitalist country, but a backward one in comparison with its neighbours. There had been no completed bourgeois revolution, with spectacular agreed dates, as occurred in France and Britain. By the 1920s, however, Spain's literacy rates were close to Italy's and France's and industrialisation was growing apace. And Catalonia, as of course its Nationalists always argue, was another country. It had a stronger bourgeoisie, an organised working class and a layer of farmers who owned their land and were relatively prosperous.

The victor of the 12 April elections in Catalonia was a party only formed the previous month, *Esquerra Republicana de Catalunya* (ERC), Republican Left of Catalonia, bringing together various left nationalist groups. 'A mushroom growth, it was a party of petty bourgeois and intellectuals with the support of the *rabassaires* whose threatened tenancies it defended. It was also the party of the national hero Macià and his lieutenant, Companys.'[2]

The support of the vine-growing *rabassaires* for the left is important in today's independence polemics. Spanish centralists often accuse Catalan historians and politicians of 'airbrushing' the traditionalist, Catholic, reactionary countryside 'out of today's nationalist historiography, bent on equating the Catalans with the progressive and the modern'.[3] They remember the Carlists, but forget the *rabassaires*.

ERC's prestige stemmed from the events of Prats de Molló, a border town in French Catalonia. In 1922, inspired by Woodrow Wilson's support post-First World War for the autonomy of small nations and particularly enthused by Sinn Fein's success in Ireland, Francesc Macià, an ex-colonel in the Spanish army, co-founded an organisation called *Estat Català* (Catalan State) to fight for Catalonia's independence. Macià had resigned from the army in 1906 in protest at the military attack on *Cu-cut*. He belonged to the activist wing of Catalan nationalism, but with a militarist outlook. At the time of the 1917 general strike, he argued for arming the people, but he lacked Layret and Seguí's belief in working-class mass action.[4] In 1926, *Estat Català* planned an invasion of Spanish Catalonia from Prats de Molló, with the idea of taking the town of Olot and proclaiming the Catalan Republic. Luckily for their physical integrity, the majority (111 people) were arrested before crossing the frontier. One of the leaders of the armed groups was Peppino Garibaldi, grandson of the hero of Italy's unification. It turned out that Garibaldi was no paladin of national liberation, but a double agent. Mussolini was informed of Macià's every move and in turn informed the French authorities and the Spanish dictator. At his Paris trial, Macià turned the farce of the failed invasion into a propaganda triumph. *La cause catalane* was headlines across Europe. Macià was able to read a long speech in court. The conspirators, he said, represented 'the survival of the spirit of oppressed Catalonia'. The participants were found guilty, but sentenced to exile from France and such brief prison terms (two months for Macià and a 100 franc fine for possessing a firearm without a licence) that they were released at once. Seen as a quixotic idealist, the elderly Macià (he was 67 in 1926) had become enormously popular in France.

Five years later, the failed insurrectionist Macià was President of the *Generalitat* by electoral means. On 14 April 1931, Lluís Companys announced from Barcelona Town Hall Catalonia's independence with Macià as President. The politicians then crossed the square and Macià proclaimed from the balcony of what was then the *Diputació* (Regional Council) headquarters and at once became again (as it is now) the *Palau de la Generalitat* the foundation of 'the Catalan state, which we will cordially seek to integrate into the Federation of Iberian republics'.[5] It was, wrote Andreu Nin, who had returned to Catalonia from nine years in Russia in September 1930, 'the most revolutionary act that occurred on April 14'.[6]

That very afternoon, the *Sindicat Lliure* was closed down. Political prisoners were released from the men's prison. The building was set on fire and in the chaos, nearly all the prisoners escaped. A group of armed women and men marched at 10pm on the women's prison on *carrer* Santa Amàlia, took it by force, destroyed the records and chapel and released the prisoners. The nuns who ran the jail were unhurt. According to Josep Fontana, one prisoner hid in the nuns' rooms because she did not wish to be released.[7] Some police stations and right-wing newspapers were attacked, but incidents were relatively few. The Catalan Republic was born in peace and hope.

The central government took fright at Catalonia's secession and sent a delegation by plane to Barcelona. Macià and the parties integrating ERC backed down amicably and accepted a statute of autonomy to be worked out within a federal Spain. The reason given for retreating from the Unilateral Declaration of Independence was to abide by the August 1930 Pact of San Sebastián, which Macià had signed along with Spanish Republicans and Socialists. At the time, the step backward seemed unimportant: they could sort out the details of a federal Spanish state later. In the ten days after 16 April 1931, a group sent to a hotel in Núria in the Pyrenees composed the Catalan Statute. Independentists' enthusiasm soon dribbled away, as this draft approved in Catalonia was then not debated in the divided Spanish parliament until summer 1932, by which time a head of steam had been built up throughout Spain against Catalan rights and federalism. The statute that Spanish President Azaña finally pushed through in late 1932 was a watered-down version: it contained only 18 of the Núria Statute's 51 articles. Catalonia was to be an autonomous region, and not a state within an Iberian federation, as had been posited in 1873 and as the Núria Statute had proposed.

Macià and ERC missed their opportunity on 16 April. The independence of Catalonia had lasted two days (it had lasted eight under Pau Claris in 1641). The founding member of both Spain's Communist Party and its Left Opposition (ICE) Juan Andrade (1898–1981) explained:

There is only one way a revolutionary movement, which comes to power through elections, and which is being pushed forward by the masses, can consolidate itself: by taking radical measures *immediately*. This it failed to do. The bourgeois forces were demoralised; measures to reform the basic structures of the state, the army, the land could have been taken straight away. Failure to do so allowed the bourgeoisie to reorganize, to begin the counter-attack...[8]

The lost opportunity would return to haunt the Catalan Government in 1934, when it was imprisoned and Catalonia's autonomy was suppressed. Nevertheless, 14 April opened a pre-revolutionary period in Spain leading to the full-scale revolution that would erupt in Catalonia on 19 July 1936 in response to Franco's uprising.

The CNT

The main forces representing the working class in 1931 were the Socialist UGT, whose base consisted of the more skilled and conservative workers, and the CNT, overwhelmingly the majority union in Catalonia. At its 1931 plenum, the CNT claimed 291,150 members in Catalonia; in 1933, 208,821; and in 1936, 134,381.[9] Like all organisations, the CNT exaggerated its membership figures. In fact, dues-paying membership was very low. However, the CNT's influence was much greater than its numerical membership. The CNT was quite different from the bureaucratic UGT, which had lost credibility because of its support for Primo de Rivera. The highly moral anarcho-syndicalist CNT, banned under the dictatorship, had no paid officials, no strike fund. It was the revolutionary mass union of the Catalan and Spanish working class.

The CNT was divided between its more moderate leadership and the more 'purist' and radical Federation of Iberian Anarchists (FAI) founded in 1927. Both the 'moderates' and the FAI, however heroic and committed, were grievously anti-political. Of this contradiction, for which the Catalan working class paid dearly, Maurín wrote severely in 1935:

> Anarchism, despite appearances, is not really revolutionary because it sets unattainable objectives ... Our anarchists have received from Bakuninism the narrow ideas of a sect and that it can reach anarchy in brief moments, jumping over historical stages as if in a fairy tale.[10]

For Maurín, the FAI were dogmatic, putschist and had no strategy for winning the masses of the CNT and outside it to revolutionary action. He polemicised: 'Socialists and Communists are enemies, because they are not anarchists; peasants struggling to gain land are bourgeois ... the [Catalan] national liberation movement is reactionary ... Sectarianism leads anarchists to not wanting to see reality.'[11]

Maurín's strictures are largely borne out by the accounts below: of anarchists holding back the 1931 strike wave; repeatedly calling mass insurrectionary strikes without proper preparation; and refusing to take part in joint action with other forces, as in October 1934 in Catalonia. These disastrous policies contributed to its falling membership and influence, only restored by the outbreak of Civil War in 1936.

July to September 1931 saw an explosion of labour struggles in Catalonia, even broader than at the end of the First World War. In August alone, there were 41 strikes and 40,000 engineering workers were out for a month.[12] These strikes are often cited as evidence of how anarchist extremism made life impossible for the new government of Republican reformists. In fact, some strikes were often supported by ERC and bourgeois Republicans. In the dispute with the US-owned *Telefónica* company, the workers' demands were little different from the demands of the Republican–Socialist alliance before 14 April. It was the first time ever that workers had a Government that was more on their side than on the bosses'. Logically, in a situation of low pay, the growth of unemployment (Spain was not exempt from the international crash of 1929) and rent rises, workers were out to recover ground lost during the dictatorship.

Despite the initial enthusiasm for the Republic, Government reactions to the strike wave brought rapid disenchantment. Long-time Socialist bureaucrat Largo Caballero was Minister of Labour and used his position to favour the UGT. The CNT's assembly-based decision-taking and direct action clashed with Socialist gradualism, with all its apparatus of arbitration tribunals. *Crisol*, a left-Republican paper in Madrid, compared the CNT with the Nazis. The Socialist press said the CNT were merely 'gunmen' (*pistoleros*), this with quite some cynicism since some of the gunmen of the illegalised *Sindicat Lliure* had found refuge in the UGT. When in June 1931 CNT members protested against dismissals at a box factory near Barcelona docks, the UGT members who had replaced the sacked CNT members opened fire on the demonstration, wounding 13 people. They could be *pistoleros* too.

The CNT leadership, in fact, tried to contain this strike wave. With their customary wariness of economic strikes, they adopted an approach of wait and see what happens with the new Republic. Instead of attacking the economic system and political strategy of the Republican Government, they attacked individuals such as Largo Caballero as 'immoral' and 'saboteurs'.

The CNT postponed textile and construction strikes in May, arguing that the proletariat should reserve its strength for revolution and not provoke state repression. Ealham quotes the CNT's paper *Solidaridad Obrera* as saying that the union was being 'overrun by the masses'.[13] It was not just the moderates who sought to hold back economic strikes. FAI militants did so in the CNT's construction union, where they had a majority, because they were awaiting the right moment for a revolutionary general strike.

Despite the best efforts of the CNT leadership, the strike wave expanded: the telephone company, docks, engineering, textiles and transport all saw mass strikes in the first months of the Republic.[14] CNT pickets did not play about. Scabs were beaten up. Direct action, backed by widespread support in working-class neighbourhoods, fruit of two decades of education, mutual support and propaganda, defeated many bosses. In a particularly violent barbers' strike, barbershops were smashed up and the strikers won not just a wage rise but also recognition of the union and its job pool, that is, any vacancies were to be filled from the CNT's list of unemployed members. Recognition of the CNT's right to fill vacancies was an important element of workers' control, creating loyalty to the union and neutralising scabs.

At the same time as the workplace strikes, a massive rent strike started in July, with demands for 40 per cent reduction in rents and for the unemployed to live rent-free. By August, there were 100,000 on rent strike in Barcelona and surrounding towns. Largo Caballero called the strike 'absurd'. Repression was fierce and, by December, the strike was broken. Nevertheless, rent strikers often reached agreement for reduced rent with landlords, who preferred less rent to none at all.

The central government used methods against the strikers that differed little or not at all from those of previous regimes. In a few short months, a serious breach opened up between the Republican Government and the Catalan working class. Strike leaflets and posters were illegalised. A group of children were arrested for heckling a *Telefónica* scab in Barcelona's Rambles. On 23 July, two Assault Guards were seriously injured when trying to detain activists at the offices in Clot of the CNT's Textile

Union. On the same day, six anarchists were killed by police in a battle at the Raval office of the Construction Union. The agreement giving victory to the engineering union at the end of August was torn up by the bosses in October, as the tide of strikes began to ebb due to repression and exhaustion. Such was the pre-revolutionary atmosphere that even the doyen of the Catalan conservative press *La Vanguardia* criticised the bosses for threatening 'civil peace' and reported that the majority of Barcelona's citizens had no respect for the police.[15]

There was another reason for the breakdown of working-class trust in Macià and ERC: racism against immigrants from southern Spain, especially from Murcia. The economic slump of the early 1930s led to large numbers of unemployed workers in the Barcelona area. Sections of ERC, in the *Generalitat* and the City Council, responded by demon-ising them as the sources of crime and disease. People were begging and sleeping in the street. Migration led to disorder. This 'invasion' had one tragi-comic solution. A train was hired by the *Generalitat* to return unemployed migrants from Barcelona's Sants station to Murcia. Free drink and food for the journey was provided. The train filled with volunteers. At La Bordeta, just outside Barcelona, the train stopped, very possibly sabotaged. When it got going again, the passengers had disappeared back into the city with their free meals. The shameful behaviour of the 'left' nationalists echoed what had happened 100 years before, when the Baron de Meer had called the *miserables*, the jobless poor fleeing famine, society's 'dregs'. The CNT had no such prejudice. It opened its ranks to all workers, Catalonia-born and immigrant, employed and unemployed.[16]

There were two main consequences of the 1931 strike wave. One was lasting distrust among workers of the Socialist–Republican government in Madrid, which would lead to mass CNT abstention in the 1933 elections ('Against elections, social revolution', was their notoriously abstract slogan at the time), which assisted the right winning power. The other consequence was that the CNT shifted again towards being a union organised from the bottom up and moderate leaders lost influence and/or were replaced.

As explained in Chapter 8, the CNT's strength was much broader than in the workplaces. It was deeply rooted in working-class neigh-bourhoods in the main cities, where the police did not dare to enter except in large groups, where families were defended from eviction for not paying rent, where *ateneus* gave classes in everything imaginable and food was distributed free to the unemployed. This educational and self-defence tradition did not stop because the Republic had arrived. Spain's 1931–1933 Republican government was engaged in reducing Church power over education, introducing agrarian reform, approving divorce and votes for women over 23, and trying to modernise the army from the top down. Fatally, these often well-meaning liberal reformers had no grasp of working-class urgency for bread and jobs NOW, not in an undefined future. For the FAI, eyes fixed on revolution, parliament was a 'brothel'.[17]

Revolutionary Gymnastics

The principal division in the union was clarified on 31 August 1931, when thirty leading CNT members signed a manifesto. These *treintistas*, '*thirty-ists*', were members of the more moderate leadership (though not only) and hit back against militants of the base and the FAI who were arguing for immediate insurrection. With reason, the *treintistas* believed that immediate revolution was not on the agenda. In the strike wave, the working class was fighting to defend its interests and not for revolution. A longer period of education and propaganda was required before the working class was ready to sweep away the bosses. 'We want a revolution that springs from the people, not a revolution that a few individuals can make,' the *treintistas* argued.[18] The FAI and militant sectors involved in strike organisation attacked the *treintistas* as reformists and traitors to anarchism. At the April 1932 Catalan congress at Sabadell, following the *treintistas*' rejection of 'revolutionary gymnastics' and the removal of their leader Ángel Pestaña as CNT national secretary, the *treintistas* walked out. They were then expelled, which lost the CNT statewide some 70,000 members, though most rejoined at the outbreak of war.

Nevertheless, the more radical sectors did not disagree that the working class was not ripe for revolution. The disagreement centred on how to educate the class. FAI leader Ricardo Sanz said:

After seven years of clandestinity, the members generally did not know where they were going or what they wanted. In such a situation, what was needed was practice, exercise, revolutionary gymnastics. We were the motor or spark that could get these gymnastics going…[19]

In January 1932, the 'revolutionary gymnastics' took the form of an attempted insurrection in the small Catalan coalfield round Fígols. Fed by tough conditions in the mines, the strike spread rapidly to neighbouring towns such as Berga and Manresa, but failed to spark off a revolutionary uprising. The FAI did not seem too disturbed by failure: it saw such an insurrection as part of the learning process that would educate the working class in the need for revolution. However, though such events hardened conscious militants, they lost popular support.

In January 1933, a further insurrectionary adventure in Catalonia failed, but the slaughter of 22 anarchist-led peasants who rose up in the Andalusian village of Casas Viejas rocked the Azaña coalition. Spring 1933 saw as broad a strike wave as in summer 1931. In April in Catalonia, Cardona's potash miners and Barcelona's dockers and building workers were out. These strikes combined with a huge campaign for the release of the CNT's 9,000 prisoners throughout the state. One should add that some 400 workers had been killed and 2,000 wounded in clashes with the army and police in the first two years of the Republic. This fed into an active 'No Vote' campaign in the November elections. Durruti asked the CNT's giant anti-election rally in Barcelona's bullring on 5 November: 'Workers, you who voted yesterday without considering the consequences, if they told you the Republic was going to jail 9,000 working men, would you have voted?'[20]

By autumn 1933, after just 30 months the Republic was worn out. Prime Minister Azaña had forced through the watered-down Catalan Statute, but had failed in agrarian reform. The attempted reform had only inflamed rich landowners while at the same time dashing the hopes of landless labourers. Azaña's coalition of liberals and socialists, searching for reforms while maintaining class peace, was enormously appealing to the middle sectors of society, but these middle sectors were shrinking amidst political radicalisation. Azaña's policies were squeezed into failure as class war was placed by both left and right at the centre of the political agenda.

Workers Alliance

In the Spanish elections of 19 November 1933, the left-Republican vote collapsed. Lerroux, the one-time 'Emperor of the Parallel', the former radical republican leading workers away from both anarchism and

Catalanism, came to power as leader of a right-wing coalition that set about reversing all the progressive legislation of the previous two years. In the November 1933 elections Gil Robles' Catholic-monarchist CEDA echoed Hitler's style and language: 'Its election posters appealed to voters to "save Spain from Marxists, Freemasons, Separatists and Jews" and its press reminded voters that Hitler had come to power legally.'[21]

The anarchists responded by further revolutionary gymnastics, an uprising on 8 December 1933. Some leading FAI militants, such as Garcia Oliver, opposed it, arguing lack of preparation and that repression had taken its toll on the movement. In four days, the insurrection was crushed after heavy street fighting in Aragon. Other areas supported the uprising, but did not themselves rise up. The failed insurrection weakened the CNT and FAI, though did not break their fighting spirit. Andy Durgan summarises the consequences of these 'abortive uprisings',

> ...called by relatively few activists without consulting the membership in any serious way. The result ... was hundreds of casualties and arrests, the closing down of many union centres, a steep decline in dues-paying members and exacerbation of existing divisions in the workers' movement.[22]

The failure of the 1931–1933 reformist government, combined with the rise of Hitler, pushed the Socialists leftwards. Gil Robles was seen as a Spanish version of the Austrian chancellor Dollfuss, who shelled workers' flats when crushing red Vienna in February 1934.

These factors and the clear lack of preparation in the disastrous Aragon uprising led to the formation of the *Alianza obrera*, the Workers Alliance, an attempt initiated by the BOC and supported by the Left Socialists to unite the working class in an extra-parliamentary front against fascism. Characteristically, the CNT kept its distance: only in Asturias did they join the Alliance. When the CEDA entered the Government of Lerroux's Radicals in October 1934, the Alliance was forced to react. The General Strike called by the Socialists went off half-cock: Largo Caballero's revolutionary rhetoric was no substitute for organisation on the ground. In Asturias, however, the Workers' Alliance took over the region, and began to organise the economy. For two weeks they held off the army, led by Franco. Hundreds of workers were killed in fighting, tortured and/or executed summarily. The crushing of the Asturian uprising was a decisive step towards Civil War: the left saw in the operations of Franco's Army of Africa what they could expect if revolution did not succeed.

In Catalonia, the *Generalitat*, under Lluís Companys (Macià had died on Christmas Day 1933), had several conflicts with the central government. The key conflict was that the *Generalitat* had passed legislation giving *rabassaires* ownership of land if they had cultivated it for 15 years. This was a crucial question, as the new vines introduced after the phylloxera epidemic of the 1880s had a much shorter life than the previous ones. *Rabassaires'* tenancy agreements depended on the life of the vines. Fifty years, with the accepted idea of planting shoots from the old vine that made the life of the vine almost infinite, was very different from the 15-year leases the landlords wanted.

ERC had a majority in the *Unió de Rabassaires*, the vine-growing tenant farmers' union founded in 1922 and strong in the provinces of Barcelona and Tarragona, though during the Republic the BOC was to challenge ERC's control. The Lerroux government, in alliance with Catalan landowners, opposed the Catalan legislation. Under pressure from the *rabassaires* on the left and from the paramilitary separatists of *Estat Català* led by Josep Dencàs on the right, and having to respond to the Workers Alliance's General Strike, Companys reluctantly declared 'a Catalan state within the Spanish Republic' on 6 October. The CNT did not support this 'repetition as farce of Macià's gesture in April 1931'.[23] The BOC and other forces attempted to develop an insurrectional General Strike in some areas of Catalonia, but without the participation of the CNT or practical support of the *Generalitat*, it failed. This disaster led to the imprisonment of the entire *Generalitat* government, the suspension of Catalan Autonomy, press censorship and eviction of hundreds of *rabassaires*.

After the defeat of October 1934, the pressure of the working class for unity led to the formation of the Popular Front, known in Catalonia as the *Front d'Esquerres*, Left Front, for the elections of February 1936. The BOC and the smallish group of Trotskyists of *Izquierda Comunista* (Communist Left) were also impelled by these events to overcome harsh polemics and move towards revolutionary unification. The POUM would be born at a meeting in the Barcelona suburb of Horta in September 1935.

The Popular Front won the elections of February 1936 on a formal programme little different from that of 1931. The context was very different, though: years of frustrated reform had disappointed and radicalised most sections of the workers' movement; the threat of fascism was much more real; few thought that the right would accept any new attempt to implement the reforms introduced in 1931–1933. This was the case: the military were plotting for a coup. Calvo Sotelo, who had been Primo de Rivera's finance minister and led the monarchist *Renovación española* in the state parliament, 'openly declared himself a fascist and called on the army to "deal furiously" with the "enemies of Spain"'.[24]

In the February 1936 elections, the *Front d'Esquerres*, led by ERC, won 59 per cent of the votes in Catalonia, against 41 per cent for Cambó's *Front d'Ordre* (Front for Order), a higher proportion for the left than in Spain as a whole, where the Popular Front won narrowly (48 per cent against 46.5 per cent). The openly Spanish-nationalist right wing, whether the CEDA, *Renovación Española* or the *Falange* of José Antonio, the dictator Primo de Rivera's son, had minimal support in Catalonia, whose political map was quite different from the rest of the state's (as it is today). Immediately following the elections, the 3,000 Catalan prisoners detained in October 1934 were released. Among them, Companys (who had been sentenced to 30 years for 'military rebellion') and the *Generalitat* government returned in triumph, with the Catalan Autonomy Statute restored. The only exception was Josep Dencàs of *Estat Català*, who had aspired to be the Catalan Mussolini and fled into Roman exile in October 1934.

After February 1936, ERC followed a moderate line, supporting the Spanish Popular Front government in order to avert the threat of military rebellion. The Catalan parliament was placid in comparison with the incendiary rhetoric of the Spanish *Cortes*. Catalonia seemed an oasis, but this was misleading, because the CNT's strength was not reflected in the parliament. Madrid in these months, from February to July, suffered many more street clashes and murders, mainly provoked and committed by the far right. The CNT had reoriented from ultra-left insurrectionism to a line more in favour of working-class unity. In this tense calm, both the CNT and the POUM were preparing for extra-parliamentary resistance to the coming *coup d'état*.

REBEL PORTRAIT: BUENAVENTURA DURRUTI

Buenaventura Durruti was bank-robber, trade-union leader, orator and natural leader of the masses. Incorruptible revolutionary, alongside his intimate friend Francisco Ascaso, he became a romantic hero, both at the time and in later generations.

Durruti was born in León in June 1896. One of a numerous family, he wrote in 1927 to his sister Rosa: 'From my most tender childhood, the first I saw around me was suffering, not only of our family but also of our neighbours. Intuitively, I was already a rebel. I think that my destiny was decided then.'[25]

Aged 14, he left school to become an apprentice mechanic in the workshop of a socialist. He joined the UGT in 1913, but was rapidly disappointed with its gradualism. His first strike was in solidarity with miners. The Civil Guard came looking for him and he fled the city. He found a job on the railways, where he was active in the General Strike of 1917 and was expelled from the UGT. From December 1917 to January 1919, he stayed in France to avoid military service. He returned to a job in La Felguera, a major industrial centre in Asturias, and joined the CNT. Arrested for desertion from the army, he escaped and fled again to France.

In 1920, he was drawn to Barcelona like many anarchists from around the state because of its revolutionary activity. In 1922, he founded the group *Los Solidarios* with Garcia Oliver, Ascaso and Ricardo Sanz. They were a group of young men (Durruti was among the oldest) with long experience of poverty, struggle and unstable jobs. Their ideology was against ideology and for action. 'As self-styled "avengers of the people" *Los Solidarios* prioritised armed struggle above all, believing that freedom had to be fought for, gun in hand.'[26]

They raised funds for the CNT by robbing the Bank of Spain in Gijón. In response to the murders of Salvador Seguí and other anarchist leaders, *Los Solidarios* decided on reprisals. On 4 June 1923, two men killed the Cardinal of Saragossa. Durruti was not one of the two, but fled with Ascaso, who was, to Chile, where they robbed a bank. Back in France in 1925, they were imprisoned, but finally released after an international campaign.

After the fall of the monarchy, Durruti returned to Barcelona. Despite their famed intransigence, *Los Solidarios*, now known as *Nosotros*, were not members of the FAI at this time. Like other anarchists, they welcomed the Republic. Durruti, as late as September 1931, praised Macià for his 'inherent goodness ... purity and integrity'.[27] He probably liked the attempted invasion of 1926 and saw Macià as a man of action.

After the December 1933 insurrection, Durruti and other anarchists were deported to the Spanish colony of Guinea. The victory of the Popular Front in February 1936 saw him back in Barcelona. Prominent in the street fighting after 18 July, he lost his intimate friend Ascaso, killed in the 20 July assault on the Drassanes barracks. Durruti was one of the anarchist leaders who met Companys on 20 July and supported (some say, he proposed) the setting up of the Central Anti-Fascist Militia Committee. In the first weeks and months of the war, Durruti and his group clashed sharply with the FAI and CNT leaders. Durruti wanted all arms and all leaders to the front. The anarchist leaders argued they were more useful defending anarchist power against political manoeuvres in Barcelona and its neighbouring cities.

The very first act of the Anti-Fascist Militia Committee was to form what became known as the Durruti Column with the aim of liberating Saragossa, an anarchist stronghold that had fallen to the fascists. Some 2,000 volunteers left Barcelona on 23 July 1936. What the column lacked in arms and artillery, it made up for in enthusiasm. Durruti himself rode in a Hispano Suiza from the Barcelona factory rapidly converted into an armoured car. Just before leaving, Durruti gave his most famous interview to the Canadian journalist Pierre van Paasen, who remarked on his quiet and serious mien while he explained the millenarian vision of anarchism:

> We have always lived in slums and holes in the wall ... It is we who built these palaces and cities, here in Spain and in America and everywhere. We, the workers, can build others to take their place. And better ones! We are not in the least afraid of ruins. We are going to inherit the earth ... The bourgeoisie might blast and ruin its own world before it leaves the stage of history. We carry a new world here, in our hearts.[28]

The column freed numerous villages on its way towards Saragossa, encouraging collectivisation and preaching libertarian ideas. It was halted some 30 kilometres from Saragossa, which became the war's front line for the next two years. This allowed Barcelona – unlike Madrid, which had Franco's armies on its doorstep – to breathe freely in the rearguard. Other columns, of ERC, of the POUM, of the Communists, of more anarchists, followed. The columns' advance led to the Council of Aragon, a huge experiment in collectivisation of the land, until it was dismantled by the Communists in 1937 (see Chapter 10).

Durruti took his column to defend Madrid in early November. There he was shot in the chest on 19 November (no one knows by whom: stray bullet? enemy sniper? political assassination?) and died the following morning.

Death consolidated his legend. His funeral demonstration in November in Barcelona was huge. Most commentators say it was the

Figure 8 Buenaventura Durruti's commemorative slab
in the Montjuïc cemetery, Barcelona. 'We Carry a New
World in Our Hearts' (Dámaso Martín)

biggest ever seen in Barcelona until the anti-war demonstration of 15 February 2003. Even Antonov-Ovseenko, the Soviet consul sent by Stalin to Barcelona to destroy anarchist and POUM power, felt he had to attend. The Via Laietana was renamed the Via Durruti.

Gerald Brenan wrote: 'Durruti was a powerful man with brown eyes and an innocent expression.'[29] He was a man of action who wasted few words. There are several anecdotes adorning his legend. In the early 1930s, he and his *Nosotros* comrades often met at *La Tranquilidad*, a bar run by an Aragonese anarchist (as Ealham notes, the least tranquil café on the Paral·lel):[30]

A young beggar with a defeated air came into the bar asking for money. When he approached Durruti's table the bar went silent. Durruti looked the man intently in the eyes and then pulled out his pistol and slammed it on the table, saying: 'There, take my gun. Go to the bank.'[31]

Instead of following FAI members like his old *solidario* colleague Garcia Oliver into the Republican Government in September 1936, Durruti chose to fight on the Madrid front. He told van Paasen: 'I do not expect any help for a libertarian revolution from any Government in the world. … We expect no help, not even from our own Government, in the last analysis.'[32]

Though he was in his early career a gunman, believing in exemplary minority action against members of the ruling class, he became an inspirational leader of the mass movement. A worker himself, he was adored by the revolutionary working class for the sharp clarity of his ideas and his honesty in putting them into action.

He had a political after-life in *The Friends of Durruti*, founded by former members of his column in March 1937 to oppose anarchist collusion in government and to resist incorporation of anarchist militia into the regular army. In the Barcelona May Days of 1937, they broke with classic anarchism by moving towards the POUM's position and arguing that the working class had to seize political power. But they were too small a group to influence events.

10

Catalonia, Cradle of the Spanish Revolution: 1936

The working class, arms in hand, halted fascism in Catalonia on July 19 and crudely posed the problem of power.

Andreu Nin[1]

At 4am on Sunday 19 July 1936, the factory sirens in the entire Barcelona area began to howl in a prearranged signal calling workers to resist a military revolt. The summons to action followed several days of maximum alert before the threat of an imminent coup. Anarchist action groups had spent these days of preparation watching barracks, making grenades and collecting arms, sometimes by assaulting police or, on one daring occasion, raiding the prison ship *Uruguay* moored in Barcelona harbour.

As workers tumbled out of bed before summer's early dawn, barricades were going up all over the city to prevent the military occupying strategic buildings and working-class neighbourhoods. After heavy fighting, in which workers and the Catalan police halted the soldiers marching on the city centre at several key points, by mid-afternoon, it was clear that the coup had failed.

Shivers of triumph run through the city, cars and trucks full of workers, men and women, soldiers with their fists in the air, cheering. There are no trams – the electricity's down – and no petrol. The bars are closed, dead horses litter the Plaza de Cataluña. But the air has turned to rejoicing. Ambulances come and go, the only bells in the city. Churches begin to burn.

'What do you expect!' someone says. 'They're easier to see than the banks, and they burn better!'

Not one shop looted, not one hold-up, not one food store attacked, not one outrage in all the delirious city.[2]

By the end of the day, the rebels were in a desperate position, holed up in the Drassanes (the medieval shipyards between the Paral·lel and Rambla) and the Sant Andreu barracks on the other side of the city. At midnight on 19–20 July, the Sant Andreu barracks were taken by CNT activists and some 90,000 rifles seized.[3]

Memory Wars

Over 80 years on, the Spanish Civil War is the terrain of ferocious memory wars. In the Spanish state, right-wing propagandists posing as historians, openly promoted by ex-Prime Minister Aznar and his conservative Partido Popular (People's Party), place the start of the war in the Asturias workers' revolt of October 1934. Thus, they exonerate the CEDA, the monarchists of Calvo Sotelo, the Falange and the army from responsibility for the rebellion of 18 July 1936. These good old soldiers were merely responding responsibly to the chaos of anarchist revolution.

More insidiously, because at first glance it seems so fair, the right and parts of the Socialist Party argue today that there were terrible things done on both sides and the best thing to do is to forget the whole unfortunate business and get on with life in the new post-Franco democracy. Terrible things were indeed done on both sides. War is not gentle. The questions are: who was responsible? Who benefited? The answers are simple: those who rebelled to install a military-fascist regime were responsible. Major capitalists and landowners benefited. And, as is recognised by a swathe of historians from mild conservatives to the revolutionary left, the Franco side conducted torture and murder as a question of policy, whereas the many fewer killings on the Republican side mainly took place in the first weeks of angry, 'uncontrolled' revenge and were never sanctioned as policy by leaders. Any equals sign placed between the two sides is an attempt to falsify history.

The fascination with the Spanish Civil War is rooted in that it was not only a war. It was a testing ground for the fascist powers. It was the crucible of left-wing strategies: every possible idea was tested in practice. It was the romantic cause that rallied the world's working class and intellectuals: 'Spain in 1936, like Spain in 1808, was converted into the centre of the world's passions and disappointments.'[4] Huge solidarity movements and the International Brigades were organised to defend the Republic against fascism.

Most of all, most inspiring, 1936 stands alongside the Paris Commune and the Russian Revolution as Europe's most thorough-going social revolution. Unlike the first two, the Spanish Revolution took place in an industrialised, modern country. The POUM leader Andreu Nin, who knew something about the Soviet Union because he had lived there from 1921 to 1930, said that the 'stupid … Spanish military' had provoked 'a proletarian revolution more deep-going than the Russian one itself'.[5] Nin was referring to the mass armed participation in defeating the coup in Catalonia and the self-organisation of the working class that followed, collectivising workplaces and marching on Saragossa. Some 80 per cent of Barcelona's workplaces were collectivised in the first weeks after 19 July; some 40–50 per cent, in the rest of Catalonia.

As well as the memory wars between right and left, between the ruling class and the working class, the war and revolution posed important disputes of tactics and strategy within the left. The first historians of the war were mostly foreigners, for the simple reason that under Franco Spanish historians could not investigate properly. Valuable work was done by these historians to unearth facts that Franco propaganda had buried. Overwhelmingly, however, the best-known of them have defended the Popular Front against the anarchist or POUM perspectives. English-language Civil War historians such as Hugh Thomas and Gabriel Jackson or, more recently, Helen Graham and Paul Preston have seen the Spanish Revolution as an obstacle to winning the war. Their view is shared by most of a new generation of Spanish historians. In recent decades, they have fetishised the figure of Juan Negrín, who became prime minister of the Spanish Republic in May 1937 with Communist Party support after the Revolution was crushed.

Fighting in the Streets

In Catalonia the victory over the military uprising on 19 July 1936, opened a full-scale revolution that was defeated with the reconstruction of Republican order in two key periods: the tumultuous first eleven weeks of the war and then the street fighting from 3–7 May 1937.

Throughout the Spanish state, in the places where the generals' uprising was defeated, it was by mass action led by groups of armed workers (with the exception of the Basque Country). This is not to say that sections of the Civil Guard, army and police (as was the case in Catalonia) did not remain loyal to the Popular Front government, but the workers' organisations were the decisive force.

The leaders of the military uprising could rely on very little support in Catalonia. Cambó's right-wing coalition, the *Front d'Ordre*, had won a considerable 41 per cent of the Catalan vote in the February 1936 election, but however right-wing the *Front d'Ordre* was, it was ruled out of any possible alliance with the army because of its Catalanism. This is not to say that Franco did not accept money from Cambó and much of the Catalan bourgeoisie, as a *quid pro quo* for recovering their properties after the war. The heirs of the *Front d'Ordre* are still alive and kicking. They ran the *Generalitat* under Jordi Pujol (president 1980–2003) and now, on the boards of big business, vigorously oppose the independence movement.

The anarchist-led groups that had assaulted weapons stores and barracks to arm the working class were decisive. The workers' victory brought confidence to at once collectivise workplaces and challenge the power of the *Generalitat* governed by ERC, which had opposed the distribution of arms to anyone except 200 members of its own youth section. Collectivisation was necessary in many cases because bosses had fled. It is also noteworthy that Catalonia (unlike Valencia) saw not just a big-city revolution: there was also a majority in several rural areas (particularly round Lleida) against the military uprising. The *rabassaires* and other peasants had understood which side they were on through the conflicts over property contract laws mentioned in Chapter 9.

On the afternoon of Monday 20 July, while the barricades still dominated the main avenues and the smell of gunpowder still drifted down the alleys of the Old City, the exhausted anarchist leaders, 36 hours or more without sleep, met with President Companys. This dramatic meeting reads today as a piece of theatre that encapsulates the basic problem of the Catalan revolution. The CNT controlled the city: the Drassanes had fallen that morning. Militants of other organisations, the POUM, Communists and ERC members, had taken part in the fighting, but the CNT was dominant.

Companys, well aware he had lost the monopoly of armed force that maintains the capitalist state, invited the CNT leaders to the *Palau de la Generalitat*. In an exercise of 'brinkmanship', to use Chris Ealham's term, he made a famous speech that seems to risk all, but more than anything shows how well this former labour lawyer and friend of Layret and Salvador Seguí understood the CNT. This is the version, probably embellished but more or less accurate, that appears in the memoirs of Joan Garcia Oliver, who was present:

> Today you are the masters of the city and of Catalonia ... You have conquered everything and everything is in your power. If you do not need me or want me as President of Catalonia ..., I shall become just another soldier in the struggle against fascism. If, on the other hand, you believe in this post ... I and the men of my party ... can be useful in this struggle.[6]

The CNT had spent two days fighting in the streets. They felt exultant. They did not believe in taking power. They were not Marxists, who had understood after the defeat of the Paris Commune that the old state power had to be destroyed. They were proud to be anarchists, uncorrupted by power. Feeling 'strong as a lion', the Catalan CNT suffered, said Asturian POUM leader Ignacio Iglesias, from a 'superiority complex'.[7] One of their theorists, Diego Abad de Santillán, wrote: 'We did not believe in dictatorship when they exercised it against us, and we did not want it when we could exercise it to the detriment of others.'[8]

Lenin would have turned in his mausoleum and Trotsky cursed when he heard about it – don't these people know you have to conquer state power?! But the CNT was the CNT. They could point to the degeneration of proletarian dictatorship in the Soviet Union under Stalin. The German anarchist Helmut Rüdiger, IWA (International Workers Association) representative in Barcelona and member of the Durruti column, wrote, referring to the possibility of seizing state power: 'Don't let's fool ourselves. If the CNT had had such a programme before 19 July, it would not have been the CNT, but a Bolshevik party.'[9]

The Central Anti-Fascist Militia Committee (CCMA) was set up at the famous meeting with Companys. This 'democratic collaboration' against fascism was then rubber-stamped at a rapidly convened anarchist assembly. Dual power was established in Catalonia, but it was a strange dual power. The two opposing power blocks collaborated. The anarchists dominated the CCMA, while Companys stamped the *Generalitat*'s seal on what the Committee decided. Companys had diverted the CNT from consolidation of the revolution ('going all the way', in Garcia Oliver's words) to fighting fascism. As Miguel Romero explained: 'It was a double power, but completely asymmetrical: the socially and militarily strong power is politically weak; the socially and militarily weak force is politically strong.'[10]

It was a type of dual power that was not dual power because the CNT and FAI did not pose an alternative power to bourgeois power – a kind of proletarian dictatorship that was no dictatorship because the anarchists abhorred all dictatorship. The CNT felt it could just ignore the *Generalitat*. This allowed Companys, supported by the Spanish Government and, crucially, by the Catalan communists of the PSUC, newly formed through a merger of Communists and Socialists just a few days after the military rebellion, to spend the next two months manoeuvring skilfully to restore power to the *Generalitat*.

The CCMA and its numerous branches throughout Catalonia could not be called Soviets either. 'The CCMA, which had the appearance of a revolutionary body, was a trade union-dominated government and war ministry in all but name, and it allowed the anarchists to participate in power without compromising their anti-statist principles.'[11]

The agreement between Companys and the anarchist leaders in no way reduced the initial energy of the Revolution. Going beyond any government agreements, local revolutionary committees re-organised life throughout Catalonia, especially in the working-class quarters. Everyone lived in the streets. Spontaneous orators would draw a crowd. Flags and posters covered walls; demonstrations were constant. Mansions of the rich and classy restaurants were occupied, the latter often converted into cheap eating-houses. The political organisations took over the best hotels for their headquarters. They occupied the offices of right-wing papers: the POUM used the presses of the Carlist *El correo catalán* for its main paper *La batalla*; the PSUC's *Treball* was printed in the workshop of the defunct Catholic daily *El matí*. No bourgeois was seen on the streets. It was easy to believe falsely that the proletarian revolution was won.

Creative and Chaotic

Many readers will be familiar with Orwell's description: flags and posters everywhere, churches gutted, no tipping, no 'Señor' or 'Don' (everyone was 'Comrade'), workers who looked a foreigner in the eye, no suits or jewellery, no private cars, posters and slogans on every wall – and he arrived five months after 19 July, on 26 December 1936, when revolutionary fervour was already in decline.[12] There are many other accounts that give the feel of what it was like to live this revolution, accounts that take readers into working-class quarters and workplaces, where Orwell did not tread. Here are some stories.

Trains became free, so revolutionary tourism was not just foreign sympathisers turning up to write articles: workers who had never been out of Barcelona would get on a train and travel to, say, Valencia, walk around for a few hours, talk to people (in a revolution you can talk to anyone in the street) and come back. Other free travel was more dangerous: the bourgeoisie's cars were acquired and tearaways with no experience painted them with slogans and drove them at high speed. Barcelona's *Gran Via* became a racetrack and the Les Arenes bullring at the end of it became a cemetery for wrecked cars.

People who had never spoken found a voice. Andreu Capdevila, CNT activist in the British-owned Fabra i Coats textile factory in Sant Andreu, explained that, as soon as the factory was collectivised: 'It was amazing, everyone turned into a parrot, everyone wanted to say what he or she felt. They obviously felt themselves in charge now and with the right to speak for themselves.'[13]

The collectivised entertainments industry was one of the few to show profits. Prices were cut and workers packed out cinemas, theatres and the opera house. A single wage was introduced for all theatre workers, as in most sectors. This ideal was not always realisable, as this anecdote shows. The tenor Hipólito Lázaro was due to sing at the Tívoli theatre. He stood up and told the company, 'We're all equal now and to prove it, we all get the same wage. Fine, since we're equal, today I am going to collect the tickets at the door and one of you can come up here and sing.' The workers' council running the theatre had to cede Lázaro a higher wage.[14]

The 7,000 Barcelona tram-workers had 700 trams painted red and black (CNT colours) and operating on the rails only five days after 19

July. Workers re-laid tramlines torn up for barricades. They repaired 100 trams previously deemed unfit for service. All this phenomenal effort was done with voluntary overtime by workers committed to collectivised transport. In each of the last four months of 1936, revenue increased over the last four months of 1935. How was this achieved? By raising fares? No! Fares were reduced, with the introduction of a standard charge however far the passenger travelled (this is still the case today), in order to favour workers travelling from the outskirts. 'Such reductions in fares would have resulted in losses under the previous administration, but the suppression of capitalist profit and of high salaries for ... executives and technicians actually made it possible to show an operating surplus.'[15]

I am fond of the story of the greyhound racing section of the CNT entertainments union. Here the old managers and trainers were kept on, the dogs were taken over and bred and everyone was paid the same 15 pesetas a day. Betting continued and the popular sport made such profits that they lent 100,000 pesetas to the cinema section to buy foreign films.[16]

If the ideal of equal wages for all was not always attainable, if less conscious workers worked less and production dropped when capitalist discipline eased, if sometimes the former boss was kept on as managing director because he knew best how things worked, if women were still paid less than men, nevertheless every workplace saw assemblies and the majority feeling that the company now belonged to the workers. The alienation of work was overcome.

Though full equality of pay was not always achieved, gaps between skilled and unskilled workers and between men and women narrowed. Conditions in workplaces improved: hours were cut, the rhythm of work was slowed and canteens became cheaper. Sometimes new showers were built or crèches opened. Sick pay and holiday pay were often introduced for the first time. In the collectivised and merged (doing away with wasteful capitalist competition) beer factories, a yearly suit was added to the wages.[17] The enthusiasm of revolutionary change, nurtured for many years by anarchist propaganda, turned the world upside down.

Workers' management was not easy. Workers' control was *relatively* easy, that is, monitoring bosses' every move; but workers' management, that is, running the place without bosses, was a leap into the unknown. And it was especially hard when ERC and the PSUC were doing everything in their power to limit and control collectivisations.

The situation in these first weeks of revolution was both highly creative and extremely chaotic. The mass movement overwhelmed both the CNT and POUM. Indeed, it wasn't until the end of August that the CNT formally called for collectivisation. As the example above of the loan lent by the greyhound collective to the film collective suggests, you can't run an advanced economy on the basis of individual enterprises doing what they want. Juan Andrade wrote of 'economic cantonalism', whereby in some enterprises workers raised their wages, while in others they worked longer hours for nothing to keep up production.[18] As the communists and POUMists (and many anarchists, too) insisted, there had to be overall planning. One example showed what was possible: as there was no armaments industry in Catalonia, this had to be urgently invented from scratch by adapting engineering plants to alternative production. And this meant direction from above, even though clever adaptations could be devised from below by skilled workers. Fraser narrates how CNT metal-workers collaborated with the *Generalitat*'s War Industries Commission, set up in August 1936, to bring an expert from Oviedo and to nationalise 'twenty-four engineering and chemical factories turning out shells, explosives and armoured vehicles ... Pastry-kneading and beer-bottle corking machines were amongst the machinery pressed into service'.[19]

All this economic change was taking place in a war situation: international capitalism froze bank accounts, cancelled orders, impeded supplies. One direct example: Catalonia's textile manufacture was devastated by the lack of imported raw materials and the war cutting off at least 50 per cent of the internal market in Spain. The turn to making uniforms for the army helped keep the industry afloat.

Another large problem for the economic and political transformation of Catalonia was that the most class-conscious militants left for the front. Durruti disagreed with other anarchist leaders over whether it was more important to get to the front and take the CNT bastion Saragossa; or to stay in the rearguard and fight to keep the revolution on course. The most energetic and idealistic youth rushed out of the factories and *barris* to volunteer for the columns. Parties set up recruiting posts. They were overwhelmed by volunteers. More experienced activists, hardened in strikes where use of guns and grenades was common, acted as instructors.

As these columns reached Aragon, they collectivised villages and assisted in collectivisation already under way. This was not forced collectivisation, as had occurred in Stalin's Soviet Union. There was a long tradition of anarcho-syndicalism in Aragon, not just in Saragossa but also in the countryside. Undoubtedly, there were cases of peasants reluctant to collectivise their land, who were forced to do so or, at least, felt obliged to do so – but this was not the norm. Gaston Leval and his translator to English, Vernon Richards, argue that the columns had little effect on collectivisation, which was achieved by those actually working the land. It's more accurate to say that the combination of the arrival of anarchist columns from Valencia and Barcelona and the anarchist base already existing in many villages led to the collectivisations.

These were economic collectivisations, that is, fertilisers, seeds and machinery were held and bought in common and produce was sold in common. By July 1937, shortly before the *Consejo de Aragón* (Council of Aragon) and its collectives were suppressed by Negrín's counter-revolutionary government, there were at least 800 agricultural collectives in Valencia, Aragon and Catalonia – fewer in Catalonia, where peasants were more prosperous – involving some 400,000 people.

The CNT and POUM were also overwhelmed by the spate of killings in the first months of the war. Some 1,300 religious personnel (priests, nuns, monks) were killed in Catalonia. These were members of the oppressive Catholic Church: Jews and Protestants were not molested. In addition, numerous bosses were 'taken for a ride' and dumped by the side of the road with a bullet in the neck. Personal vendettas were settled, too. Every morning corpses were found by l'Arrabassada, the pretty rural road that winds through the Collserola hills behind Barcelona to Sant Cugat. Traditionally, anarchists have been blamed, but reality was more nuanced. There were anarchists, known as the *amargados*, the embittered, who believed that all right-wingers should be physically eliminated (something of a mirror image of Franco's position). However, anarchist leaders, including intransigents like Durruti, were against the killings. Frederica Montseny of the FAI wrote that the killers showed 'a lust for blood inconceivable in civilized society'.[20] It is true that, when the Durruti or other anarchist and non-anarchist militia columns took a village, they did often kill the priest or village boss. If you imagine the decades of abuse and violence, often including rape or theft of land, then such killings appear justified. In addition, village dignitaries were often captured arms in hand after fighting the militia columns. In the cities, particularly unpleasant landlords, rent collectors or bosses who had not fled were shot. The CNT's main sin in this respect was that it accepted people in good faith. It was open to anyone who professed agreement with its aims. This made it an easy refuge for any thug, murderer released from prison at the start of the Revolution or even fascist.

The *Generalitat* issued safe-conducts to numerous right-wingers: more than 11,000 escaped to France. All the trade union and political organisations fought to control the killings. The Popular Tribunals set up in Andreu Nin's brief time as Catalan Minister of Justice brought down the numbers radically. The killings, and even more so the exaggerated reports of the killings and abuse of clergy, damaged the Republic's and the Revolution's images. For instance, the millionaire bootlegger Joseph Kennedy, father of the president, was able to use the killings of priests to mobilise a Catholic lobby in the USA to prevent Roosevelt supplying aid to the Republic.

Many activists were also politically concerned by the killings. Murders and disorder terrorised members of the middle class, throwing such sectors as shopkeepers and office workers into the arms of the PSUC or open counter-revolution. Fraser cites Saturnino Carod, leader of an anarchist column in lower Aragon, who 'demanded that all lives and all property – not only religious – be respected. The column's task was to fight the enemy in open combat, not take justice into its hands'. Carod harangued the townspeople in the square at Calaceite after the church had been burnt: 'Do not believe that by burning churches ... tomorrow everyone will feel himself, herself an atheist. The more you violate their consciences, the more they will side with the church.'[21]

Saturnino's was not a universal view. The CNT was extremely moralistic, seeing the world in sharp black and white. The Church corrupted workers' minds. Therefore, priests should be eliminated and churches demolished.

Revolutionary Strategy and Suicide

In this revolutionary situation, the POUM was conscious of its enormous responsibility. As revolutionary Marxists, their leaders understood the political orientation of the PSUC and Stalin's emissary Antonov-Ovseenko.[22] The PSUC's support for Stalin's concept of the Popular Front, a broad alliance to defeat fascism that included bourgeois forces, meant that from the start it organised to crush 'revolutionary excess'.

The PSUC argued that it was not the time for revolution: Catalonia, and the Spanish state, was at the democratic stage, waging a war for bourgeois democracy against fascism. Its hostility to the POUM was exacerbated by the latter's criticisms of the start of the Moscow trials in August 1936 and its defence of the Old Bolsheviks on trial and of Trotsky against Stalin's trumped-up charges.

The POUM's programme was that of revolutionary Marxism. They fought for a democratic and socialist revolution. They believed that many of the unresolved tasks of the bourgeois revolution, such as land reform, separation of Church and State, the independence of women or the emancipation of the oppressed nations, could only be completed by the proletariat. The bourgeoisie was no longer a progressive force: fearing working-class power, it was driven to the fascist solution.

The POUM's activists fought at the front and fought alongside the CNT to deepen and extend the Revolution, but it was too small to influence events decisively. Its most controversial move was to agree to the dissolution of the Central Anti-Fascist Militia Committee (CCMA) and enter the *Generalitat* government in late September 1936. This, along with its signing of the Popular Front electoral agreement in January 1936 and its later failure to try to take power in May 1937, were the three principal reasons why Trotsky and the small group of Fourth Internationalists in Barcelona (about 30 'Bolshevik-Leninists') characterised the POUM as 'centrist', that is, revolutionary in language and reformist in practice.

On 26 September, the *Generalitat* formed a new government under Josep Tarradellas (who appears again 40 years later in Chapter 11) of ERC. It included members of the CNT and Nin on behalf of the POUM. These were remarkable events. Anarchists entered a government and revolutionary Marxists joined a bourgeois government. The main anarchist paper *Solidaridad Obrera* justified the *volte-face* as follows:

> The Government ... is no longer a force oppressing the working class, just as the state is no longer the organism separating society into classes. And both will oppress the people still less when people from the CNT take part in them.[23]

After joining the government, Nin accompanied Companys to Lleida, where the POUM was the main force in the local Committee, and persuaded it to dissolve. There is controversy on this mission of Nin. Some commentators say that Nin was shouted down; it seems, though, that the Committee accepted the proposal with no or little protest. The argument of the revolutionary forces for joining the government was that this would not reduce the power of the working class, but would help overcome disorganisation and 'legalise' the conquests of the masses. Indeed, on 24 October, a decree promulgated by the Tarradellas government did legalise the collectivisations of companies with over 100 employees or whose bosses had fled or been declared 'seditious', surely the most radical measure ever taken by a bourgeois government. This decree disguises, though, the real content of the dissolution of the CCMA and its local committees. Miguel Romero summarised: 'In reality, what had happened was that revolutionary power had recognised the legitimacy of Republican power and, by so acting, had committed suicide.'[24]

The new government represented the return of Republican authority that Companys and the PSUC had been striving for. While the CNT and POUM presented the dissolution of the CCMA as a merely technical move, the PSUC had it clear. The editorial of its main paper, *Treball*, stated: 'This Government has the duty to pull Catalonia up out of the paralysis to which irresponsible experiments of puerile revolutionarism have condemned it.'[25]

It is important to understand the context to the POUM's fateful step. Its militants were under extreme pressures of isolation and persecution. The POUM had seen before the war how the CNT's membership was falling and opted to have the members of its union the FOUS (Workers' Federation for Unity), which was, with some 50,000 members at most, much smaller than the UGT and CNT, enter the Socialist UGT. This was in hindsight a mistake, though very understandable: many members of the FOUS had previously been excluded from the CNT because they were Marxists. In the chaos and exultation of the first weeks of war, the CNT grew enormously, while the Catalan UGT, after the founding of the PSUC in July 1936, fell under the control of Stalinism. The POUM believed that, for the working class to seize power, it had to win the CNT to its positions. It ceaselessly called on the CNT to reorient towards taking state power. However, unable to work shoulder to shoulder with the bases inside the CNT's component unions, its influence was reduced and these calls were abstract.

The other great pressure on the POUM was their awareness that isolation would lead to repression by the Communists, whose power in the army, police and government was growing. The POUM was rightly concerned that the supply of arms, food and pay to its militia on the Aragon front could be cut off. It was clear from early on that Soviet aid was not distributed equitably: no Soviet arms reached POUM and anarchist columns on the Huesca front.

In December 1936, the Catalan government was reorganised: the POUM was excluded. Formally, the PSUC was also outside the government, but all three UGT representatives were PSUC members. The CNT, lamentably, saw the question as a row between two types of communists and accepted the POUM's exclusion. The CNT did not understand that they and the revolutionary masses that they led were the ultimate target of the PSUC.

The May Days

With the hindsight gained by reading history books in comfortable rooms, we can say that the revolution was over on 26 September, when the CNT and POUM entered the *Generalitat* government. It didn't feel like that at the time – not to the militia fighting the fascists, the workers pushing forward with collective organisation in factory and *barri*, nor to later observers like George Orwell. Politically, though, 26 September was a defeat.

Throughout the state, the war did not go well that winter. The militia columns that had left Barcelona in euphoria in July were bogged down some 30 kilometres from Saragossa and on the hills around Huesca. Extremadura and most of Andalusia fell to Franco's forces. Planes strafed columns of refugees fleeing Málaga along the coast road after it fell on 7 February 1937. Nevertheless, Madrid's resistance inspired the left worldwide and the Republic won the Battle of Guadalajara in March 1937. Morale remained intact, but the lesson that popular mobilisation was key to victory, particularly in the defence of Madrid, was downplayed. The Communists, along with the centre and right of the Spanish Socialist Party, were insistent that a traditional army had to be built to defeat Franco. They were surely right that, in a conventional war, militia columns had little possibility of defeating a disciplined army supplied by Mussolini and Hitler. However, the Communist line of constructing a hierarchical, traditional kind of army instead of building one on the model of the Red Army under Trotsky meant that the revolutionary spirit that was the Republic's greatest asset was broken. A more centralised army was needed, but one based on the revolutionary militia, not on their destruction.

In the rearguard, in revolutionary Catalonia, the situation was deteriorating in early 1937. The building of a regular army, by which the militia columns were converted into units of the Popular Army from October–November 1936 onwards, caused resentment in the POUM and CNT. There were also rows about food: the CNT accused the Communist Joan Comorera responsible for supplies of creating scarcity and favouring the PSUC. On several occasions in the early months of 1937, there were armed clashes as CNT militants in Barcelona seized food supplies.

Serious conflicts also arose on the question of 'public order'. In February 1937, the *Generalitat* ordered the dissolution of the armed working-class patrols and the unification of all the police forces. A few days later it ordered that all explosives and arms should be handed in, measures ignored by the POUM and CNT.

What was one of the last opportunities to reverse the trend towards the strengthening of the government and weakening of the revolutionary forces, was the formation in February by the POUM and anarchist youth organisations of the Revolutionary Youth Front. It was a huge step: the first time that a part of the CNT accepted the need for a united front. The Revolutionary Youth Front's aim was to defend the gains of the revolution and liquidate 'the remains of the bourgeois past'. The CNT, though, did not support its youth section's 'too political' initiative.

In contrast, to show the gulf between the revolutionary forces and the counter-revolutionary PSUC, it is worth quoting the aims of the JSU, the PSUC's youth organisation:

1. To defend the Democratic Republic.
2. To be the 'government' youth, acting and being the support of the legitimate government of the Republic.
3. To defend the unity of all anti-fascist youth in the service of national independence [referring to Spain, not Catalonia] and oppose ultra-revolutionary Trotskyist phraseology.[26]

The witch-hunt against the POUM, slandered constantly by the PSUC as 'Trotsky-fascists', 'in Franco's service' and 'fifth columnists', was steadily increasing in virulence.

All these tensions building between the working-class organisations erupted into a decisive mini-civil war within the Civil War in Barcelona from 3–7 May 1937. On 3 May, three truckloads of assault guards under Catalan police chief Rodríguez Salas, a PSUC member who was a former anarchist, moved to take over from the CNT the telephone exchange building on Barcelona's central Plaça de Catalunya (the building's still there – now a mobile phone shop). The CNT refused to leave. This was the spark that ignited the tension of the preceding months. Barricades went up all over the city. The POUM joined the CNT on the streets. The balance of forces was in the revolutionaries' favour. The question of reversing the counter-revolutionary advances, to defend the revolution, was posed. However, the anarchist ministers intervened decisively to demobilise the resistance. Five thousand assault guards sent by the central government to defeat the revolutionaries arrived on 7 May. The CNT accepted the promises of Companys that there would be no reprisals. With no guarantees at all, they laid down their arms on 7 May: 218 people had died in the fighting.

The consequences of the May 1937 defeat of the Revolution were far-reaching. The government of the left socialist Largo Caballero fell on 15 May and Juan Negrín became the Spanish prime minister in a government with a stronger Communist presence and no anarchists. The losers of the May Days were not just the CNT and POUM, but also Catalan autonomy. The central government intervened the powers of the *Generalitat* on 5 May, suppressing the 1932 Statute of Autonomy. In October 1937, Negrín moved his government from Valencia to Barcelona, making the city the capital of the Spanish state for the only time in history. He made clear his attitude to Catalan nationalism: 'I am not making war on Franco to allow a stupid and provincial separatism to sprout in Barcelona ... I am making war for Spain ... and for its greatness ... There is only one nation: Spain.'[27]

It is a typical view of both right- and left-wing PSOE (Spanish Socialist Party) members. It harks back to the top–down Jacobinism of the Cadiz constitution of 1812. A strong centralised state was needed – whether in the nineteenth century to carry through the bourgeois revolution, or in 1937 to fight fascism. It is a view echoed by the Socialist Party today.

The Nationalist Left

Esquerra Republicana was still in government, but its political power had been removed. Unlike other middle-class Republican parties in the rest of Spain, ERC had a mass base and had won three of the four elections in Catalonia since 12 April 1931. The election it narrowly lost was the state one in November 1933, which ushered in the two years of right-wing government, but ERC still governed in Catalonia. Its membership was varied – remember it was a coalition of parties – ranging from Communists to *Estat català* and its leader Josep Dencàs who supported Mussolini.

ERC's greatest social achievements were in education, health and culture. The draft Statute of Núria wanted powers for education to be fully transferred to the *Generalitat*. In the 1932 fudge passed by the Spanish parliament, responsibilities for education were shared. This meant that, though Catalan was recognised as a co-official language in Catalonia, most schools continued to teach in Spanish. Nevertheless, 50 per cent of all teachers registered for the *Generalitat*'s courses in written Catalan. The 1930s left a legacy in the *escola catalana* (Catalan schooling), basically a successful attempt to change the rigid tradition of memorising like parrots, Catholic precepts and harsh discipline. The *escola catalana* prioritised the Catalan language, secular beliefs and the use of reason not punishment. To some degree, the schools overlapped with the anarchist schools such as the *escola natura* (Nature School) in the Barcelona *barri* of Clot, financed by the CNT's textile union. Here some 250 children of anarchists were taught a rebel, anti-capitalist culture and taken out of the slums to summer camps in the Pyrenees.

Books (up from 308 titles published in 1930 to 865 in 1936) and magazines in Catalan flourished during the Republic. Daily papers in Catalan rose from ten in 1927 to a remarkable 25 in 1933.[28] The new medium of radio popularised the language, too. The linguistic clashes promoted by the Spanish right today in Catalonia were largely absent in the 1930s. People talked naturally in Catalan and were keen to learn to write it correctly.

Usually, in accounts of this great proletarian revolution, the national question fades towards unimportance. Defeating Franco is the main challenge; Durruti's column is far more exciting than the education system. However, the complexity and interlinking of the national and

Figure 9   Mural in Girona to commemorate Antònia Androher (1913–2007), one of the founders of the POUM in 1935. As Councillor for Education and Culture on the Girona City Council from October 1936, she organised free, universal schooling in Catalan (Chris Bambery)

class questions are key to understanding Catalonia. Catalan politics was posed in national terms: Cambó's right-wing *Lliga* was Catalanist, however subservient the Catalan bourgeoisie was to Primo and Franco. Before 1939, open proponents of Spanish nationalism were in an extreme minority in Catalonia. This differed sharply from the rest of

1930s Spain, where the left Republican parties (like President Azaña's) had little mass base, the Socialist party was largely Spanish nationalist and the right was sympathetic to fascism. Thus, Catalan nationalism shifted all of Catalonia's politics to the left.

A telling example of the difference can be seen in the preparations against the probable *coup d'état*. In the months after the Popular Front victory of February 1936, it was common knowledge that the army was going to rebel. Despite this, two of the leading conspiring generals were sent by the Spanish government to ideal destinations – for the generals. Franco was posted to semi-exile in the Canary Islands, where he was close to the Army of Africa, and the main conspirator Mola was sent to Pamplona, where Spanish reaction had its only mass base, the Carlist volunteers in their red berets. In contrast, in Catalonia, ERC was careful in its anti-coup preparations and made sure that coup supporters were marginalised. This meant that the head of the army in Catalonia, Llano de la Encomienda, did not support the uprising. General Goded had to fly in from Mallorca to take charge – with unfortunate results for both the rebellion and him.

The End

The main victim of the May 1937 defeat was the POUM, illegalised on 16 June. Most of its leaders were jailed. Andreu Nin was kidnapped from the Rambles, tortured and murdered by Soviet agents near Alcalá de Henares. Foreign POUM supporters like Kurt Landau or the young Scottish working-class leader Bob Smillie were killed. The Soviet Union wanted to set up Moscow-style trials in Catalonia, but Spain was not Russia: though the Revolution had been defeated, the working class had not been crushed.

Throughout the summer of 1937, the Council of Aragon and the agricultural collectives it organised were disbanded – a process graphically shown in Ken Loach's *Land and Freedom*. Politically, the CNT continued its evolution from purity to pragmatism, entering an alliance with the UGT and accepting the need for centralised, top–down organisation.

The war continued with Franco's superior forces advancing. Franco wanted the war to last in order to crush the opposition totally. This was to be the definitive victory over communism and the liberal democracy that permitted communism to breed. In autumn 1937, the Republic lost the north of Spain. Over the winter of 1937–1938, the Republicans took Teruel then lost it in February. Franco now advanced through Aragon and reached the sea at Vinaròs on 15 April 1938, dividing the *països catalans* in two by cutting off Valencia from Catalonia. That same month, his army entered Catalonia and took Lleida. Mass bombardments by Italian aircraft based in Mallorca of Barcelona and industrial towns in its hinterland started in March. The March 1938 bombings were mainly of working-class areas: there were still bomb sites in Barcelona's Raval quarter in the 1980s. 'Between 1937 and 1939, aerial bombardment killed 2,428 people and destroyed around 1,500 buildings in the "city of evil".'[29]

The 'city of evil' was Barcelona, but Tarragona was, in proportion to its size, the Catalan city most punished by the bombs. Tarragona's oil tanks burned for three nights after being bombed on 19 July 1937. From April 1937 to January 1939, the city suffered 144 bombardments: 230 people were killed and 350 wounded out of a population of about 38,000. In the last year of the war, hunger accompanied the bombs and the approach of the fascist army in gnawing away at Catalonia's civilian population's morale. Masses of refugees fleeing Franco's advance stretched diminishing resources and increased despair.

Novels can catch better than history this suffering of a people. In the last year of the war, hundreds of thousands were scrabbling to survive, particularly women, responsible for holding together families in the rearguard. Mercè Rodoreda's classic *In Diamond Square* tells the story of Natàlia, who struggles to keep her mental health in the war-torn city and to feed her children when her husband dies at the front. Rosa Maria Arquimbau shows a different kind of working-class woman, Laura the independent seamstress, in *Forty Lost Years*. A free and practical spirit, Laura knows how to be 'nice' to members of the 'patrol gangs' in order to get hold of food for her parents. These complex and beautiful novels catch the felt experience of the poor, the obverse of the images of exultant revolutionary change.

Franco turned his attention to Valencia, but was stopped by stubborn resistance on the XYZ defensive line. Then his armies were diverted by the Republican offensive on the River Ebre (Ebro). The Battle of the Ebre, fought through the summer of 1938, was the last great effort by the Republican Government. Negrín's final throw of the dice depended heavily on Catalan recruits, including many adolescents, the *quinta del biberón*, the 'children's levy'. The Republican troops crossed the Ebre on 25 July 1938 and advanced at first, but Franco brought reinforcements from the Valencia front and used superior air power. After 115 days of fighting, the battle was lost on 16 November 1938, with over 20,000 deaths on the Republican side. No human or material strength was left in Catalonia.

When your enemy has superior air power, artillery, tanks and training, the strategy of attempting to win a major battle by frontal assault is dubious. Guerrilla warfare was not encouraged, despite its long history in Spain. Franco's rearguard was not sympathetic to him and guerrillas would have found a large sea to swim in. The military historian Antony Beevor thought that a strategy of 'short, sharp probing attacks' and guerrillas where the terrain favoured them, combined with defensive lines, could have tied down Franco's armies and allowed the Republic to survive till the Second World War – Negrín's aim.[30] Why did he not adopt such a strategy? Mainly because of the dynamic of the war, which had shifted from revolution from below to Stalinist control. Guerrilla warfare frees fighters from tight military control. It would have also clashed with the Republican Government's wrong-headed policy of trying to win France and Britain's support by convincing them that the war was democratic, not revolutionary.[31]

Barcelona fell on 26 January 1939, followed by a huge exodus over the French frontier of soldiers and civilians. It was the bleakest of midwinters. There is no precedent in Spanish history. Due to the centuries-long struggle by Spanish nationalists to purify the race by expelling Moors and Jews and to unify the country in Catholicism, by force if necessary, numerous exiles fled Spain in every century; but there was no mass exodus to compare with the estimated 465,000 who crossed the French frontier between mid-January and the arrival of Franco's troops at La Jonquera on 10 February. Many went on to other countries and many returned to Spain, but an estimated 182,000 stayed in France. About 9,000 were deported to the Mauthausen concentration camp, of whom 7,000 died. Spanish fighters were prominent in the French *maquis* and were among the first to liberate Paris in August 1944.

Two months after the fall of Catalonia, the war was over. At the other end of the *països catalans*, on the quay at Alacant (Alicante), some 15,000 troops were trapped. A few committed suicide. Most were disarmed, beaten up and sent to concentration camps.

REBEL PORTRAIT: FREDERICA MONTSENY

Frederica Montseny was born in 1905 into an anarchist family. Her parents edited a libertarian journal *La revista blanca* in which she herself wrote. She published some 50 short novels aimed at working-class women, the first in 1920. Later, in exile, she wrote a number of books on famous anarchists, anarchist ideas and her own life.

It was her gifts as a speaker that brought her to prominence once the CNT was legalised in 1931. In 1986, I heard her, now blind and walking with difficulty, bewitch a Barcelona audience with her rhetoric. She toured Spain and France as a keynote anarchist speaker throughout the 1930s. By 1936, she was a member of the national councils of both the CNT and FAI. She celebrated 20 July in Barcelona with idealism and eloquence:

> The day faded gloriously, amidst the glow of the fires, in the revolutionary intoxication of a day of popular triumph … The city had quickly become the theatre of the revolution unleashed. Women and men, systematically attacking monasteries, burnt everything inside them, including money. Absolute generosity, grandiose faith in victory and revolution.[32]

Fewer than three months after this paean to revolution, she was one of the four anarchists who joined Largo Caballero's Madrid government and so contributed to the resurrection of state power and the confusion of the CNT masses. She betrayed a lifetime's militancy against state and government. She justified it on 3 January 1937: 'The anarchists have entered the government to prevent the Revolution from deviating and in order to carry it further beyond the war, and also to oppose any dictatorial tendency, from wherever it might come.'[33]

Montseny was the first woman to be a minister in Spain. In her brief seven months as Minister of Health and Social Affairs, she was responsible for promoting sex education, organising refuges for orphaned children and dining rooms for pregnant women, and proposing alternative work for prostitutes. The Abortion Act she put forward was opposed by the majority of the cabinet and never passed. There was only time for one refuge and one dining room to be opened before the events of May led to the fall of Largo Caballero and her own removal as minister. After leaving the government, she returned to arguing that only libertarian revolution could achieve the projects she had proposed in government.

Speaking at a meeting in Barcelona on 11 April 1937, Montseny had to taste the bitter pill of being heckled by the Friends of Durruti for betraying anarchism. Three weeks later, she and the other anarchist ministers used their influence to get the CNT to lay down their arms in the May Days conflict. The apolitical ultra-leftism of July 1936 had led to its sad corollary: opportunist collaboration with the state.

Women's lives were changed profoundly by the revolution. The prominence of women such as Montseny or the Communist *Pasionaria* helped challenge traditional roles. The anarchist organisation *Mujeres Libres*, Free Women, was a huge step forward in the self-organisation of women. Chris Ealham tells a fascinating story that reflects not only the power of *Mujeres Libres*, but the reality of anarchist organisation. On 19 July, a crowd attacked Barcelona's women's prison on the *carrer* Santa Amàlia, as they had done on 14 April 1931, and freed the prisoners. Some of these were anarchists; many were women forced by poverty into prostitution. This time, unlike 1931, several of the warder-nuns who were notorious for cruelty were killed. The CNT placed a notice on the roof: 'This torture house was closed by the people.' Then, an assembly of *Mujeres Libres* discussed what to do with the building and voted to demolish it. On 21 August, the Construction Union of the CNT carried out this task. First-class anarchist coordination.[34]

The brief flowering of *Mujeres Libres* at the start of the revolution should not deceive us into thinking that the CNT was a feminist organisation. There was a wide gap between revolutionary rhetoric with its posters of smiling militia women, and practice. Catholic sexual education was not easily thrown off. Mary Nash, in her *Rojas*, explains the phenomenon of the Catalan abortion law, passed by the *Generalitat* in December 1936: the first country in Western Europe to do so. The CNT activist and doctor, Félix Martí, close collaborator of Montseny, drafted this progressive law. However, very few women took advantage of the legislation to have official, safe abortions because the subject was still taboo. Attending a hospital was too public an act. Women's support networks of backstreet abortions continued to be preferred.

A public debate could have made abortion more acceptable, but the Act was dictated (ironically) from above by decree and, extraordinarily, *Mujeres Libres* did not even discuss the Abortion Law in its propaganda.

Their educational programmes focused on maternity, childcare and basic anatomy.[35]

Though Dr Martí was a pioneer in women's health, he and the CNT were not supporters of women's liberation, as we might understand it today. He wrote in 1935: 'Proper sexual education for the new generations will eliminate … homosexual deviation. Each man will have in his mind no other image than that of a sweet, self-denying woman.'[36] No paladin of gay liberation, either! As Mary Nash explains so clearly, mere months of revolution could not overturn centuries of patriarchal practice and propaganda.

Frederica Montseny died in Toulouse, where she had spent her decades of exile, in 1994. On her and her FAI colleagues falls the responsibility of having abandoned the Revolution to support the return of capitalist order in 1936–1937. Not wanting the dictatorship of the proletariat, tragically this sector of anarchism ended up supporting the dictatorship of the capitalists. Montseny was also a powerful advocate for women's rights, whose few months as minister laid the basis for future agitation and legislation after the dictatorship.

11

Defeat of the Dictatorship

Comrades, if you are longing
for free spring-times,
with you I want to walk.

Lluís Llach, *Abril 74*

The story of the Spanish Transition of the 1970s starts in the terror of
Franco's victory in 1939. When Catalonia fell in January, most soldiers
and activists fled to France. Many, particularly children, the malnour-
ished and the wounded, died, shoved into beach concentration camps
such as Argelers (Argelès), with no protection against winter weather
and no sanitary facilities except the sea. The camp was opened on 1
February. By 10 February, 180,000 people were living on the beach.
The guards, billeted in the fortress of Cotlliure, were Senegalese, tall
black men, different and indifferent to the Catalans' suffering. As the
Valencian novelist (and camp internee) Max Aub put it, 'there is absolute
equality between internees and guards. Neither know why they're
here'.[1] Emissaries from the Franco government visited the camps and
promised no reprisals if soldiers returned. Most did return and tens
of thousands of them then died in prisons and concentration camps.
Franco's infamous retrospective 'Law of Political Responsibilities' made
any previous support for the Republican Government a crime.

Many had stayed in Catalonia, thinking they were safe as they had not
been activists, but they had underestimated the new regime's determination not just to root out anarchism, communism and separatism, but
also to silence all democrats. Franco saw nineteenth-century liberalism
and parliamentary democracy as the breeding ground for atheism,
masonry and anarchist revolution. All the Spanish state suffered the
horrors of the dictatorship, but Catalonia suffered particularly, as it was
the centre of both revolution and secession. In 1938, Franco had made

his intentions clear: 'We want absolute national unity, with just one language, Castilian Spanish, and one personality, Spanish.'[2]

I asked Professor Paul Preston about the particular violence of Franco's occupation of Catalonia. He told me:

> The depth of anti-Catalan sentiment created in the rebel zone was reflected in the repression unleashed … The extent of a near-racist hatred was revealed after the occupation of Tarragona on 15 January 1939. At a celebration in the Cathedral, the officiating priest shouted during his sermon: 'Catalan dogs! You are not worthy of the sun that shines on you'.[3]

A regime of terror was installed, with the populace encouraged to denounce their neighbours (often with the enticement of acquiring their property) and constant executions, many at Barcelona's *Camp de la Bota*, now the site of the classy beach-side Fòrum neighbourhood. Since 2019, an impressive monument records the names of the 1,706 people known to have been executed there. The last victims were five CNT militants as late as February 1952, although most executions took place before 1943 when Franco still thought that the Nazis would win the war. Pere Ribot, curate at neighbouring Sant Adrià in 1941, remembered: 'My alarm-clock was when at 7 in the morning they shot the condemned. And each day I knew how many had died by the sound of the *coups de grace*.'[4]

The *Camp de la bota* was not the only mass execution site in Barcelona. In a quarry half-hidden behind the Montjuïc hill, columns record the names of those tossed into a mass grave after being executed in the moat of Montjuïc castle. President Lluís Companys was handed over to Franco by the Vichy government and shot there on 15 October 1940. He is said to have faced his death with calm, barefooted on the Catalan earth and shouting ¡*Visca Catalunya!* True or not, it is a story of courage that inspired Catalans to survive the bitter decades to come.

Historians give varying figures for the numbers of people executed in Catalonia after the Civil War. Conxita Mir found that, after the fall of Lleida in April 1938, 558 people were executed after summary military trial, 148 were executed without trial and 169 prisoners were killed.[5] Solé i Sabaté, after extensive research, calculated some 3,385 throughout Catalonia, two or three in each village in order to maintain the populace cowed; other historians estimate more.[6]

Figure 10   2019 Wall naming the 1,706 people executed at the Camp
de la Bota, Barcelona, from 1939 to 1952 (Marisa Asensio)

The 1940s were years of well-calculated sadism. As after 1714,
Catalan autonomy and culture were suppressed. The *Generalitat* was
abolished. The Catalan language became illegal in schools and in public.
All names had to be in Spanish. Not even tombs could be inscribed in
Catalan. Civil servants, including teachers, were sacked and new ones
appointed according to their loyalty to the regime. Church processions
and military parades with fascist salutes occurred daily. Falangist and
religious insignia replaced all signs of the Republic.[7] The prisons were
packed: new ones were improvised. Prisoners died of disease and hunger.
The general populace lived in poverty, hunger and fear. Tuberculosis
was rife.

There was another Catalonia. The bourgeoisie were delighted to
return from France and Burgos to occupy again the houses and factories
they had lost. Many of these ex-*Lliga* members became stalwarts of the
Franco regime. Wages were low and workers obedient. Cambó spoke for
'Franco's Catalans' in 1943: 'I repudiate the regime ... but the important
thing is the maintenance of internal order and the prevention of another
Civil War and the only person who can guarantee this is Franco.'[8]

Resistance

All the defeated parties attempted, courageously but to little effect, to maintain clandestine organisation within the country. Anarchist and communist guerrillas, the *maquis*, tied down the Civil Guard in the Pyrenees, but had little or no contact with the working class. In October 1944, in the euphoria of the liberation of Paris, the Communists led 2,500 soldiers into the high Pyrenean valley, the Vall d'Aran. The invasion was a debilitating, demoralising failure. The PCE had confidently expected an uprising throughout Catalonia in response to their army, but – and this would be a consistent weakness of the PSUC/PCE in the following decades – the leadership in France and Moscow had not fully grasped the reality of life within Spain, that is, the extent of the defeat and the extenuation of the working class.

The earliest recorded workers' resistance took place on 8 May 1945, when several factories stopped work and trams halted in silent celebration of Hitler's defeat. A similar anti-fascist protest took place at the Maquinista locomotive plant (now a shopping mall) in Sant Andreu, Barcelona, on 15 August 1945, when Japan surrendered and the afternoon shift of 1,800 people did not turn up. In general, though – and this would be the pattern of working-class resistance right through to the 1970s – protests and strikes were over concrete questions of wages and conditions. Valiant political activists promoted such actions, which only took on an explicitly political content following the customary police repression. The first major strike started in the Manresa textile factory Bertrand y Serra in January 1946. The owners refused to pay the local holiday on 24 January to celebrate Franco's 1939 occupation of the city. The women workers, led by Joana Picoy, entered the factory, but did not start the machines. Each shift did the same. Other factories in the city followed suit. The women, present at their posts but not working, resisted the attacks of the feared armed police, the *grisos* (*greys*, because of their uniforms), and the inducements of the Civil Governor. Some shops in the city closed in solidarity. After a week, on 31 January, the women won not only their demand, but also a wage rise.[9]

The years 1946 and 1947 saw a number of protests: as many as 47 textile companies and 17 engineering plants took action against starvation wages in the former year. Even the bosses' organisation in Sabadell recognised that these actions were 'due to the steady increase in the cost of living'. They were protests of desperation, but also motivated by hope that Franco might follow the fate of Mussolini and Hitler.[10] In contrast, 1948 and 1949 saw no conflicts at all: fatalistic despair had set in.

In 1950, a semi-skilled textile worker had to work eight hours to buy a dozen eggs; an unskilled worker, eight hours for a kilo of bread. As hunger was rife, theft from workplaces was common practice and socially condoned.[11] Frying pans hanging from balconies in many neighbourhoods protested silently that there was no cooking oil and the pans were empty.[12] Just to make ends meet, people were often working 60-hour weeks.

The most famous struggle of these hungry years was spectacular: the 1951 Barcelona tram boycott. Extreme poverty combined with two other factors to create the conditions for the boycott. In 1948, the Communist Party had abandoned guerrilla struggle to concentrate on underground organisation in the workplaces;[13] and in Madrid, tram fares were lower, which was perceived as clear discrimination. Despite Franco's best efforts, the national question refused to disappear.

In this context, the announcement in February 1951 that tram tickets were to rise by 20 *céntimos* was explosive. In the first week of March, the overwhelming majority of the population refused to travel on public transport. Empty trams passed thousands of workers walking miles to work. Trams were stoned or burnt. Police baton-charged crowds. On the afternoon of Sunday 4 March, the authorities laid on special free trams at the Les Corts football stadium to take home the crowds after the Barcelona Santander match. Though it was pouring with rain, no one boarded them.

On the Tuesday, the vertical union, membership of which was compulsory for workers and management alike, convened a meeting of 2,000 work-place representatives. According to a participant cited by Sebastian Balfour:

[The provincial boss] ended by singing *Cara al Sol* (the Falangist hymn), and told the audience to go home because the meeting was over. But nobody moved from their seats. Then the real meeting began. For four hours ... one speaker after another coming forward to give an improvised speech.[14]

The meeting called a general strike before being removed from the premises by the Armed Police. The next day, Wednesday 7 March, the authorities cancelled the fare rise. But the protest did not end there: the following Monday, some 300,000 workers did strike against arrests during the boycott and paralysed the city for three days. They won. Those arrested were released and the Civil Governor, City Mayor, police chief and the boss of the vertical union were all sacked.

Despite the hopes raised among the opposition, the Barcelona events did not augur the collapse of the regime, just about to be bolstered by the 1952 military treaty with the USA, which signified the end of its international isolation. It would be twenty years before the opposition could muster again such broad mass protests.

Wriggling into Every Crack

Unrest swept the universities in 1956. A generation that had not known the Civil War, sons (mainly) and daughters of both victors and vanquished, agitated for the right of assembly and election of representatives. The movement led to the founding of the FOC (Front Obrer Català – Catalan Workers' Front), which argued that socialist revolution was on the agenda, unlike the PSUC, the Catalan Communist Party that was fighting fiercely to defeat the regime, but with the lesser perspective of a democratic republic. The student revolt of 1956 was also significant because a large minority of university students broke with the regime. By the 1960s, Barcelona university was a semi-free enclave. The political activist and novelist Manuel Vázquez Montalbán (1939–2003) told how he was being chased after a demonstration and slipped into a class of several dozen students. Armed police flung open the door and aggressively asked if anyone had just entered the classroom. No one, neither teacher nor students, betrayed the presence of the sweating Vázquez Montalbán. Many of the 1956 student activists would become the lawyers, scientists, journalists, bank-workers and teachers who founded professional associations and took part in the mass actions of the 1970s.

On 12 March 1956, the large engineering factories of Barcelona, Pegaso, La Maquinista and Olivetti, and its major textiles plants such as Fabra y Coats and La España Industrial came out on strike. As well as the customary arrests, beatings and prison sentences, two wage rises that year led to the restoration of average earnings to the purchasing power of 1936! Another figure shows the poverty of the Spanish state: in 1935 Spain's GDP per capita was 67.3 per cent of the Western European average; in 1960, it was 50.8 per cent.[15] In 1958, the Collective Bargaining Act ceded the right to elect union representatives – within of course the state-run vertical trades union: all independent unions were illegal. The opposition, particularly the Communist Party, seized this opportunity and many members were elected as representatives. 'It went against the grain to participate in these state-controlled structures,' said Cipriano García, a leader of the workers' struggle in Terrassa, 'but I think we were right. We had to wriggle into every crack that opened in the system'.

On 20 November 1964, while the dictatorship was still congratulating itself on 'twenty-five years of peace and plenty', 300 workers met in the church of Sant Medir in the Barcelona quarter of Sants to formally found the *Comissions Obreres* of Catalonia. These *Workers' Committees* were something more than a trade union: they were 'a social and political movement to coordinate workplace struggles'. The four central points of the platform agreed at Sant Medir combined basic economic demands – a minimum wage for eight hours work and a sliding scale of wages to defend purchasing power – with political demands: the right to strike and freedom to organise.

The use of churches as meeting-places was particularly painful for Franco, whose attempt to eradicate left-wing ideology rested on an official doctrine of a united Catholic Spain. Now leftist priests and Christian organisations were working alongside the godless Communists. They were even meeting in churches, some of which had only recently been rebuilt after their destruction by atheists in the Civil War. Sant Medir itself was one such – re-opened in the 1950s. This key site of the anti-Franco struggle is a strikingly eccentric, brown concrete building with Dalinian egg-like domes on top.

During the first two decades of his dictatorship, Franco followed an economic policy known as 'autarky' or self-sufficiency. It was a total failure. By 1959, the regime was facing collapse. The World Bank warned the Spanish state that it was only two months from bankruptcy.[16] Despite its grandiloquent rhetoric of national independence and empire, the regime was forced to open Spain's doors to foreign investment. These capitalists couldn't believe their luck: not only were wages lower than anywhere else in Western Europe (except Portugal), but unions were illegal and workplace discipline was guaranteed by the police. Like China's in the 1990s, Spain's economy began to expand by some 10 per cent a year throughout the 1960s. The chaotic and unregulated industrialisation drew migrants into Catalonia's cities from hungry southern Spain. From 1960 to 1970, Badalona grew from a population of 92,000 to 163,000; L'Hospitalet from 123,000 to 242,000.[17] A peasantry and rural proletariat that was easily controllable by rural bosses and the Church became inhabitants of the outlying suburbs of the expanding cities. Many became aware of their collective power in both the factories and the new neighbourhoods. Despite continuing vigorous repression, the economic boom after 1961 meant that wages improved: 'State-owned enterprises and private sector industrialists were prepared to pay to avoid interrupting valuable production.'[18]

Residents' Associations

In the 1940s and 1950s, most migrants from the South lived either as subtenants to people from the same villages who had emigrated earlier or in self-constructed shanty towns on the outskirts of the cities. Some of these shacks, in Barcelona's Guinardó park for example, lasted until the 1990s. In Sabadell, hundreds of people lived in home-made caves dug in the banks of the River Ripoll until the end of the 1950s. In the 1950s and 1960s, speculators like Juan Antonio Samaranch, the falangist who became President of the International Olympic Committee, started building tower blocks, often unconnected to roads or basic services. Density of population was very high: in the *Ciudad Satélite* estate in Cornellà, just south of Barcelona, in 1970 each person had on average only 10 square metres of living space.[19]

At first, migrants were set only on survival but, in the mid-1960s, neighbourhood committees began to be organised. From 1969, these local committees blossomed into the *Associacions de veïns* or Residents' Associations, which became a huge neighbourhood movement in the 1970s. Carles Prieto, one of the leaders of the Residents' Association in Sants, told me:

People working in factories and involved in struggles for higher wages ... wanted to introduce into the areas where they lived the successful ways of organising they'd experienced at work. A SEAT worker earning good wages at the end of the 1960s just wasn't going to go on living in a shack without running water.[20]

In 1969, a new law partly legalising Associations, a wave of workplace repression and 'the influence of the Paris May', in Prieto's view, helped the Residents' Associations spread quickly throughout Barcelona, its surrounding industrial cities and the inland cities of Terrassa and Sabadell, in both workers' and more middle-class quarters, in both immigrant areas and traditional Catalan areas. Just as the factory *Comissions* had been built painstakingly, often by taking up very basic questions such as the conditions of the toilets; so the Residents' Associations focused first on 'non-political' questions such as paving the streets or rubbish collection.

The mayor of Barcelona from 1957–1973 was José María Porcioles. He was closely linked to the Banco de Madrid, which was connected with the Franco family: one of its main shareholders was the father of Franco's son-in-law. This bank, despite its name Barcelona-based, was founded in 1954 in Porcioles' office, when he was a notary before becoming Mayor. Porcioles and his cronies so enriched themselves in the speculative development of the 1960s that a new word was coined to describe corrupt building practice: *porciolisme*.

So blatant was corruption under Porcioles, riding roughshod over the regime's own urban planning laws, that he was finally removed by Madrid in 1973. The Residents' Associations, with their consistent exposures of building scandals, had helped create the climate for Porcioles' fall. Carles Prieto explained:

> The fall of Porcioles gave people confidence. In Sants, we had meetings of up to 150, most of them overjoyed just to be able to speak and hear Catalan in public. And in 1974 we won the battle with our alternative for the Plaça de Sants. We defeated the idea for a fly-over and we got the old tram depot, the *Cotxeres*, converted to a Community Centre. After that, the tide turned. The mass of local people openly supported us.[21]

Freedom, Amnesty, Statute

By the early 1970s, there were Residents' Associations in every *barri* of Catalonia's towns and cities. The Residents' Associations and *Comissions*

Obreres were the major forces organising mass pressure from below. However, a specific element of the transition in Catalonia was the demand for national rights. In November 1971, the *Assemblea de Catalunya* (Assembly for Catalonia) was formed on the PSUC's initiative. It was an umbrella organisation for illegal political parties, unions and professional associations. Its four main points were amnesty, introduction of democratic rights, re-establishment of the 1932 Autonomy Statute as a step towards self-determination and coordination with the opposition in the rest of the state.

The *Assemblea de Catalunya* had extraordinary success in mobilising under the famous slogan *Llibertat, Amnistia, Estatut d'Autonomia* (Freedom, Amnesty, Statute of Autonomy). Socialist groups, several far-left groups, the dominant PSUC and a swathe of local neighbourhood organisations and individuals united in the *Assemblea*. It had over 40 branches throughout Catalonia, which meant that when its elected leaderships were arrested in 1973 (113 people) and 1974 (67 people), it continued to function. You cannot so easily behead an organisation whose strength is in its feet.

After Franco's death in November 1975, the *Assemblea* organised mass demonstrations on 1 and 8 February 1976, and the huge march of several hundred thousand at Sant Boi on 11 September that year. Sant Boi, a town in the 'red belt' round Barcelona, was chosen, for sure because it was a centre of workers' struggle, but also because it was the birthplace of Rafael Casanova, the Chief Councillor of Barcelona during the 1714 siege.

The *Comissions Obreres*, dominated by workers who had migrated from other parts of the Spanish state to Catalonia in the 1940s, 1950s and 1960s, driven by hunger and hope, took on board the demands of the Assembly of Catalonia. The *Comissions* saw support for Catalan rights as an integral part of the anti-Franco struggle. In both the Basque Country and Catalonia, the national question energised the anti-fascist struggle, to make these two historic nations the most militant in the Spanish state.

The autochthonous and immigrant working class united in these years. At Sant Boi in 1976, Basque, Galician and Andalusian flags were waved alongside the Catalan ones. The PSUC and *Comissions Obreres* had mobilised their bases from the immigrant cities of the 'red belt'. Home-made placards declared: *Andalusians salute you on this historic day. Long live Catalonia!* The loss of 1970s unity is deeply mourned in the current independence struggle, where so many Spanish-speaking families have been pulled behind the Spanish nationalism of the Socialist Party and *Ciutadans* (see Chapter 12).

The workers' movement had not been a straight line of increasing struggle, but rose and fell through the 1960s as victories and repression alternated. By the early 1970s, strikes and demonstrations were common all over Spain. The international context was important. Paris '68, Italy '69, Britain '72, especially the Portuguese Revolution in 1974 and the ongoing resistance of Vietnam made these years ones of rising class struggle and optimism, only dented by Pinochet's 1973 coup in Chile.

Within Spain, the ailing and ageing dictator appointed Carrero Blanco as prime minister in 1969, with the brief to defeat the workers' movement. Carrero's first move was the show trial of 16 members of the Basque urban guerrilla organisation, ETA, in December 1970. He failed. Massive national and international demonstrations forced Carrero to commute the six death sentences. Despite heavy news censorship, activists in Spain delighted to hear of Spanish Embassies in various European cities in flames. Carrero, remembering Martínez Anido and the *Sindicats Lliures* of the 1920s, resorted to 'unofficial' gangs (members of fascist organisations and 'off-duty' policemen) to intimidate strikers and demonstrators. It became standard practice: 127 people were killed by police or fascists in 1975–1983.[22] These murders should not obscure the day-to-day violence of capitalism in 'peacetime': many more workers died at work. For instance, in 1972 alone, there were 236,050 recorded workplace accidents in the Spanish state and 424 deaths.[23]

In 1973, Carrero attempted another show trial in Madrid, this time against the *Comisiones Obreras* leaders. They were jailed, but ETA's widely celebrated assassination of Carrero on 21 December 1973 changed everything. The state, deprived of its strong man, responded like a thwarted child by executing the Catalan anarchist Salvador Puig Antich in March 1974, but was torn between the hard-line 'bunker' who wanted no change at all and 'reformists' within the Franco apparatus, who understood that the ruling class's economic privilege and power would be endangered unless concessions were made to the opposition.

After Franco's death in November 1975, his successor King Juan Carlos, while swearing loyalty to Franco, sided with the reformists. He did not want to end up like his brother-in-law Constantine, kicked out of Greece on the fall of the dictatorship in 1974. Juan Carlos installed

Adolfo Suárez as prime minister in July 1976. Suárez succeeded in organising general elections in June 1977, a new, more democratic constitution backed by referendum in 1978, and municipal elections in 1979, which marked the end of the main political changes of the 'Transition'.

In later years, the new post-79 democracy exalted Juan Carlos, Suárez and General Gutiérrez Mellado, the Head of the Army, as the three great democrats who engineered a Transition that avoided the risk of Civil War. The truth is different. As Abril Martorell, one of Suárez's ministers explained, 'Though it's true that the Transition was agreed between a few individuals acting on their own, the force that obliged them to agree was in the streets.'[24]

In the 1970s, fear was still general, but anger and disgust at the regime inspired a generation of activists to continue to risk their lives in struggle, thus forcing political change from below. A powerful example was the police killing of Manuel Fernández Márquez, one of 2,000 construction workers on strike at the Sant Adrià del Besós power station (Barcelona), on 3 April 1973. In the 1960s, such state violence would probably have driven the strikers back to work, but not only did Fernández Márquez's murder fail to break the strike, but workers' rage led to a general strike of solidarity in the nearby towns of Cerdanyola and Ripollet, extended by the *Comissions Obreres* networks.

There is no room here to explore the ins and outs of the workers' struggles of these years and the variations in the kind of industry. Terrassa and Sabadell, for instance, were wool towns, though this changed with the introduction of synthetic materials in the 1960s. In contrast, the towns in the *Baix Llobregat* (the lower Llobregat river – from Martorell to the coast) developed only in the 1960s and were dominated by multinational-owned engineering firms. The *Baix*, as it was known, became the centre of class struggle in Catalonia from 1970–1977, with three general strikes in 1974–1976.[25]

In the *Assemblea de Catalunya* and the workers' movement, the PSUC was the dominant force. The PSUC was the Catalan Communist Party, in constant tension with the PCE, who saw it as the Catalan 'section' of the PCE. In the 1950s the PCE/PSUC had adopted a policy of 'national reconciliation' to reach a parliamentary democracy, which meant workers linking with the 'progressive bourgeoisie' against the Francoists. It was a rerun of the 1930s Popular Front. This policy ran into sharp contradictions when workers went on strike and found that the bourgeoisie they were meant to be courting relied in practice on Franco's police. The PCE/PSUC's reformist policy gave rise to successive splits. By the 1970s, though the PSUC maintained its leadership and prestige in the opposition, the far left (mainly Maoist), organised in several groups seeking socialist revolution and not bourgeois democracy, numbered tens of thousands. One of these was the PSAN (Socialist Party for National Liberation), but it remained small: just as in 1936, the question of defeating fascism took precedence in activists' minds over independence. Nevertheless, the PSAN, with its propaganda linking socialist revolution and the independence from Spain of all the *països catalans* (Catalan Lands), was a powerful ideological influence decades later on the CUP.

These years of political ferment also saw the birth of a women's movement. Property rights (women had none under Franco: rather, women were men's property), divorce, abortion and family planning were issues carried by women into the mass organisations. Pickets in support of prisoners were often led by women. May 1976 saw the founding of an autonomous women's movement, with 2,000 women meeting at the *Llars Mundet* in Horta, Barcelona (an orphanage on the site of what was a concentration camp in the years immediately after Franco's victory). Basic women's rights became part of the agenda of most of the left, while many young women were beginning to discuss oppression and sexuality.

For gays and lesbians, the struggle was still more uphill. The FAGC (Gay Liberation Front of Catalonia) was boldly founded in the month of Franco's death, November 1975. The first Gay Pride demo brought together 5,000 people in 1977, risking arrest as homosexuality was illegal till 1979. Many male homosexuals were in jail as common criminals under the Law against Social Dangers (they did not benefit from amnesties for political prisoners). Much of the radical left did not support gay rights. ORT (Maoist) leader Manuel Guedán said: 'It is an alteration of sexuality ... it is not normal or natural.'[26] Guedán apologised and rectified later. At the time, influenced by China or Castro, many leftists saw homosexuality as a 'bourgeois deviation'. It would take many years before left organisations integrated gay rights into their programmes and practice.

196

SEAT and Roca

A list of strikes during the 1970s includes every major workplace in Catalonia.[27] I've selected struggles in Catalonia's two largest factories, the SEAT car plant (in the Zona Franca, Barcelona) and Roca Radiadores (in Gavà), to illustrate three key points: the power of the workers' movement in the transition, the political weakness of its leadership and the numerical weakness of the far left.

In October 1971, 7,000 workers at the car manufacturer SEAT occupied the Zona Franca plant. This was the first major struggle at the state's biggest company, founded in 1950, whose General Manager was a military officer. The workers' demands in 1971 were multiple, but focused on winning readmission for workers sacked for union activities. The police used tear gas and charges on horseback, but the workers defended themselves with high-pressure hoses and other tools of the factory. It took the police thirteen hours to seize control. Three workers were wounded by gunfire and one, Antonio Ruiz, died twelve days later. In Sebastian Balfour's words, 'The October struggle at SEAT radicalized somewhat the climate of public opinion. It also provided a model of struggle for many militants outside the plant'.[28] Repression defeated one struggle, but lit up later ones.

A vital lesson of this 'success in failure' was that, to reduce the influence of the far left, the Barcelona *Comissions* leadership went so far as to dissolve the committee coordinating the engineering sector. The PSUC thus impeded coordination between SEAT and other plants, which reduced the possibilities of extending the struggle.[29] The PSUC feared that workers' struggle coordinated from below might outflank their strategy of workers' pressure to negotiate collective agreements and could even skip out of their control into a general strike.

Another effect of the SEAT occupation and the workers' eviction was that many bosses began to see police brutality not as an aid but a hindrance. More and more often, bosses negotiated directly with the *Comissions* elected by the workers, in order to avoid strikes and conflict that would lead to damaged machinery and lost production. The 1971 occupation at SEAT cost the company some 2,000 million pesetas.

When today you land at Barcelona airport, you are in the ex-industrial town of El Prat. Nearby are Gavà, Sant Boi, Viladecans and Sant Vicens, industrial towns in the Baix Llobregat. Roca was a particularly large factory, with some 4,800 workers who manufactured radiators at Gavà. Direct democracy through frequent assemblies, with the revolutionary left playing a leading role, sustained the longest strike in the Transition. The 1970s Transition was not the 1930s: there was no pre-revolutionary situation despite the enormous social and political upheavals. The struggle at Roca, however, shows how the struggle could have been pushed forward, to make a Transition much more favourable to working-class interests.

Roca was a later struggle than the SEAT occupation. 1976 saw throughout the Spanish state the greatest number of strikes of the entire Transition, as workers fought against rising prices and sensed, where organisation was strongest, that the dictatorship without its dictator was tottering.

There were two major strikes at Roca in 1976, one starting in March and lasting 42 days, the other starting on 8 November and lasting 95 days. What differentiated the two struggles was the self-organisation of the workers in the second strike. After the 42-day strike, activists started to organise separately from the delegates of the vertical union, elected every four years. They considered that more direct democracy was needed and organised factory assemblies in each section. The assemblies elected directly between 43 (at the start) and 60 (later) representatives, who then forced the vertical union to resign (some honest delegates had already become directly elected representatives) and won a tense recognition battle from the bosses. Fernando Palomo explained how trust and confidence were created:

> The conditions of work were infrahuman in many respects. Many Roca workers died of silicosis. In fact, during the time we were on strike, once or twice a month the entire workforce would march in demonstration to a funeral. There were terrible conditions, of health and also rhythm of work and everything. All this unites people, doesn't it? If in addition at breaks or lunch, we talk … information and this and that. An atmosphere of comradeship is created and seeing the representative who you've elected, you say, 'I want him to represent us and he, well, we'll follow him wherever.'[30]

To British workers, the figure of the directly elected representative is familiar as the shop steward. At Roca, however, the 'shop stewards' were elected in assemblies under illegal conditions. Democracy was more direct.

The 95-day strike was provoked by the management, who dismissed a leading activist while the reps were still preparing the strike. During the 95 days, the workers withstood constant police attacks on picket lines and demonstrations. Live bullets were fired into workers' houses, many grouped in an estate near the factory. The workers were nearly all male, but the women of their families also demonstrated.

As at SEAT, the question of solidarity was key. In fact, the workforce returned after 95 days because solidarity was falling. *Comissions Obreres* did support the strike, but it was a passive support. The workforce went directly to neighbouring factories in the Baix Llobregat, asking for financial support and solidarity action. Such a huge strike, widely covered on television and in the press, could decisively have changed the balance of forces if the *Comissions* had worked to bring out other factories in a one-day (or more) general strike.

Fernando Palomo summed up the political possibilities thwarted:

> The Baix Llobregat at that time was a domain of the PSUC and the traditional *Comissions Obreres*. Our strike didn't please them and they fucked us over as much as they could, they put every kind of obstacle in our way ... It's understandable because here there was an important political question. We were in a transition process, the leadership of the Communist Party had pacted with sectors of the army and Church and the powers that be for national reconciliation and democratic change. Any strike outside this framework could damage their strategy. In addition, conflict was enormous at that time, there wasn't a day without a strike in the Baix Llobregat and, well, this could lead to Roca setting a precedent of combativity and different, new forms of organisation outside the control of the PSUC's apparatus and that damaged them.[31]

The 'different, new forms of organisation' were forms of direct democracy: all decisions were taken in assembly and only the elected shop-floor delegates would negotiate with the company, not *Comissions Obreres* on their behalf; the strikers' organisation of self-defence against the police; and their direct appeals for solidarity, using union structures where possible and going beyond them when necessary.[32]

Of all the strikes in the Transition, Roca's was the most radical.

The Return of the Generalitat

The results of the first democratic elections,[33] on 15 June 1977, were quite different in Catalonia from those in the Spanish state overall, where Suárez's improvised coalition the UCD (*Unión del Centro Democrático*) won. In Catalonia, the Socialists won 28.56 per cent of the vote and the PSUC, 18.31 per cent, with Suárez's UCD on 16.91 per cent and Jordi Pujol's right-wing Catalan nationalists on 16.88 per cent. The national question and the high level of workers' struggle meant that Francoism was marginalised more in Catalonia than in the rest of the Spanish state (excepting the Basque Country). Many of those capitalists who had supported with cash and raised arms General Yagüe's entry into Barcelona in January 1939 transformed themselves into lifelong Catalanists once the end of the dictatorship could be glimpsed on the horizon.

The year before the 1977 elections, Suárez had contacted through intermediaries Josep Tarradellas, resident in France and President of the *Generalitat* in exile since 1954. Now, Suárez acted quickly to avert the danger of a Government in Catalonia of the parties based on the working class. Just twelve days after the elections, Tarradellas landed in Madrid and negotiated directly with Suárez and the king. The PSUC and Catalan Socialists entered a state of suicidal hypnosis. They complained, but did nothing, while Suárez and Tarradellas (who represented no one) agreed to reinstate the *Generalitat* under a regime of Autonomy yet to be negotiated. The Catalan right celebrated this as the triumphal return of an historic institution, but this was a smokescreen concealing that the *Generalitat* was restored with no democratic legitimacy or any real content of self-government. Dramatically, the PSUC accepted this, no longer seeking the 'rupture' with Francoism they had fought for since 1939, but a transition controlled by King Juan Carlos, Suárez and his ministers, all Franco supporters until the day before. Language suffered the stress of political surrender: the PSUC called their new policy a 'pacted rupture'.

On 11 September 1977, Catalonia saw the biggest demonstration since the funeral of Buenaventura Durruti 41 years before. Whistling and placards against Tarradellas were heard and seen everywhere – one popular chant was: *No volem titelles. Fora Tarradellas (We don't want puppets. Tarradellas out)* – but everything was already decided. On 23 October, Tarradellas returned to Catalonia as president. All parliamentary parties entered his unelected government, including the PSUC: its version of the Italian 'historic compromise'. The PSUC collapsed in 1981–1982.

Though too weak to change events, the revolutionary left did not accept these manoeuvres. The LCR summarised the significance of the role of Suárez's 'Viceroy' Tarradellas like this:

> For the 'Catalan opposition' and particularly the large workers' parties, Tarradellas meant ceaseless affronts and headaches. But essentially he was a relief, for he created the possibility of diverting the attention of the workers' movements towards a third party in discord. This enabled them to camouflage better their capitulation to Suárez's plans.[34]

The Catalan right showed once again that it preferred direct negotiation with Madrid in order to maintain its influence and businesses, against the will of the people of Catalonia that had been expressed clearly in the June election.

Suárez had tamed Catalonia. At the same time as the return of Tarradellas he was negotiating the 'Moncloa Agreements', in which Communists and Socialists accepted the pegging of wages below inflation in return for promises of social legislation that were never fulfilled. The path was cleared for the approval in referendum of the monarchical Constitution in December 1978.

In a 68 per cent turnout, 90.46 per cent of Catalans voted Yes to the new Constitution (pompously called the *Carta Magna*), even though it specified that Spain had to be a monarchy, the state's unity was guaranteed by the army and mergers or close links between different Autonomous Communities were forbidden. Several such articles were dictated directly by the army and monarchy. Since 1978, the massive Catalan vote for the Constitution has often been wielded as a stick to try and silence its left-wing opponents. The vote for the Constitution can more properly be interpreted as a vote against a possible coup or new Civil War and for democratic peace, however limited, after years of dictatorship and struggle.

It was a vote under pressure and with scant prior debate. All the media and parliamentary parties pressed for a 'Yes' vote. In short: 'The authoritarian conditions that in 1977 and 1978 shaped and curtailed the writing and approval of the Spanish constitution to a large extent invalidate the constitution's legitimacy as a democratic framework.'[35]

Demands of the years of struggle, such as self-determination, demilitarisation or the cleansing of Francoists from public institutions (police, judiciary, civil service), were overlooked.

REBEL PORTRAIT: LLUÍS LLACH

Lluís Llach is a singer-songwriter with a powerful voice and lyrical, melodious compositions, but has no doubt about his purpose: 'My singing has always been political'; and 'Singing in Catalan means being an activist.'[36]

Born in 1948 in the town of Verges in the Baix Empordà, Llach first sang in public in the choir of the imposing Dance of Death performed there every Easter Thursday since medieval times.

Llach became in 1968 one of the youngest of a 1960s group of singers known as the *Setze jutges*, Sixteen Judges. The *jutges* were leaders of a huge cultural movement known as the *Nova Cançó*, New Song, that

Figure 11   Lluís Llach revolutionising the public with his look
(Dámaso Martín)

bound together masses of young people against the dictatorship. The *Setze jutges* aimed to rescue Catalan culture from the silence imposed by Franco; and to create an alternative to commercial (mostly anglophone) pop.[37]

The *nova cançó* was influenced by French anarchist singer-songwriters such as Leo Ferré and Georges Brassens. It fed and was fed by Catalan youth's growing rejection of the dictatorship. It was also a movement that bound together the Catalan lands: Maria del Mar Bonet comes from Mallorca, Raimon and Ovidi Montllor from Xàtiva and Alcoi, respectively, towns in the *país valencià*. And all these singers performed in Catalan throughout the Spanish state to the acclaim of mass audiences – impossible to imagine today, when that anti-Franco unity between peoples has been smashed.

Llach's success was immediate. His *L'estaca*, The Stake, inspired by May 1968, was chanted by tens of thousands against the regime, not just in concerts but also at demonstrations. This anthem of collective resistance has the brilliant simplicity of a children's song:

> If I pull hard this way
> and you pull hard that,
> the stake will surely fall, fall, fall
> and we'll all be free.

Llach was offered a juicy recording contract in 1968 if he sang in Castilian. He refused the carrot and the stick struck: in 1969, he was banned for four years from live performance, bizarrely 'for revolutionizing the public with his look'. Just before the ban, he was forbidden to sing *L'estaca* in a concert at Barcelona's *Palau de la Música*. The whole audience sang the song while he quite legally remained silent on stage (though, no doubt, looking). The anecdote shows the power of a mass cultural-political movement. Despite having no television or radio time, despite being banned from performing, the *Nova Cançó* singers and their songs were widely known and their records sold.

Llach left for France, where he was also acclaimed. In 1975, after his return to performing within Spain, he reached a peak with *Viatge a Ítaca*, Journey to Ithaca. It is a complex composition, led by Llach's soaring, operatic voice:

Més lluny, sempre aneu més lluny
Further, move always further on
from the today that enchains you,
and when you reach freedom
set out again on journeys anew
… Be quite clear, don't stop.

Odysseus' journey back to Ithaca was long and hard. One's life journey is long and full of obstacles to overcome. To reach your destination is not enough; you must keep moving forward. His public understood perfectly Llach's poetry and rich song, in the common coded language needed under a dictatorship.

One of the songs on *Viatge a Ítaca* was *Abril 74*, in celebration of the Portuguese revolution. In Lisbon, Llach found the freedom that was lacking in Spain.

> I lived that environment very intensely, as I saw myself as a sort of accomplice … I remember a tremendous chaos and, what's more, the people used songs as tools of struggle.[38]

Viatge a Ítaca sold 150,000 copies; his next LP, *Campanades a morts* (*Chimes for the Dead*), even more. *Campanades* protested and mourned the notorious police assault on a strike meeting inside a church in Vitoria (Basque Country) in March 1976. Five people were shot dead. Llach raged against the 'Murderers of reason, of lives'.

Llach, like Raimon, Bonet and Ovidi Montllor, did not accept that the coming of democracy was the end of struggle, as post-Franco capitalism desired. Catalonia had to move 'always further on'. In 1979, he sang *No és això, companys* (Not this, comrades), insisting against the new strait-jacketed democracy:

> It wasn't for this, comrades,
> … that so many flowers died …
> Maybe we have to be brave again
> and say no, my friends, it's not this.

Llach's own voyage was as long and hard as Odysseus' from Troy to Ithaca. Born into a Francoist family and as a child entranced by the

Falange's imagery and display, he became (and still is) a paladin of gay rights, a cultural-political leader against the dictatorship, an opponent of NATO and militarism, activist in solidarity with Palestine, Kosovo and Africa, and a fighter for the independence of Catalonia. And a great composer and singer, revolutionising Catalonia not only with his look but also with his words and voice.

12

This Difficult Spirit: From Autonomy to Independence

Déu nos do la gosadia
de la sang independent,
i aquesta ànima difícil,
i aquest llavi malcontent.

God grant us the daring
of independent blood
and this difficult spirit
and this discontented lip.

Josep Carner[1]

On 19 May 1960, a group of Catholic anti-Francoists stood up during a packed concert in Barcelona's Palau de la Música Catalana and sang the banned *Cant de la Senyera* (*Song to the Catalan Flag*), a patriotic poem by Joan Maragall set to music.

The symbolism of the occasion was powerful. It was the hundredth anniversary year of the birth of Maragall, a poet of freedom in nature and joy in life. Maragall (1860–1911) was a key historical reference for the protesters: Catholic and Catalanist, he had opposed the Church's and Prat de la Riba's repressive line after the *Setmana tràgica*. Someone of profound religiosity, Maragall fought to renew the Church and the society it dominated; just as those reciting his poem were fighting against Franco's brutal national-Catholicism. In addition, the Palau de la Música, a magnificent *modernista* concert hall, was where in 1909 the first project for an Autonomy Statute had been presented. And, most important, Franco himself was on a visit to Catalonia.

The year before, the same group of Catalan Christians had organised, alongside other forces, a successful campaign to boycott *La Vanguardia*, Barcelona's main daily paper, because of its editor Galinsoga's infamous insult: 'All Catalans are shit'. The boycott lost the paper some 20,000 subscribers and many more readers. The regime removed Galinsoga in February 1960. (Up to the 1960s, the regime appointed – and dismissed – the editors of all newspapers published in Spain).

Jordi Pujol

After the events of the Palau de la Música, Jordi Pujol was arrested – although he had not been present; he was beaten up and sentenced to seven years in jail. He had written the leaflet that the protesters scattered over the stalls of the Palau de la Música, but the sentence was as much for the successful Galinsoga boycott as for the Palau events.

Pujol spent 30 months inside. In 1980, in the first post-dictatorship elections to the Autonomous Government of Catalonia, this conservative Catalan nationalist, his reputation bolstered by his anti-Franco activities, beat the socialist Joan Reventós against expectation to become president, a position he then held, winning six successive elections, until 2003. Pujol's victory was received with relief in Madrid: strange as it seems today, a possible Socialist government was seen as much more Catalanist and thus dangerous than a Pujol regime. Pujol won, despite having been one of the main negotiators, alongside Tarradellas, for the 1979 Statute of Autonomy, based on the 1932 Statute and widely criticised for its limitations. The negotiators accepted a swathe of amendments to the original draft. As Kathryn Crameri summarised: 'It was carefully tailored so as not to give the autonomous community any powers which might in the future prove threatening to the Spanish state.'[2]

The nations within the Spanish state were not recognised as such, just as had occurred with the 1932 trimming of the Núria Statute. Aspirations to greater autonomy were reduced still further after the attempted coup d'état of 23 February 1981. This failed to reinstall a dictatorship, as Tejero the Civil Guard colonel who led the assault on the Madrid Cortes wanted, or even change the government, as the king hoped. Its success lay in the shadow it cast over the LOAPA (Organic Bill to Harmonise the Autonomic Process), approved in 1982. This Act of Parliament gave equal status to all 17 Autonomous Communities. It became known as café per a tots (coffee for everyone), because areas of the state such as La Rioja that had never aspired to either devolution or nationhood were treated just the same as the historic nations of Galicia, the Basque

Country and Catalonia. The LOAPA was designed to impede any demands for greater recognition of national rights.

During his decades in power, Pujol was Janus: with one face he assured his voters that Catalonia was advancing in the control of its resources, while with the other he reassured the PSOE and PP governments that he could be relied on to ensure the economic and political stability of Spain. He shared the PP and PSOE's neoliberalism. With over 50 per cent, Catalonia has the highest proportion of private schools in Europe. Many of these (the *concertades*) are religious and are financed by the Autonomous Government. Since the 1980s, privatisation of public corporations (water, municipal workforces, sections of the Health Service etc.) has been promoted.

Pujol and the coalition he led, *Convergència i Unió*, could conceal their common right-wing interests with Spanish governments behind important Catalanist measures. His governments founded the autonomous television channel TV3 and Catalunya Ràdio; they subsidised press and books in Catalan. Most importantly, linguistic immersion in the schools meant that all schoolchildren learnt Catalan.

Pujol pressed Madrid constantly for more devolved powers. Catalonia gained over 100 transfers of control during his governments. The dream of Capmany or Prat de la Riba that Catalonia could lead the Spanish state politically as well as economically was not Pujol's. Instead, Pujol became a kingmaker in Madrid, first of all lending *Convergència i Unió*'s votes to keep Felipe González in power in 1993 and then supporting Aznar and his PP in 1996. Support did not come free. Pujol negotiated greater investment in Catalonia and transfers of power. Pujol was a high-class horse-trader. The need for *Convergència*'s votes hadn't prevented Aznar's over-excited followers on election night in 1996 chanting:

Pujol enano,
habla castellano
(Pujol dwarf/speak Spanish)

Pujol was short of stature. The crude insult wouldn't have bothered him. He knew that what Galinsoga had shouted in public many in power in Madrid thought in private, even though Aznar absurdly claimed he spoke Catalan in intimate conversations.

Pujol's 1980 victory was a surprise to many because the nationalist right had not been so prominent in the anti-Franco struggles as the Communists and the *Assemblea de Catalunya*. Under Franco, Pujol and his followers emphasised 'Building the Country', which was understood as re-constructing Catalan cultural and financial institutions. The Socialists and Communists had won a majority in the 1977 statewide elections but, by 1980, the high level of class struggle had dropped and unemployment was rising. The *desencís* (disenchantment) of the 1980s was setting in. This decline in struggle favoured Pujol. Moreover, he knew rural Catalonia profoundly: his combination of anti-Franco credentials and Catholic, conservative politics was a winning formula. In addition, the PSUC that had won 18 per cent of the vote in the 1977 general election collapsed in 1981, splitting into Eurocommunist and pro-Soviet parties.

Despite being the author of a 1958 pamphlet that saw the mass post-Civil War immigration of Andalusians to Catalonia as a serious threat to the national reconstruction of Catalonia ('[their] natural ignorance leads to mental and spiritual wretchedness'), Pujol as President was canny enough to avoid explicitly racist division. He insisted that anyone who lived in Catalonia was Catalan and launched a massive and successful 'normalisation' programme in the 1980s to teach both Catalans (who spoke Catalan, but had not been taught to write it) and immigrants the language. His election slogan was an inclusive 'In Catalonia, everyone has a place'.[3] He then came up with the famous 'Everyone who lives and works in Catalonia is Catalan'.[4] Catalan became the normal language in schools and the autonomous administration, although the press and television continued to be read and seen mainly in Spanish and continue so to this day (some 75 per cent for television viewing).

Esquerra Republicana could not hide the ugly side of their nationalism as well as Pujol did. In 1980, their votes gave Pujol the presidency in exchange for their leader Heribert Barrera becoming president of the parliament. Barrera had a long history of racism, dating from the 1930s, when he was closer to Macià's *Estat català*, some of whose leaders ended up admiring Mussolini, than Companys' left social democracy (see Chapter 9). There are numerous pearls from Barrera:

'American negros have a coefficient lower than whites'.
'I prefer a Catalonia as it was in the Republic, without immigration'.

'We may have overcome Andalusian immigration, but I don't know if we will be able to cope with immigration from South America and the Maghreb'.[5]

Migration from southern Spain had soared in the 1950s and 1960s. By 1970, 37.6 per cent of the Catalan population had been born outside Catalonia. Over 700,000 Andalusians settled in Catalonia from 1940 to 1970.[6] Some Catalan nationalists saw this as a plot to undermine Catalan language and culture by introducing more Spanish speakers to Catalonia.[7] In reality, migration was a result of uneven development: poverty in southern Spain and the relative wealth of Catalonia. At the time, the regime's desire to divide the two sections, migrant and autochthonous, of the working class largely failed. It would be later, in the second decade of the twenty-first century, when independence struggles were on the rise, that the state was successful in pulling many workers behind a Spanish nationalist political project, a neo-Lerrouxism led by *Ciutadans*, founded in 2006. This was possible because decades of Pujolism, followed by Artur Mas's severe cutbacks in social spending, allowed *Ciutadans* to identify Catalanism with a self-serving, racist Catalan ruling class.

Pujol survived a powerful campaign orchestrated from Felipe González's Socialist Government when the *Banca Catalana* that he had founded collapsed among accusations of corruption in 1984. Pujol used the attacks from Madrid to reinforce his prestige in Catalonia. He and Catalonia held the moral high ground, he claimed, against this 'dirty trick'. Henceforth, Pujol (and his successor Artur Mas) habitually defended themselves from attacks in Louis XIV style ('l'état, c'est moi'), that is, by claiming that criticism of him was really an attack on Catalonia.

In 2014, Pujol fell off his high pedestal. He was forced to admit that, for over 30 years, he had evaded taxes on 4 million euros held secretly in Andorra. Subsequent police investigations found that 69 million euros 'of unknown origin' had been found in various foreign bank accounts belonging to Pujol and his family. The report of the investigating judge in July 2020 concluded that there was sufficient evidence to put Pujol, his wife Marta Ferrusola, and their seven children on trial for belonging to a criminal organisation guilty of fraud and money laundering. Despite this, it is still common to hear nationalists argue that Pujol shouldn't be criticised too severely, because criticism provides ammunition to anti-Catalanists and because he is the 'father of modern Catalonia' who did a lot of good for the country during his presidency. The reverse is true. If you refuse to criticise a corrupt leader, then you are accepting that an independent Catalonia will be corrupt. And doing good for the country? Pujol's enthusiastic neoliberalism maintained poverty and deepened inequality, laying the material basis for the rise of *Ciutadans*.

Education is today a particular battleground. Spanish centralists see the 40 years of Catalan control of education as forty years of indoctrination of children in myths of Catalan superiority, laying foundations for independence. The *Generalitat*'s education and culture programmes 'did much to propagate the idea that … [Catalans] were inhabitants of a distinctive nation', in John Elliott's words.[8] In truth, such programmes were mainly correcting the four decades of Francoist indoctrination at the barrel of a gun. And, of course, Catalans *are* inhabitants of a distinctive nation.

Statute

When the Socialists wrested the *Generalitat* from Pujol's *Convergència i Unió* in 2003, the new President Pasqual Maragall proposed a new Statute for Catalonia to improve on the 1982 LOAPA's *cafè per a tots* and revived the call for a federal Spain.[9] Aznar, who was President of the Spanish Government from 1996 to 2004 and held an absolute majority from 2000, was attempting to recentralise the state and make Madrid not just the political capital it had been for five centuries, but also Spain's economic centre. The Autonomous Communities that controlled 20 per cent of public expenditure in 1982 controlled 51 per cent (both figures exclude pensions) by 1998.[10] Maragall sought to both extend devolution further and reassert Catalonia's economic dominance; whereas Aznar wanted to reverse the devolution of powers and promote Madrid's new-found economic strength.

Maragall, who enjoyed enormous prestige as the mayor of Barcelona from 1982 to 1997, a period that included the 1992 Olympic Games, was talking of a Europe of the Regions ('our new homeland is Europe'), a challenge to Aznar's vision of a strong, centralised state. Globalisation was changing the balance of forces. The Catalan bourgeoisie was not now so dependent on selling its goods within the Spanish state. Spain's membership since 1991 of the EU opened up Europe as a market. At the same time, Catalan business wanted to keep its competitive edge over Madrid. This revolved round three central infrastructure demands: an AVE (High-Speed Train) not just to Madrid, but also to London, Milan and Paris; an airport that could be an international hub, without everything (such as, for example, flights to New York) passing through Madrid;[11] and the Mediterranean rail corridor from southern Spain through Valencia and Barcelona and into France.

The PP detested Maragall's government and project. In opposition in the state after March 2004, it launched a campaign in the rest of Spain to boycott Catalan products and collected 4 million signatures against the Statute. The boycott had a practical effect: Catalan products lost sales in the rest of Spain. However, the world market compensated. *Cava* (sparkling wine), for instance, found new markets: Freixenet had big success (undercutting champagne prices) in the rest of Europe and the USA.

Zapatero, the Socialist prime minister in Madrid from 2004 to 2011, promised that he would respect the vote of the Catalan Parliament, which in 2006 passed the Statute, involving better financing and greater autonomy, by 90 per cent of the votes (all but the PP). In June 2006, it was approved in referendum with 74 per cent voting 'yes', though on a low (49 per cent) turn-out.

Then Maragall's statute ran into quicksand, not unexpectedly, in the Spanish parliament. Zapatero reneged on his promise. The PP and many of the PSOE's leaders objected strongly to the definition of Catalonia as a nation. It ended up being a 'nationality'. The PP took the statute to the Constitutional Court, a Conservative body that wields the 1978 Constitution as a shibboleth to halt progressive legislation.

In 2010, four years after the PP's appeal against the *Estatut*, the Constitutional Court deleted 14 of the Statute's clauses and amended 27 others. This was especially outrageous because some of the clauses deleted had already been approved in, among others, the Valencian and Andalusian Autonomous Communities' statutes. Clauses giving Catalonia greater judicial independence and setting a minimum level for state spending in Catalonia were struck out.

On 10 July 2010, hundreds of thousands demonstrated against the sentence in Barcelona behind the slogan *Som una nació. Nosaltres decidim* (We're a nation. We decide). Only 16 per cent of Catalans found the

Constitutional Court sentence 'fair'. Sixty-one per cent found it unjust. After the demonstration, Catalans' support for independence leaped to 47 per cent. During the Pujol years, this figure had vegetated at around 10 or 15 per cent, a significant if small minority. Now, any advance in autonomy had been blocked by the state. Where else to go but to secede? At this juncture, events began to run out of control for both Pujol's *Convergència i Unió*, returned to power in 2010 under Artur Mas, and the PP, who defeated the PSOE in the 2011 Spanish general election. A profound grass-roots rebellion in Catalonia began to mobilise the 45–50 per cent of Catalans that the polls showed in support of independence.

To step back in time a moment, this mass independence movement was also fed by the many and varied anti-capitalist mobilisations since the 'Battle of Seattle', a demonstration against the World Trade Organization (WTO) in December 1999. For a few years, every meeting of the world's main economic and financial institutions was besieged by mass demonstrations. Catalans participated in Davos, Prague, Nice (where trades unionists also marched in force), Geneva and Edinburgh, among other places. In July 2001, in demonstrations against the G-8 in Genoa, Berlusconi's police killed Carlo Giuliani and beat up hundreds of demonstrators. The quite conscious assault on the right to protest halted the dynamic of the movement.

Demonstrators had real victories: in June 2001, for instance, the World Bank cancelled its 'Summit against Poverty' in Barcelona because of the threat of mass mobilisation. These anti-globalisation and anti-capitalist mobilisations spilled over into the international movement to stop the 2003 invasion of Iraq, which the Spanish Government supported. In the Barcelona anti-war demonstration of 15 February 2003, with at least a million marching, even members of Pujol's government felt obliged to take part.

Though these movements declined, as mainly student demonstrators did not have the power to halt imperialist war or overthrow the World Bank, WTO or the International Monetary Fund; and reformist leaders like Susan George were not prepared to call for more demonstrations after the police riot at Genoa, they left confidence in the validity of mass mobilisation and widespread questioning of capitalism. In 2011, throughout the Spanish state, the 15-M (15 May or *indignados* = the indignant) movement occupied the main squares of the state's cities for several weeks. They were reacting to the austerity measures adopted by Zapatero's Socialist Government in 2009 and by Mas after coming to power in Catalonia in 2010. At that time, Mas loved to boast that Catalonia was ahead of the state government in the public sector cuts it had made. These cuts and wage freezes were to be deepened by the PP that won the state general election in November 2011.

Grass-Roots Rebellion

The decade-long mobilisations against capitalist globalisation, imperialist war and austerity that involved millions in the Spanish state fed into the reactions to the liquidation of the Catalan *Estatut*. It was no secret that Spain's Constitutional Court was going to strike down clauses. Thus, before the Court's verdict, a grass-roots movement, led by the anti-capitalist CUP (Popular Unity Candidacies) and ERC, began to organise local consultative referendums on independence. The first consultation took place on 13 September 2009 at Arenys de Munt, where 41 per cent of the electoral roll voted. The question at Arenys, followed with slight variation by succeeding consultations, was: 'Do you think that Catalonia should become an independent, democratic and social state based on the rule of law, as part of the European Union?'[12]

The last consultation was in Barcelona in April 2011. In the eighteen months in between, a national coordinating committee was organised and an estimated 60,000 volunteers took part in the campaigns. On 12–13 December 2009, 160 small town councils all round Catalonia organised votes. A second wave of 77 towns voted on 28 February 2010. On 25 April, 210 towns and villages voted. Throughout Catalonia, some 15–20 per cent of the electoral roll voted in these referendums. The result was always a Yes to Independence as the vast majority of participants were independence supporters. What was important, though, was not the result but the mobilisation.

The independence movement had taken off. *Convergència*, the main party of the Catalan bourgeoisie, was pushed into support for independence if it was not to be outflanked. In part, this was a smokescreen: Artur Mas was diverting attention from serious corruption scandals in his party and from outrage at his austerity policies. Spanish centralists wield *Convergència*'s corruption as a weapon against the independence movement, making out that the whole movement is corrupt. In fact, it has been a movement driven from below since the first consultation at

Arenys, dragging Mas along. He was the dog tied to the back of the cart, not the pony trotting out in front.

The *Diada*, Catalonia's national day to commemorate the defence of Barcelona against the Bourbons in 1714, saw million-plus demonstrations on 11 September 2012, 2013 and 2014. On 9 November 2014, the *Generalitat* finally organised a Catalonia-wide referendum. It was illegalised by Spain's constitutional court, but went ahead as a consultation with no legal standing. There were two questions: 'Do you want Catalonia to be a state?' and 'Do you want this state to be independent?'

If it seems strange to think a state might NOT be independent, the reason can be found in history, when often a 'Catalan state' had been proposed within a federation of Iberian peoples, as in the 1873 Republic. Eighty per cent of 2.3 million voters voted Yes–Yes (the electoral roll in 2010 in Catalonia held 5.3 million people). The referendum was a festive occasion. It showed the force of the movement. It also showed that the conservative pro-independence parties were not prepared to break with Spanish constitutional legality by organising a binding referendum.

Pressure continued. The 'binding' referendum was to come on 1 October 2017, under Mas's chosen replacement, the journalist and Mayor of Girona, Carles Puigdemont, leader of a government of coalition between *Convergència* and ERC. Mas had been forced out by the refusal of the CUP to accept as President someone so closely involved with cuts and corruption.

Europe's Biggest Anti-Capitalist Organisation

The CUP won 336,000 votes, 8 per cent of the total, giving it ten members of parliament in the September 2015 Catalan elections. It had become the biggest revolutionary force in Europe. Its involvement in local struggles in the villages, towns and cities of Catalonia gives it a strong base, made visible in the independentist *casals* (bars/organisation centres) in every village and city neighbourhood – heirs of the anarchist *ateneus*. Decisions are taken by assembly. For many years, it did not stand in parliamentary elections, as it was healthily aware of the danger of institutional politics separating it from its local bases. In 2012, it stood for the first time in Catalan elections. November 2019 was its first participation in a Spanish state election.

Other sectors of the left often attack the CUP for being nationalist, like its allies on the independence question, ERC and the various parties into which *Convergència* has been shattered by the force of the independence movement. There is an important difference between being nationalist and independentist. The CUP and its voters are socialist internationalists fighting to create a democratic Republic, where social services will be expanded not cut, jobs created by public spending and doors opened to refugees. This is not to say that there are not nationalists in and around the CUP, but it is essentially independentist, internationalist and feminist.

Sexual politics came to the fore in these years, reflecting a new wave of politicised young women. CUP leader Anna Gabriel dared to question the nuclear family and sowed terror in conservative hearts with her magnificent reprise of the international challenge to patriarchy: 'We are the daughters and grand-daughters of the witches you were unable to hang.' This was a quite different Catalonia from Pujol's. As president, he had called on women to sweep the streets in front of their houses.

Another aspect of the CUP's 2015 advance in votes, seats and influence was its irruption into the 'red belt' around Barcelona, the neighbouring cities where many migrants from the rest of Spain lived and who had voted massively for the PSUC and the Socialists in the Transition. Its ability to integrate other forces into its candidatures won in 2015 the mayorship of Badalona, Catalonia's third city, from the racist PP leader Xavier Garcia Albiol, challenging the Socialists and the PP who, after the collapse of the PSUC, liked to claim the 'red belt' as their own, independence-free fiefdoms.

1 October 2017

When Puigdemont took over from Mas in January 2016, he promised a binding referendum in 18 months. It came after 21, but no one was complaining about the time scale. Summer 2017 saw rising tension that reached a peak in September. The central government took control of Catalonia's finances. On 6 September, the legislation permitting the 1 October referendum was agreed in the Catalan parliament: all the opposition parties walked out. On 20 September, the Civil Guard and Catalan police, the *Mossos*, raided several departments of the Catalan government and arrested various senior officials and politicians. Masses filled the streets. Anna Gabriel (CUP) said it was a coup against the Catalan government. Carme Forcadell, President (speaker) of the Parliament, denounced the PP for effectively introducing a state of emergency, with constitutional guarantees suspended. Two huge grass-roots organisations, *Òmnium cultural*, whose roots go back to the 1960s struggles against the dictatorship's persecution of Catalan culture, and the ANC (*Assemblea nacional catalana*), founded in 2011 by activists of the local referendum movement, were both pushing for independence. In the evening of 20 September, their two leaders, the pacifists Jordi Cuixart (*Òmnium*) and Jordi Sànchez (ANC), known as the two Jordis, stood on top of a Civil Guard car to appeal to the 40,000-strong crowd to disperse. The protesters were preventing the judicial officers and police who had searched the *Generalitat*'s Finance Department from leaving. The two Jordis were arrested a month later, charged with sedition, not granted bail and eventually sentenced to nine years for organising the 20 and 21 September demonstrations.

As 1 October approached, 10,000 Civil Guards were drafted into Catalonia. These cops were often seen off from their home bases with chants of *¡A por ellos!* (Go get them!). They were heirs of the troops brought by ship to smash the *Setmana tràgica* uprising. Many slept on a boat in Barcelona harbour, colourfully and absurdly painted with the cartoon character Tweety Pie. With surrealist creativity, *Piolín* (Tweety Pie) was adopted as a symbol. 'Free Tweety Pie' slogans mocked the police on social media, T-shirts and posters. Humour apart, police raids were constant. Polling papers were found and confiscated. The CUP offices were raided. Websites were blocked.

The independence movement reached its peak – so far – on the weekend of Sunday 1 October 2017, day of the independence referendum. In a triumph of local, non-centralised organisation (speciality of the CUP), polling stations, mainly schools, were occupied on the Friday night or Saturday morning to prevent them being secured by the police.

Aníbal, a CUP leader in Barcelona, told me:

We approached the local school on Thursday. They were cautious: they told us they had no authorisation to open the school all weekend. We held an assembly in the schoolyard on Friday and, lo, I found on the ground an envelope with a set of keys and a note explaining the alarms. We slept there Friday night.[13]

Figure 12   Human tower in a pro-independence demonstration
(Paul Ambrose)

On the Saturday, there were widespread rumours that the Catalan government, under political, judicial and police pressure, were going to call off the referendum. The CUP stood firm. Throughout Catalonia, thousands occupied the polling stations before the vote. The government realised it could not cancel the vote without losing all credibility.

Sunday 1 October was election day. Aníbal continued:

At 5.30 on Sunday morning a car drew up and an elderly man carried in the urns and voting papers. His legs were trembling with pride as everyone applauded. We organised a defence team, led by trade unionists from all round the state who had come to support us. We were concerned police agents might infiltrate us to mess up the voting process. A bit later, a pair of *mossos* [cops] strolled up and asked 'What's going on?' 'A chess tournament,' we answered.

The voting was very moving. Huge numbers of people. A lot of very old people, people in wheelchairs. Tears in people's eyes. We had news of other polling stations being attacked. Riot police vans stopped. When they saw the number of people lined up, arms linked, to defend the vote, they drove off. Numbers were key. We had about 300 people protecting the polling station. I believe the cops didn't dare attack us.[14]

The same story was repeated all over Catalonia. In some places, the police did attack. At the Guinardó Health Centre, Barcelona, police in full riot gear assaulted the long queue waiting to vote, 'deliberately knocking people down, young and old, some over 80', Leo told me. 'Little by little they cleared people from the square, forced the door and entered the building, which was the most frightening moment.'[15] Front pages and television news headlines all round the world showed armed, masked, unidentified cops hurling people to the ground, even downstairs, for the crime of trying to vote. Rioting police smashed windows and beat demonstrators with batons. New Zealander Dr Helena Catt, who led the 17 accredited international observers, said: 'We saw numerous and repeated violations of civil and human rights.'[16]

Sandra White, member of the Scottish Parliament and one of the international observers, said:

> The brutality in Catalonia I have never seen the like of and I hope never to see that like again. I absolutely implore the EU, Europe – you cannot stay silent on this. If you stay silent you're complicit in the attacks that were put upon the Spanish people.[17]

Forty-three per cent of the electoral roll voted, some 2,275,000 people; and the police prevented an unknown number of other votes. Some 800 people were injured. To the rage of the Spanish state, despite the police attacks, the response of voters and demonstrators was peaceful. The state desires and provokes violent confrontation in order to paint dissidents as terrorists. It did this anyway, but less convincingly. The referendum plunged the Spanish state into the worst political and constitutional crisis since the 1981 coup. The Spanish Deputy Prime Minister Soraya Sáenz de Santamaría confused her desire with reality by announcing that evening: 'There has not been a referendum or the appearance of one.' She was forgetting her own police's figures: it had closed 79 out of 2,315 polling stations.

Adrià Carrasco (see also *Repression*), an ecology activist from Esplugues, summed up the importance of 1 October:

> A lot of people thought there was nothing to be done, that no matter how much you organise, you can't beat the system. And that day [1 October] was the evidence that this is a lie and that people organising is the only way. As a country, it is one of the greatest exercises of disobedience, organisation and even victory for the people we have ever lived through.[18]

On Tuesday 3 October, a one-day general strike of protest closed Catalonia, even though the two main trade unions gave only passive support. This was the first mass strike against state repression since the time of Franco. It was organised by small, combative unions, which meant it went a lot further than the symbolic stoppages proposed by Òmnium and the ANC. The strike was angry and militant. One example of many was a trick played by farmers. They announced that their tractors would cut the motorway to France at the La Jonquera frontier. Civil Guard vans rushed there to prevent the blockage. The police were delighted to reach the frontier before the tractors. Then the farmers emerged to close off the motorway behind the Civil Guard, who were trapped, feeling frustrated and foolish, for much of the day between the frontier and the tractors. Heavy tractors are a great weapon to have on your side in a worker–peasant alliance.[19] Aníbal Basora summarised:

> If we want to put it in epic terms, in the strike of 3 October, when millions of persons were blocking communications, the Spanish state and Catalan elites lost control of Catalonia for a few hours, something that had not occurred since May 1937.[20]

The Puigdemont government was now caught between its 1 October mandate and its fear of committing the illegality of a Unilateral Declaration of Independence (UDI). The CUP pushed for an immediate UDI.

On 10 October, Puigdemont signed a declaration of independence, but suspended its application in order to give time for 'dialogue'. His delaying tactic only showed the *Generalitat*'s weakness, as the central government had no intention of talking. Amid mass pressure and mounting tension, the parliamentary majority declared independence on Friday 27 October.

The Declaration was a damp squib. Puigdemont did not proclaim Independence from the balcony of the *Palau* to the crowd packing the Plaça Sant Jaume, as Macià had done. There were no fireworks of celebration. Independence did not last for Pau Claris' week (1641), nor for Macià's two days (1931). The third Catalan Independent Republic lasted for one hour, as the state government at once implemented direct rule through the Spanish Constitution's Clause 155. The Catalan Government was sacked.

It became clear that Puigdemont's government had no plan to implement the independence they had declared. The mass of independence supporters in the streets were disconcerted. On the Saturday, Puigdemont gave an appearance of normality, photographed with his family at a Girona restaurant, but however much you eat out in autumn sunshine, a UDI is hardly normal. That weekend, he meekly left the country along with five members of his government.

On the Monday morning, we were confounded to see that the remaining *consellers/eres* did not go to work in defiance of Spanish Prime Minister Rajoy's suspension of Catalan autonomy. They did not call on the mass movement to defend the new Republic against Rajoy's police. They accepted their dismissal. Was there an alternative? A vigorous call to defy 155 and occupy the *Generalitat* offices, with the *consellers/eres* defended by large crowds, would have put the new state into practical existence. Its leaders gave up without even testing the waters. The sad and farcical situation recalled Companys' formal support for the October 1934 revolt, but then he did nothing to actually win and ended up in jail. The *Generalitat* had no strategy for victory and no confidence in the mass movement.

Repression

On announcing the suspension of Catalonia's autonomy, Rajoy convened Catalan elections for 21 December 2017. His ploy backfired, as the three

Catalan pro-independence parties won 47.7 per cent of the vote and 70 of the 135 seats. *Ciutadans*, under their militantly right-wing leader Inés Arrimadas, won most seats, but the new government was formed with a coalition between the absent Puigdemont's *Junts per Catalunya* (Together for Catalonia) and ERC.

The members of the government who had not gone into exile were arrested. Of the Number Ones for the two main Catalan nationalist parties, Puigdemont was at Waterloo (would he be Wellington or Napoleon?) and Oriol Junqueras of ERC in jail in Madrid. Not only were six of Puigdemont's *consellers/eres* and Carme Forcadell the president of the parliament imprisoned – first without bail though they had committed no violent crimes and then sentenced to draconian prison terms – but there was also large-scale repression of mayors (some 800) and local activists. At the time of writing, in early 2022, there are about 3,500 people tied up in court cases arising from 1 October or subsequent disobedience – 316 for blocking roads.

Before October 2017, Committees for the Defence of the Republic (CDRs) sprang up across Catalonia, with the aim of defending the vote. After October, the CDRs mobilised frequently to cut roads, block rail tracks, picket any appearance of the Spanish authorities and agitate against repression and for independence. When the Catalan leaders were imprisoned, while their middle- and upper-class supporters took to wearing yellow ribbons, the CDRs sought to disrupt the state. Particularly popular was their occupation of motorways on the day of heavy traffic returning from the Easter holidays in April 2018. Instead of halting traffic with a roadblock, they raised the toll-booth barriers to allow everyone to drive through without paying.

The Spanish state in the months after 1 October lost the propaganda war on various fronts: beating up elderly voters on 1 October, failing to get Belgium, Germany, Switzerland or Britain (Clara Ponsatí in Scotland) to extradite Puigdemont and his *consellers/eres*, failing to stop Puigdemont and other exiles from taking up their seats in the European Parliament, failing to defeat the movement in elections or crush it on the streets.

However, the struggle for independence will not be lost or won in propaganda wars in Europe, important though these are. The key is the mass movement and, inevitably, the CDRs declined through late 2018 and 2019 after months of mobilisation. Under the brilliant name

Tsunami Democràtic, the movement rose again in late 2019 to protest the prison sentences of the main independence leaders. About 25,000 people surrounded the *Camp Nou*, Barcelona's football stadium, when Real Madrid, closely identified with Spanish nationalism, visited. Movements rise and fall anyway; but the decline is also due to the skilful use of repression by the Spanish Government.

On Tuesday, 10 April 2018, just after the CDRs had damaged profits by letting motorists through the toll barriers for free, police burst into the house of Tamara Carrasco in Viladecans and arrested her on terrorism charges. 'There were snipers on the roof, the Catalan police blocked the traffic and then 20 Civil Guards entered my house,' Tamara Carrasco explained.[21] Other activists were also arrested in carefully orchestrated scenes of police overkill, filmed and photographed for television and press consumption.

For several days, the state news was all about Tamara Carrasco as leader of a terrorist cell. Proof of terrorism was leaked: a map of the location of a Civil Guard barracks was found in her house. It transpired it was a Google map printed off for a demonstration in front of the barracks.

After three days in solitary confinement in Madrid, Tamara Carrasco was subjected to house arrest for a year before the charges of 'rebellion, sedition and terrorism' were dropped in May 2019, reduced to 'inciting disorders'. Chris Bambery, 'Public Point of Enquiry' for the British All-Party Parliamentary Group on Catalonia, wrote after visiting Tamara Carrasco under house arrest: 'Tamara says the CDR is a decentralised organisation with local groups taking their own collective decisions and the idea she is some puppeteer pulling the strings is a fantasy.'[22]

The purpose of the repression is twofold: to insist throughout Spain that the Catalan movement has to be repressed because it contains dangerous cells of terrorists, like the dissolved Basque urban guerrilla group ETA. This strategy of fear brings an avalanche of votes for the right. And second, the repression has serious political, psychological and social effects on the movement. Repression costs people their jobs. It costs money for lawyers. Repression is a warning to protest movements ... *any of you can be dragged out of bed by 20 Civil Guards bursting into your home in the small hours.* With snipers on the roof. And television cameras jostling for space outside.

In October 2020, all charges against Tamara Carrasco were dropped.

On the same day, 10 April 2018, police came for Adrià Carrasco (no relation) in Esplugues. His mother warned him and he was able to make a cinematic escape, leaping from his bed out of the back window and eventually finding his way to Belgium. Like Tamara Carrasco, he was accused of terrorism. A thousand days later, all charges were dropped and he returned home.

Spanish Policy

The rise of *Podemos* on the left, and *Ciudadanos* and then the fascist Vox on the right, ended the cosy bipartisanship of the PP and PSOE that endured from 1982 to 2015. Both these parties, mired in corruption scandals, pursued similar neoliberal policies of privatisation and deregulation. The rise of *Podemos*, as it came out of the mass struggles of the 15-M, contributed to the crises of the state. Multiple crises combine. It is an economic crisis, after the crash of 2008. It is a social crisis, with mass impoverishment after both the PSOE and PP imposed austerity, while huge sums were paid out to rescue the banks. It is a climate crisis, which is still hardly talked about despite the storms and droughts that increasingly ravage the peninsula. It is a crisis of the monarchy, as King Juan Carlos was forced to resign in 2015 and retreat to exile in 2020. The end of bipartisan government meant that the emperor, Franco's chosen heir, could be seen without his clothes, receiving enormous commissions paid into tax havens on business deals for Spanish firms. It is a crisis of the courts, too. Brave, independent judges exist, but too many follow the governments' bidding.

It was a crisis of legitimacy of the entire system. The biggest crisis was the Catalan crisis.

It is worth breaking down the main arguments wielded by the Spanish government against independence. The most common one is legalistic. The referendum contravened the 'indissoluble unity of the Spanish nation', expressed in the Spanish Constitution of 1978. Clearly, no secession from a state that wants to maintain the union is legal. In the Spanish case, the constitution was an agreement reflecting the balance of forces in 1978. There's no reason it can't be altered over 40 years later to allow a referendum. In fact, it was amended in 2011 to affirm that repayment of public debt (mostly to German banks) took priority over any other state spending.

The second argument of unionists is that only 48 per cent of Catalan voters supported independence parties in the 2017 election, though these won a narrow parliamentary majority. Thus, the pro-independence government is accused of fracturing society and causing conflict. The fracture, if there is one, is the reverse. Fomenting anti-Catalanism and refusing to discuss the question politically have fostered conflict in Catalan society. Unionists have gone quieter on this argument since pro-independence parties won 52 per cent of the vote in the February 2021 election.

A third argument is that only the Spanish population as a whole is entitled to vote on Catalan independence. This denies Catalonia the right to national self-determination, a democratic right widely accepted in international law. Spanish Governments insist, though, that Catalonia is not a nation.

The fourth argument is that independence will bring financial ruin to Catalonia. The possibility of independence led 1,500 Catalan companies, encouraged by the PP, to change their official addresses to other parts of the state. These threats and many companies actually moving have caused real anxiety in Catalonia about current and future jobs and prosperity. However, after independence, capitalist companies would still want to do business in Catalonia. Being outside the EU would also, supposedly, bring ruin. But imagine the problems of communications between Spain and France if an independent Catalonia excluded by a Spanish veto from the EU imposed tariff barriers. This argument loiters in the realm of propaganda.

A fifth argument (bizarre when it comes from xenophobic ideologues) is that any movement for national independence is right-wing and anti-immigrant, like UKIP or Italy's neo-fascist *Lega Nord*. This can seem convincing because, unlike Ireland, say, in 1916 or Brittany today, Catalonia is not a poor nation within a richer state, but one of the wealthiest parts of the Spanish state. Its leaders are often accused of wanting independence to keep all their wealth and to refuse solidarity with poorer parts of Spain. This is true of its bourgeois leaders, as it was true of Cambó and his *Lliga*. As we have explained, though, the Catalan independence movement is driven from below by its radical currents.

There are two simple, but little-confessed reasons for rejecting Catalan independence. The first is that independence would weaken the Spanish state's weight within Europe, even more so as Catalan independence would probably lead to Basque independence, too. A smaller population would mean less influence. The second unadmitted reason is the same, but seen in economic terms. The Spanish state would be much poorer without two of its wealthiest areas.

To defend its privileges, the ruling class in Madrid has exerted a ruthless media battle. The whole world saw Catalans' peaceful resistance on 1 October 2017, *except* the people living in the Spanish state outside Catalonia. Spain's television and press did not show the images of police violence. Thus, the '*¡A por ellos!*' appears quite normal to masses of Spaniards who have been educated to see the independence movement as an attack on them by rich Catalans.

On 8 October 2017, under the banner *Cataluña es España*, a coalition of forces under the name Catalan Civil Society, ranging from the PSC to fascist grouplets, organised a large demonstration through Barcelona. This was the 'response' of the supposedly silent majority to the 1 October referendum and the 3 October General Strike. Participants arrived from all round the state. The Nobel Prize-winning novelist Mario Vargas Llosa was there: the referendum was 'absurd nonsense ... an anachronism'.[23] There was nothing unusual in right-wingers supporting the suppression of Catalan autonomy. This had been going on for centuries. What was shocking was to see the PSC, the Catalan Socialist Party of Maragall and the Statute, marching shoulder to shoulder with fascists, the PP and the Lerrouxist *Ciutadans*. The Maragallian idea of a Federal Spain was revealed as just an abstraction to draw people away from independence. A federal Iberia/Spain is feasible, but only *after* independence, as an accord between equals.

So, is independence possible? History shows that the fight against centralism has recurred again and again and been crushed each time: in 1641, 1714, 1939 – and now in 2017.

Today, the Spanish state is staggering from one crisis to the other, which favours a grassroots-driven independence movement. Independence won't be won by clever speeches or the wooing of Europe's leaders, who are by definition allies of Spanish governments. It will be won by the mass movement: the heirs of Pere Joan Sala, of Pau Claris' *Coronela*, of Joan Baptista Basset, Teresa Claramunt, Layret, Nin and Maurín.

This chapter, quite unlike the preceding ones, has not discussed the working-class movement, so central to the Civil War, anti-Franco struggle and the Transition. This is in part due to the changes in the composition of this movement. Its traditional bases in the factories have declined and platform capitalism (Google, Amazon, Deliveroo, Uber etc.) has created a new, often more fragmented working class. The main unions have not caught up with these changes. And it is in part due to the legacy of Pujolism, which has left many children of immigrant workers with deep distrust of Catalanism.

The challenge of independentists is to win the working class that voted for *Ciutadans* and now for the Socialist Party. This is impossible for Puigdemont and Mas, promoters of big business and cuts in social spending. Step forward the CUP and the forces around it: can we re-unite the working class, to recreate the unity built in struggle of the 1960s and 1970s?

Endwords

Spanish centralists seek to paint Catalan nationalism as backward and reactionary. A frequent example used today is that the areas of most support for the Carlist pretenders nearly 200 years ago are the same areas of mass support for independence today, that is, the Catalan countryside. The following is a quote from one of a multitude of articles in the Spanish press that link Independentism and Carlism: 'Independence ideology ... bears similarities with Carlism, the absolutist and reactionary ideology of the nineteenth century and has become the new neoCarlism.'[1]

The journalist goes on to argue that Amer, where the family of Carles Puigdemont, the President of the *Generalitat* in exile since October 2017, has had its cake-shop for several generations, was a hot-bed of Carlism. True, but it also happens that the Amer valley was where the peasant revolt led by Pere Joan Sala started. The lesson is that you should not extrapolate details of history to suit your argument.

I want to end with a long quote from the erudite historian Josep Fontana (1931–2018) that flows against the cake-shop style of argument. A long quote with a long view of history:

> Beneath daily events and the actions of politicians who believe, mistakenly, that it is they who mark the collective directions of a people, a deep and powerful current of collective consciousness circulates. This is what has allowed us to conserve our identity against all attempts to deny it. A current that at times seems hidden, but rises into light every time an obstacle needs to be confronted ... a sentiment that has lasted over time and that has come down to today in full force, having resisted 500 years of attempts at assimilation ... [and] long campaigns of social and cultural repression that are still alive and ongoing today.[2]

Who knows if independence will be won? The collective consciousness of a nation, though, will not disappear.

Appendix: Catalan Art Revolution

The early twentieth century saw a blaze of famous artists from Catalonia who lit up the world. The Catholic, Catalan-nationalist architect Antoni Gaudí (1852–1926) was revolutionary in his art nouveau buildings. The sculptor Julio González (1876–1942) made heavy iron seem to float lightly. Salvador Dalí (1904–1989) painted dreams and the contorted, melting rocks of Cadaqués. After youthful flirtation with the revolutionary left (the BOC), he became an ardent waver of flags for Franco. The surrealist painter Remedios Varo (1908–1963), born in Anglès near Girona, painted the unconscious in vivid colour. She returned from France to fight for the revolution in Barcelona in 1936.

Southern Catalonia produced two of the twentieth century's most famous painters. The young Picasso spent nine months from 1897–1898 in the remote village of Horta de Sant Joan with his lifelong friend Manuel Pallarès. Picasso was recovering from scarlet fever. In later life, he often said: 'Everything I learned, I learned at Horta.' It was an exaggeration, for sure, but shows the importance of his time painting, learning Catalan (which he spoke all the rest of his life), working on the land and enjoying the wild countryside at Horta.

Picasso (1881–1973), child prodigy, long-lived, multi-talented, the archetypical artist of the twentieth century, whose signature was worth more than any bank-note, spent his key formative years in Catalonia. His father came to teach at Barcelona's main art school in 1895; Picasso lived mainly in Catalonia from then until he left for Paris in 1904. He was sympathetic to anarchism in 1890s Barcelona and to Communism in later years. He refused to visit Spain during the Franco years. His greatest political act was to paint *Guernica* – in tribute to the emblematic Basque town destroyed by Hitler's Condor Legion in 1937 – for the Spanish Pavilion at that year's Paris World Fair. He refused payment, but the Paris embassy's cultural attaché, the writer Max Aub, insisted and Picasso received a small sum. This payment meant that the Spanish state could legally claim possession of the painting after Franco's death. It is now the main exhibit in its own room at Madrid's Reina

Sofía Museum. Ownership is disputed by the Basque government: the unresolved national question, in the Basque Country as in Catalonia, is never absent. In Bilbao's Guggenheim Museum, an empty wall awaits *Guernica*, but claims for the painting to be exhibited there have fallen on deaf ears. It is too big a money-spinner.

Joan Miró (1893–1983) was born in Barcelona, but spent his happiest years at Montroig, a town near the coast some ten miles south of Tarragona. Like Picasso, he made his name in France. Unlike Picasso, he returned to Spain after the Civil War, first to Mallorca then to Montroig.

Miró had never made any political statement before the Civil War, but contributed to the 1937 Paris World Fair *The Reaper* or *Catalan Peasant in Revolt*, a mural of a peasant in a *barretina* brandishing a sickle, a direct reference to Catalan resistance to Spanish oppression in 1640–1641. Also in 1937, he created the most famous poster of the Civil War, *Aidez l'Espagne*, showing a powerful arm and huge clenched fist in vivid red and yellow. When he was old, Miró designed the album cover for the protest singer Raimon's first album in 1965, exhibited anti-Franco paintings and joined the occupation of Montserrat monastery in December 1970 against Franco's show-trial of ETA militants.

Why did so many great artists come out of this small country at this time? Several factors create a background. Note that all these artists were radical, either of the far right (Dalí and Gaudí) or the left. This reflected that Catalonia was a country in constant argument and debate. Anarchist and nationalist ideas swirled round young artists' heads. The former inspired dreams of justice; the latter exalted medieval glory, not just in trade and conquest, but also in the Romanesque art of the Pyrenean Boí valley or the Gothic monuments of Barcelona's Old City. Catalonia drank, too, the influence of nearby France, then the world's art centre.

The most suggestive factor is given by John Berger, who explained the society and politics that created the conditions for Picasso to flower and, by implication, the other artists mentioned above. Berger argues that Picasso lived in different historical periods all at once. Spain was 'tied on a historical rack',[1] stretched like an Inquisition torture victim. Catalonia was a relatively prosperous country within a more backward state. Conservative Catholic nationalism existed in the same place and at the same time as revolutionary anarchism. A similar argument applies to the coexistence of Carlism and working-class struggle at the start of the

Industrial Revolution. Picasso brought his revolutionary art, tensed on the rack of Spain's combined and uneven development, from Barcelona to explode into the salons of Paris.

Notes

Unless otherwise stated, all quotes from texts originally in Spanish or Catalan have been translated by the author.

Introduction

1. English translation quoted in Albert Balcells, *Catalan Nationalism: Past and Present*. London: Macmillan, 1996, 9.
2. Ferran Soldevila, *Síntesi d'història de Catalunya*. Barcelona: L'Abadia de Montserrat, 1998, 108.
3. Perry Anderson, *Passages from Antiquity to Feudalism*. London: Verso, 2013 (1974), 8.

Chapter 1

1. John Payne, *Catalonia: History and Culture*. Nottingham: Five Leaves, 2004, 158.
2. Pau Casals, UN Day Concert, 24 October 1971, General Assembly Hall in New York, UN Audiovisual Library, www.unmultimedia.org/avlibrary/asset/2362/2362972/.
3. Josep Fontana, *La formació d'una identitat: Una història de Catalunya*. Barcelona: Eumo, 2014, 21.
4. To Ramon Berenguer IV is attributed a justification of his retaining the title of Count of Barcelona: 'I am one of the greatest counts in the world, whereas, if I were called king, I should be one of the least.' See Bernat Desclot, *Llibre del rei en Pere e dels seus antecessors passats*, known as the *Crònica*. Barcelona: Teide, 1997 (originally c.1285), Chapter 3.
5. Robert Hughes, *Barcelona*. London: Harvill, 1992, 109.
6. Richard Ford, *Handbook for Travellers in Spain and Readers at Home*, 3 vols, ed. Ian Robertson. London: Centaur Press, 1966 (1845), Vol. 2, 718.
7. Desclot, *Llibre del rei en Pere e dels seus antecessors passats*, Chapter 79.
8. Ibid.
9. Joan de Déu Prats, *Historias y leyendas de Barcelona*. Barcelona: Marge, 2010, 97.
10. Hughes, *Barcelona*, 113.
11. Jaime Vicens Vives, *Aproximación a la historia de España*. Barcelona: Salvat, 1970, 97.

12. Abram Leon, *The Jewish Question: A Marxist Interpretation*. New York: Pathfinder, 1970, 133.
13. Payne, *Catalonia*, 58.
14. Pierre Vilar, *Historia de España*, trans. Manuel Tuñón de Lara and Jesús Suso Soria. Barcelona: Crítica, 1978 (1947), 35.
15. Leon, *The Jewish Question*, 136.
16. Nachmanides (*c*.1194–1270) was Rabbi of Girona. He also went under the name Bonastruc çá Porta, the name now of Girona's restored *call* (Jewish quarter).
17. Leon, *The Jewish Question*, 166. Manuel Forcano, *Els jueus catalans: La història que mai no t'han explicat*. Barcelona: Angle, 2014, 189–190.
18. Vicent Ferrer (1350–1419), notorious persecutor of the Jews, is the patron saint of Valencia.
19. Sheila Rowbotham, *Hidden from History: 300 Years of Women's Oppression and the Fight Against It*. London: Pluto, 1974, 4.

Chapter 2

1. Perry Anderson, *Lineages of the Absolutist State*. London: Verso, 1979, 64–65.
2. Albert Balcells, *Catalan Nationalism: Past and Present*. London: Macmillan, 1996, 10.
3. These minutes in Latin are contained in the *Llibre del Sindicat Remença*, held in Girona's Municipal Archive, which is how the numbers and details of the meetings are known.
4. Edmon Vallès, *La Generalitat de Catalunya en la Història*. Barcelona: Caixa de Pensions, 1978, 55.
5. Jaume Vicens Vives, *Historia de las Remensas (en el siglo xv)*. Barcelona: Edicions Vicens-Vives, 1978, 141.
6. Josep Fontana, *La formació d'una identitat: Una història de Catalunya*. Barcelona: Eumo, 2014, 119–121.
7. This transition from feudalism is summarised in Perry Anderson, *Passages from Antiquity to Feudalism*. London: Verso, 2013 (1974), 203–204.
8. Vicens Vives, *Historia de las Remensas*, 101.
9. Fontana, *La formació d'una identitat*, 102–103.
10. They were the parents of Henry VIII's first wife, Catherine of Aragon.
11. Balcells, *Catalan Nationalism*, 11.
12. Anderson, *Lineages of the Absolutist State*, 64–65. It is comforting to find such a passage as this in a general study of absolutism dating from 1974 and by an author who cannot be suspected of bias in favour of Catalan nationalism.

13. Anderson, *Lineages of the Absolutist State*, 32.
14. Josep Pla, *Salt Water*. New York: Archipelago, 2020, 340.
15. Quoted in Anderson, *Lineages of the Absolutist State*, 69–70.
16. Karl Marx, *Revolutionary Spain*. Article One, 9 September 1854. *Revolutionary Spain*, 'Survey of the Revolutionary History of Spain prior to the Nineteenth Century', is the name given to a series of eight articles by Marx published in the *New-York Daily Tribune* from 9 September to 2 December 1854. They can be found at: www.marxists.org/archive/marx/works/1854/revolutionary-spain.
17. Pierre Vilar, *Historia de España*, trans. Manuel Tuñón de Lara and Jesús Suso Soria. Barcelona: Crítica, 1978 (1947), 59.

Chapter 3

1. Catalan national anthem.
2. Ildefonso Falcones' fine novel *Cathedral of the Sea* describes the building of Santa Maria del Mar.
3. Robert Hughes, *Barcelona*. London: Harvill, 1992, 141.
4. Albert Balcells, *Catalan Nationalism: Past and Present*. London: Macmillan, 1996, 12.
5. Clara Ponsatí, *The Case of the Catalans: Why So Many Catalans No Longer Want to be Part of Spain*. Edinburgh: Luath, 2020, 53.
6. These terms are often used interchangeably. However, there is a distinction between Catalan *constitucions*, which were negotiated between the *Corts* and the monarch; and the *furs* or *fueros* of Valencia and Aragon, respectively, which were rights and privileges granted by the monarch and which, therefore, could be removed by the monarch.
7. Hughes, *Barcelona*, 155.
8. Eric Hobsbawm, *Bandits*. New York: Pantheon, 1981.
9. Chapters 60 and 61 of *Don Quijote*. This second part, which contains a remarkable description of Barcelona, was published in 1614. Since the 1970s transition, there has been a left-wing cooperative bookshop and cultural centre called *Rocaguinarda* in the Barcelona neighbourhood of Guinardó.
10. Nearly all the information on women condemned as witches and poisoners comes from the special number on 'No Eren Bruixes' of the magazine *Sàpiens*, No. 228, March 2021, www.sapiens.cat/revista/no-eren-bruixes_204337_102.html.
11. 'Witches' were hanged, as they were condemned through civil courts. Only the Inquisition, which in Catalonia opposed witch-hunting, could condemn someone to death by burning.

12. Quoted in Josep Fontana, *La formació d'una identitat: Una història de Catalunya*. Barcelona: Eumo, 2014, 150–151. The context is described in John H. Elliott, *The Count-Duke of Olivares: The Statesman in an Age of Decline*. New Haven, CT: Yale University Press, 1986, 178–202.
13. Hughes, *Barcelona*, 178.
14. Fontana, *La formació d'una identitat*, 166.
15. Josep Català and Antoni Muñoz, *Absolutisme contra pactisme: La Ciutadella de Barcelona (1640–1704)*. Barcelona: Rafael Dalmau, 2008. The relevant extract from this short book is also available at *Història i Estat*, https://historiaiestat.cat/imposicio-militar-de-labsolutisme-1640-1736-3 (accessed 13 March 2021).
16. Perry Anderson, *Lineages of the Absolutist State*. London: Verso, 1979, 81.
17. Fontana, *La formació d'una identitat*, 167.
18. John H. Elliott, *Scots and Catalans: Union and Disunion*. New Haven, CT: Yale University Press, 2020, 67.
19. 'The End of Serrallonga', in Joan Maragall, *One Day of Life is Life*, trans. Ronald Puppo. Barcelona: Fum d'Estampa, 2020.
20. Jaume Cabré, *Galceran*. Barcelona: Laia, 1978, Chapter 14.

Chapter 4

1. John H. Elliott, *Scots and Catalans: Union and Disunion*. New Haven, CT: Yale University Press, 2020, 91.
2. Perry Anderson, *Lineages of the Absolutist State*. London: Verso, 1979, 82.
3. Elliott, *Scots and Catalans*, 81.
4. Joaquim Albareda and Joan Esculies, *1714: La guerra de Successió*. Barcelona: Pòrtic, 2008, 44.
5. Víctor Alexandre, 'Testigos del asedio de 1714', *Nabarralde*, 16 October 2014, https://nabarralde.eus/testigos-del-asedio-de-1714/ (accessed 25 May 2020).
6. Henry St. John Bolingbroke, quoted in Adrià Cases i Ibàñez, Oriol Junqueras i Vies and Albert Botran i Pahissa, *Les proclames de sobirania de Catalunya (1640–1939)*. Sant Vicenç de Castellet: Farell, 2009, 38.
7. Simon Harris, *Catalonia is Not Spain: A Historical Perspective*. Barcelona: 4Cats Books, 2014, 150 (Chapter 15); and Clara Ponsatí, *The Case of the Catalans: Why So Many Catalans No Longer Want to be Part of Spain*. Edinburgh: Luath, 2020, frontispiece.
8. 'Inglesos han faltat, portuguesos han firmat, holandesos firmaran i a la fi nos penjaran.' Cases i Ibàñez et al., *Les proclames de sobirania de Catalunya (1640–1939)*, 38.

9. Edmon Vallès, *La Generalitat de Catalunya en la Història*. Barcelona: Caixa de Pensions, 1978, 72. Figures are not reliable.

10. Ibid., 69.

11. Figures dance! Cases et al., *Les proclames de sobirania de Catalunya (1640–1939)*, 43, say 25,000; but Albert Carreras says 6,000, in Ponsatí, *The Case of the Catalans*, 56.

12. Edgar Allison Peers, *Catalonia Infelix*. London: Methuen, 1937, 90.

13. Cases et al., *Les proclames de sobirania de Catalunya (1640–1939)*, 43.

14. Elliott, *Scots and Catalans*, 113.

15. Josep Fontana, *La formació d'una identitat: Una història de Catalunya*. Barcelona: Eumo, 2014, 225.

16. Elliott, *Scots and Catalans*, 95. I like to quote John Elliott (1930–2022), as he was both a distinguished historian and a vociferous opponent of Catalan independence in recent times. This means that when he describes the oppression of Catalonia by Olivares or Felipe V, he can be relied on.

17. Fontana, *La formació d'una identitat*, 225.

18. To the shout ¡*Visca la terra!*, the public is accustomed to respond ¡*lliure!*, free.

19. Harris, *Catalonia is Not Spain*, Chapter 15.

20. Fontana, *La formació d'una identitat*, 232.

21. H. Rosi Song and Anna Riera, *A Taste of Barcelona: The History of Catalan Cooking and Eating*. Lanham, MD: Rowman and Littlefield, 2019, 72. A few *xocolateries* survive still in Barcelona's carrer Petritxol.

22. Alboraia is known today for its fields of *xufes*, the root vegetable used to make *orxata* (*horchata*), Valencia's famous refreshing drink.

23. Gibraltar still has a Catalan Bay, where the Hapsburg troops disembarked, on the other side of the rock from the town. To Basset and Darmstadt's conquest, the British state owes its control of the strategic rock. 'Catalan Bay' because Basset and his Valencian soldiers, as they spoke Catalan, were commonly referred to as Catalans.

Chapter 5

1. Richard Ford, *Handbook for Travellers in Spain and Readers at Home*, 3 vols, ed. Ian Robertson. London: Centaur Press, 1966 (1845), Vol. 2, 696.

2. Karl Marx, Article One, *Revolutionary Spain. New-York Daily Tribune*, 9 September 1854, www.marxists.org/archive/marx/works/1854/revolutionary-spain.

3. George Rudé, *Revolutionary Europe, 1783–1815*. London: Fontana, 1964, 211.

4. Edgar Allison Peers, *Catalonia Infelix*. London: Methuen, 1937, 97.

5. Marx, *Revolutionary Spain*, Article Two.
6. Pierre Vilar, *Historia de España*, trans. Manuel Tuñón de Lara and Jesús Suso Soria. Barcelona: Crítica, 1978 (1947), 81.
7. Marx, *Revolutionary Spain*, Article Three.
8. Marx, *Revolutionary Spain*, Article Five.
9. Ronald Fraser, *Napoleon's Cursed War*. London: Verso, 2008, 250ff.
10. Ibid., 476.
11. Ibid., 107.
12. Ford, *Handbook for Travellers in Spain and Readers at Home*, Vol. 2, 763.
13. Ibid., Vol. 2, 762.
14. Ronald Fraser's *Napoleon's Cursed War* has the great quality of using meticulous archival research to focus on local events. This richly complements the complex accounts of battles, troop movements and political manoeuvre. See Fraser, *Napoleon's Cursed War*, 107–113.
15. Josep Fontana, *La formació d'una identitat: Una història de Catalunya*. Barcelona: Eumo, 2014, 262.
16. Marx, *Revolutionary Spain*, Article Four.
17. Written in 1808 and cited in John H. Elliott, *Scots and Catalans: Union and Disunion*. New Haven, CT: Yale University Press, 2020, 138.
18. Fraser, *Napoleon's Cursed War*, 299.
19. Ibid., 310.
20. Ford, *Handbook for Travellers in Spain and Readers at Home*, Vol. 2, 763.
21. Joan Fuster, *Nosaltres, els valencians*. Barcelona: Edicions 62, 2016 (1962), 109.
22. Ferran Soldevila, *Síntesi d'història de Catalunya*. Barcelona: L'Abadia de Montserrat, 1998, 244.
23. Riego was hanged after the defeat of the liberal triennium in 1823, but his name echoes still through the *Himno de Riego* (Riego's Anthem), which became an inspiration to liberals throughout the nineteenth century and the unofficial hymn of Spain's Second Republic.
24. Joaquín Maurín, *Revolución y contrarrevolución*. Paris: Ruedo ibérico, 1965 (1935), 10.
25. Marx, *Revolutionary Spain*, Article Nine, 14 November 1854.

Chapter 6

1. Richard Ford, *Handbook for Travellers in Spain and Readers at Home*, 3 vols, ed. Ian Robertson. London: Centaur Press, 1966 (1845), Vol. 2, 719–720.
2. Joaquín Maurín, *La revolución española*. Barcelona: Anagrama, 1977 (1931), 120.

3. Josep Fontana, *La formació d'una identitat: Una història de Catalunya.* Barcelona: Eumo, 2014, 265.
4. Eric J. Hobsbawm, *Industry and Empire: From 1750 to the Present Day.* London: Penguin, 1971, 56 (opening line of Chapter 3, 'The Industrial Revolution: 1780–1840').
5. Augustus Hare, *Wanderings in Spain*, quoted in Rose Macaulay's *Fabled Shore: From the Pyrenees to Portugal.* London: Hamish Hamilton, 1949, 73.
6. 'Raval' means suburb and is the neighbourhood of old Barcelona outside the medieval city walls, between the Rambles and the Paral·lel. It was where the first factories in the city were built.
7. Jaime Vicens Vives, *Aproximación a la historia de España.* Barcelona: Salvat, 1970, 143.
8. Ibid.
9. Information summarised in Joan de Déu Prats, *Historias y leyendas de Barcelona.* Barcelona: Marge, 2010, 147; and J.M. Huertas Claveria, *Obrers a Catalunya: Manual d'Història del Moviment Obrer (1840–1975).* Barcelona: L'Avenç, 1982, 12–18.
10. Quoted in Fontana, *La formació d'una identitat*, 270.
11. Ibid., 271.
12. Ibid., 273.
13. De Déu Prats, *Historias y leyendas de Barcelona*,133.
14. Ibid., 137.
15. Ford, *Handbook for Travellers in Spain and Readers at Home*, 716.
16. Ibid., 720.
17. Marx, *The Poverty of Philosophy*, 1846, cited in Kevin B. Anderson, 'What Marx Understood about Slavery', *Jacobin*, 5 September 2019, https://jacobinmag.com/2019/09/slavery-united-states-civil-war-marx.
18. Montserrat Llorens, in Jaume Vicens i Vives and Montserrat Llorens, *Industrials i Polítics: Història de Catalunya, Volum 11.* Barcelona: El observador, 1991, Part II, 337.
19. Ibid., 309–315.
20. Joel Sans, 'Marxisme i qüestió nacional', unpublished, 10.
21. Cited in Matt Peppe, 'Cuba's Operation Carlota 40 Years Later', *Counterpunch*, 5 November 2015, www.counterpunch.org/2015/11/05/cubas-operation-carlota-40-years-later/ (accessed 8 December 2020).

Chapter 7

1. Cited in Antonio Santamaria, 'Teresa Claramunt (1862–1931), líder anarquista y pionera feminista', *Sabadell*, 13 March 2016, at www.iSabadell.cat/Claramunt.

2. Cited in Joel Sans, 'El republicanisme federal i el catalanisme en l'últim terç del s. XIX'. unpublished, 10.
3. Engels, 'Bakuninists at Work'. Engels' essay contains the oft-quoted: 'Barcelona – Spain's largest industrial city, which has seen more barricade fighting than any other city in the world.' Curiously, this praise of the city's rebelliousness occurs in a polemic attacking Catalan Republicans and anarchists for failing to support the Murcia uprising.
4. In a desperate initiative towards the end of the rebellion, the Cartagena canton petitioned President Ulysses S. Grant to allow Murcia to become another state of the United States. Grant replied politely that he would consider the proposal.
5. Cited in J.M. Huertas Claveria, *Obrers a Catalunya: Manual d'Història del Moviment Obrer (1840–1975)*. Barcelona: L'Avenç, 1982, 63.
6. Lenin, cited in Joaquín Maurín, *Revolución y contrarrevolución en España*. Paris: Ruedo ibérico, 1965 (1935), 100.
7. Huertas, *Obrers a Catalunya*, 45–47. Huertas' book is good on both figures and local detail. In the 1860 census, Spain had 4,330,594 peasants and 500,941 workers, that is, workers were few (3.2 per cent of the total population). However, they were concentrated in Catalonia, which gave them power beyond their numbers.
8. Robert Hughes has a good summary of Oller's novel; see Robert Hughes, *Barcelona*. London: Harvill, 1992, 333–334.
9. Ibid., 335.
10. Josep Llunas, blog *Prendre la paraula*, 21 April 2016, https://blocs. mesvilaweb.cat/jordimartif69/?p=276413 (accessed 16 November 2020).
11. Josep Llunas, *La Tramontana*, 30 August 1895, '#llibrenegre 30 d'agost de 1895, Llunas en defensa de la llengua catalana, fragment d'una crònica a "La Tramontana"', blog *Prendre la paraula*, 27 December 2019, https://blocs. mesvilaweb.cat/jordimartif69/llibrenegre-30-dagost-de-1895-llunas-en-defensa-de-la-llengua-catalana-fragment-duna-cronica-a-la-tramontana/ (accessed 16 November 2020).
12. Guillem Martínez, *Barcelona rebelde: guía histórica de una ciudad*. Barcelona: Debate, 2009, 224.
13. Ibid., 236.
14. Ibid., 253.
15. Edmon Vallès, *La Generalitat de Catalunya en la Història*. Barcelona: Caixa de Pensions, 1978, 89.
16. Abel Rebollo, in Joaquim Cirera Riu (ed.), *La Barcelona Rebelde: guía de una ciudad silenciada*. Barcelona: Octaedro, 2003, 240–241.

Chapter 8

1. Victor Serge, *Birth of our Power*. London: Writers and Readers, 1977 (1931), 56.
2. I have stuck with the term 'Tragic Week' because it is so well known. However, many left-wing historians reject the term because it was coined by the bourgeoisie, who lamented the 'tragic' burning of churches. Nevertheless, it was also tragic for the fighters who died, were imprisoned and were executed.
3. Nick Lloyd, *Forgotten Places: Barcelona and the Spanish Civil War*. Barcelona: self-published, 2015 (nick.iberianaturemail.com), 34.
4. Murray Bookchin, *The Spanish Anarchists: The Heroic Years 1868–1936*. New York: Harper Colophon, 1978, 149.
5. Ibid., 150.
6. Serge, *Birth of our Power*, 106.
7. Quoted in Valerie Slaughter, 'How the Workers of Spain Battled the Spanish Flu', *The Nation*, 17 December 2020. www.thenation.com/article/world/spanish-flu-unions/.
8. Xavier Diez, *El pensament polític de Salvador Seguí*. Barcelona: Virus, 2016, 267.
9. Seguí appears fictionalised as Dario in Serge's *Birth of Our Power*.
10. The Spanish flu did not originate in Spain, but was first publicised in Spain, because the countries engaged in the Europe-wide war suffered censorship. It probably originated in the United States.
11. Slaughter, 'How the Workers of Spain Battled the Spanish Flu'.
12. Wilebaldo Solano, *Biografía breve de Andreu Nin*. Madrid: Sepa, 2006, 15.
13. Vidal Aragonés, *Francesc Layret: Vida, obra i pensament*. Barcelona: Tigre de Paper, 2020, 264.
14. Andreu Nin, *La revolución española (1930–1937)*. Barcelona: El viejo topo, 2007, 30.
15. Aragonés, *Francesc Layret*, 222.
16. Francesc Layret, interviewed by *La Publicitat* on 4 June 1919. www.isabadell.cat/sabadell/historia/francesc-layret-1880-1920-diputat-per-sabadell/ (accessed 28 November 2020).
17. *Públic*, 28 November 2020. Vidal Aragonés' *Francesc Layret* is a basic source for Layret's life and politics.

Chapter 9

1. Andreu Nin, *La revolución española (1930–1937)*. Barcelona: El viejo topo, 2007, 58.

2. Raymond Carr, *Modern Spain 1875–1980*. Oxford: Oxford University Press, 1991, 125.

3. John H. Elliott, *Scots and Catalans: Union and Disunion*. New Haven, CT: Yale University Press, 2020, 157.

4. Wilebaldo Solano, *Biografía breve de Andreu Nin*. Madrid: Sepa, 2006, 25.

5. Elliott, *Scots and Catalans*, 212.

6. Miguel Romero, *La Guerra civil española en Euskadi y Catalunya*. Madrid: Crítica & Alternativa, 2006, 15.

7. Josep Fontana, *La formació d'una identitat: Una història de Catalunya*. Barcelona: Eumo, 2014, 335.

8. Ronald Fraser, *Blood of Spain*. London: Penguin, 1981, 42.

9. Andy Durgan, *Comunismo, revolución y movimiento obrero en Cataluña 1920–1936*. Barcelona: Laertes, 2016, 120.

10. Joaquín Maurín, *Revolución y contrarrevolución en España*. Paris: Ruedo ibérico, 1965 (1935), 105–106.

11. Ibid., 106.

12. Chris Ealham, *Anarchism and the City: Revolution and Counter-Revolution in Barcelona, 1898–1937*. Oakland, CA: AK Press, 2010, 80.

13. Ibid., 86.

14. Durgan, *Comunismo, revolución y movimiento obrero en Cataluña 1920–1936*, 97.

15. Ealham, *Anarchism and the City*, 89.

16. Ibid., 123–127, explains ERC's policy on unemployment.

17. Carr, *Modern Spain 1875–1980*, 127.

18. Fraser, *Blood of Spain*, 545.

19. Ibid., 546.

20. Murray Bookchin, *The Spanish Anarchists: The Heroic Years 1868–1936*. New York: Harper Colophon, 1978, 250.

21. Andy Durgan, *The Spanish Civil War*. Basingstoke: Palgrave, 2007, 18.

22. Ibid., 16.

23. Romero, *La Guerra civil española en Euskadi y Catalunya*, 19.

24. Durgan, *The Spanish Civil War*, 27.

25. Durruti, "El de la sonrisa eterna', www.lahaine.org/est_espanol.php/ durruti-el-de-la-sonrisa (accessed 23 February 2021).

26. Ealham, *Anarchism and the City*, 46.

27. Ibid., 79.

28. Nick Lloyd, *Forgotten Places: Barcelona and the Spanish Civil War*. Barcelona: self-published, 2015 (nick.iberianaturemail.com), 60. The final sentence of this quote is carved on the huge memorial slab to Durruti in Barcelona's Montjuïc cemetery: 'Llevamos un mundo nuevo en nuestros corazones'.

29. Gerald Brenan, *The Spanish Labyrinth: An Account of the Social and Political Background of the Civil War*. Cambridge: Cambridge University Press, 1978 (1943), 250.

30. Ealham, *Anarchism and the City*, 78.

31. Lloyd, *Forgotten Places*, 244.

32. Pierre van Paasen, 'Buenaventura Durruti Interview – Pierre van Paasen', *Toronto Star*, 18 August 1936, at: https://libcom.org/article/buenaventura-durruti-interview-pierre-van-paasen.

Chapter 10

1. Andreu Nin, *La revolución española (1930–1937)*. Barcelona: El viejo topo, 2007, 234.

2. Max Aub, *Field of Honour*, trans. Gerald Martin. London: Verso, 2009, 230–231.

3. Chris Ealham, *Anarchism and the City: Revolution and Counter-Revolution in Barcelona, 1898–1937*. Oakland, CA: AK Press, 2010, 153.

4. Pierre Vilar, *Historia de España*, trans. Manuel Tuñón de Lara and Jesús Suso Soria. Barcelona: Crítica, 1978 (1947), 148.

5. Nin's speech on 6 September 1936, quoted in Miguel Romero, *La Guerra civil española en Euskadi y Catalunya*. Madrid: Crítica & Alternativa, 2006, 81.

6. Ealham, *Anarchism and the City*, 153.

7. Ronald Fraser, *Blood of Spain*. London: Penguin, 1981, 184.

8. Romero, *La Guerra civil española en Euskadi y Catalunya*, 40.

9. Ibid., 41.

10. Ibid., 41. Miguel Romero (1945–2014) was leader of the *Liga Comunista Revolucionaria* and one of the Spanish state's best-known Marxist activists during the transition and democracy.

11. Ealham, *Anarchism and the City*, 154.

12. George Orwell, *Homage to Catalonia*, Chapter 1.

13. Fraser, *Blood of Spain*, 214–215.

14. Ibid., 224.

15. Gaston Leval, *Collectives in the Spanish Revolution*. London: Freedom Press, 1975, 249.

16. Fraser, *Blood of Spain*, 225.

17. Guillem Martínez, *Barcelona rebelde: guía histórica de una ciudad*. Barcelona: Debate, 2009, 296.

18. Reiner Tosstorff, *El POUM en la revolución española*. Barcelona: Editorial Base, 2009, 134.

19. Fraser, *Blood of Spain*, 225.

20. Nick Lloyd, *Forgotten Places: Barcelona and the Spanish Civil War*. Barcelona: self-published, 2015 (nick.iberianaturemail.com), 73.
21. Fraser, *Blood of Spain*, 132–133.
22. Antonov-Ovseenko's career was as follows. Military leader of the 1917 assault on the Winter Palace, colleague of Nin and Trotsky in the Russian Left Opposition until 1928, sent to Barcelona in August 1936 by Stalin to destroy the 'Trotskyist' POUM, recalled in August 1937 with mission accomplished, executed as a 'Trotskyist' in February 1938.
23. Pierre Broué, *La revolución española (1931–1939)*. Barcelona: Península, 1977, 196–197, quoting from *Solidaridad Obrera*, 4 November 1936.
24. Romero, *La Guerra civil española en Euskadi y Catalunya*, 66.
25. *Treball*, September 30, 1936, quoted by Romero, *La Guerra civil española en Euskadi y Catalunya*, 66.
26. Quoted in Romero, *La Guerra civil española en Euskadi y Catalunya*, 81.
27. Quoted by John H. Elliott, *Scots and Catalans: Union and Disunion*. New Haven, CT: Yale University Press, 2020, 217.
28. All figures on books and papers are from Albert Balcells, *Catalan Nationalism: Past and Present*. London: Macmillan, 1996, 99.
29. Ealham, *Anarchism and the City*, 172.
30. Antony Beevor, *The Battle for Spain: The Spanish Civil War 1936–1939*. London: Phoenix, 2007, 475.
31. Durgan's *The Spanish Civil War* has a good summary of the guerrilla war question, Andy Durgan, *The Spanish Civil War*. Basingstoke: Palgrave, 2007, 37. Beevor is devastating in his critique of the Republican Government's conduct of the Battle of the Ebre; Beevor, *The Battle for Spain*, 387–400.
32. Martínez, *Barcelona rebelde*, 34.
33. Quoted in Noam Chomsky, *On Anarchism*. London: Penguin, 2014, 52.
34. Ealham, *Anarchism and the City*, 164.
35. Mary Nash, in *Rojas: las mujeres republicanas en la Guerra Civil española*. Madrid: Taurus, 1999, Chapters 3 and 5.
36. Piro Subrat, *Invertidos y rompepatrias: Marxismo, anarquismo y desobediencia sexual y de género en el estado español (1868–1982)*. Barcelona: Ed. Imperdible, 2019, 13 and 54–55. This is a trail-blazing book on 'sexual and gender disobedience in the Spanish state'.

Chapter 11

1. Max Aub, *Manuscrito Cuervo: Historia de Jacobo*. Granada: Cuadernos del Vigía, 2011, 121.

2. Quoted in Montserrat Roig, *Els catalans als camps nazis*. Barcelona: Edicions 62, 2017 (1977), 33.

3. Author's interview with Paul Preston, *Catalonia Today*, September 2011.

4. Recorded on the commemorative wall at the *Camp de la bota*.

5. Quoted in Chris Bambery and George Kerevan, *Catalonia Reborn: How Catalonia Took On the Corrupt Spanish State and the Legacy of Franco*. Edinburgh: Luath Press, 2018, 8.

6. Antoni Segura, 'Catalunya, Any Zero', in Josep M. Solé Sabaté (ed.), *El Franquisme a Catalunya, 1. La dictadura totalitària*. Barcelona: Edicions 62, 2005; J.M. Huertas Claveria, *Obrers a Catalunya: Manual d'Història del Moviment Obrer (1840–1975)*. Barcelona: L'Avenç, 1982, 315; and Sebastian Balfour, *Dictatorship, Workers, and the City: Labour in Greater Barcelona Since 1939*. Oxford: Clarendon, 1989, 3. Antoni Segura's figure includes only people executed after being sentenced by military tribunals. It does not include those summarily executed in the days following the defeat.

7. Terror sometimes drifted to farce. The *Molino rojo* music hall on Barcelona's Paral·lel, imitation of Paris' *Moulin rouge*, had its name abbreviated to *El Molino*.

8. Casilda Güell, quoted in Bambery and Kerevan, *Catalonia Reborn*, 90.

9. Huertas, *Obrers a Catalunya*, 346; and Balfour, *Dictatorship, Workers, and the City*, 9–10.

10. Pere Gabriel et al., *Comissions Obreres de Catalunya, 1964–1989*. Barcelona: Empúries, 1989, 33.

11. Balfour, *Dictatorship, Workers, and the City*, 21–22.

12. Huertas, *Obrers a Catalunya*, 312.

13. Despite the PCE's formal abandonment of this policy, local *maquis* groups continued for several years, particularly those dominated by anarchists. The last of these valiant and legendary guerrilla fighters were Quico Sabaté, shot down in Sant Celoni in 1960, and Ramon Vila *Caracremada*, killed in the mountain village of Rajadell in 1963.

14. Quoted in Balfour, *Dictatorship, Workers, and the City*, 26.

15. Albert Carreras in Clara Ponsatí, *The Case of the Catalans: Why So Many Catalans No Longer Want to be Part of Spain*. Edinburgh: Luath, 2020, 73.

16. Nicolás Sartorius and Javier Alfaya, *La memoria insumisa: Sobre la dictadura de Franco*. Barcelona: Espasa, 1999, 78–92.

17. Huertas, *Obrers a Catalunya*, 306.

18. Paul Preston, *Franco*. London: HarperCollins, 1993, 701.

19. Balfour, *Dictatorship, Workers, and the City*, 54.

20. Author's interview with Carles Prieto, El Prat, October 2004.

21. Author's interview with Carles Prieto.

22. Sánchez Soler, *La transición sangrienta*, pp.364ff; Ponsatí says that 178 people died as 'direct victims of police violence' in the same period; see Ponsatí, *The Case of the Catalans*, 37.
23. Huertas, *Obrers a Catalunya*, 314.
24. Josep Fontana, 'Infrahistoria del presente', *El País*, 14 July 2007.
25. The best overview is given by Sebastian Balfour in his 1989 book, *Dictatorship, Workers, and the City*, based on numerous interviews.
26. Piro Subrat, *Invertidos y rompepatrias: Marxismo, anarquismo y desobediencia sexual y de género en el estado español (1868–1982)*. Barcelona: Ed. Imperdible, 2019, 10.
27. Gabriel et al., *Comissions Obreres de Catalunya, 1964–1989*, 203.
28. Balfour, *Dictatorship, Workers, and the City*, 176.
29. *Combate 7*, special SEAT supplement, November–December, 1971.
30. Mike Eaude, *La transició: Moviment obrer, canvi polític i resistència popular*. Barcelona: En lluita, 2016, 125. Joel Sans interviewed Fernando Palomo, member of the LCR (Revolutionary Communist League).
31. Ibid., 126.
32. Óscar Blanco, 'La vaga de Roca: autoorganització i conflicte a contratemps'. *Ab Origine* 70, February 2022. https://aboriginemag.com/la-vaga-de-roca-autoorganitzacio-i-conflicte-a-contratemps/.
33. Though the June 1977 elections are generally cited as the first democratic elections in Spain since February 1936, there were a number of impediments which limited their democracy. For example, press censorship still existed, ERC and the far-left parties were not legalised and the PCE-PSUC was only legalised two months before.
34. *Combate*, cited in *Catalunya pels treballadors*, 20.
35. Ponsatí, *The Case of the Catalans*, 38.
36. Jordi Garcia-Soler, *Crònica apassionada de la Nova Cançó*. Barcelona: Flor de Vent, 1996, 132 and 136, respectively.
37. For this section on Llach, I have drawn on Catherine Boyle's 'The Politics of Popular Music: On the Dynamics of New Song', in Helen Graham and Jo Labanyi (eds.), *Spanish Cultural Studies: An Introduction: The Struggle for Modernity*. Oxford: Oxford University Press, 1995.
38. Josep Maria Espinàs, *Lluís Llach*. Barcelona: La Campana, 1986, 63.

Chapter 12

1. *Déu nos do la gosadia*, from Josep Carner, *Bella terra, bella gent, 1918*. Found at: http://poesia-en-catala/.blogspot.com.
2. Kathryn Crameri, *Language, the Novelist and National Identity in Post-Franco Catalonia*. Oxford: Legenda, 2000, 33.

3. 'una Catalunya vàlida per tothom'.
4. 'És català tothom qui viu i treballa a Catalunya'.
5. These and more can be found in *Què pensa Heribert Barrera* by Enric Vila. Also available free at Descargamega.net (accessed 12 February 2021).
6. Albert Balcells, *Catalan Nationalism: Past and Present*. London: Macmillan, 1996, 152.
7. Between 2000 and the economic crash of 2008 the Catalan population increased dramatically again, with the arrival of more than a million Africans and Latin Americans. Right-wing nationalists feared, once more, that the Catalan language was being diluted by Spanish-speaking Latin Americans. This is not at all certain. Many of these migrants had experienced linguistic discrimination in their countries of origin and are/were open to learning Catalan.
8. John H. Elliott, *Scots and Catalans: Union and Disunion*. New Haven, CT: Yale University Press, 2020, 253.
9. President Pasqual Maragall is the grandson of the poet Joan Maragall.
10. Pasqual Maragall, 'Madrid se va', *El País*, 27 February 2001, https://elpais.com/diario/2001/02/27/opinion/983228408.
11. Airport expansion serving the bourgeoisie's apparent economic interests, in flagrant disregard of any ecological criteria.
12. 'Està d'acord que Catalunya esdevingui un Estat de Dret, independent, democràtic i social, integrat a la Unió Europea?'
13. Interview with Aníbal Besora, 27 February 2021.
14. Ibid.
15. Interview with Leo Magrinyà, 31 March 2021. The 20-minute video *1-0 Guinardó. Ni oblit ni perdó (October 1st, Guinardó. Unforgotten, unforgiven)* is worth watching on YouTube, www.youtube.com/watch?v=Bh3gTfL-2jxk&t=4s&ab_channel=CanalVisual.
16. Chris Bambery and George Kerevan, *Catalonia Reborn: How Catalonia Took On the Corrupt Spanish State and the Legacy of Franco*. Edinburgh: Luath Press, 2018, 206.
17. Quoted in Chris Bambery, *A People's History of Scotland*. London: Verso, 2018, 342–343.
18. From the video documentary by Dan Ortínez, *Dormir amb les sabates posades (Sleep with your Shoes on)*, Aixina Produccions, 2020.
19. Bambery and Kerevan, *Catalonia Reborn*, 211.
20. Email to author, 10 June 2021.
21. Chris Bambery, 'Governments Can't Remain Silent Over Tamara Carrasco', *The National*, 22 December 2018, www.thenational.scot/news/17315483.chris-bambery-governements-cant-remain-silent-tamara-carrasco/.

22. Ibid.

23. P. Unamuno, 'Vargas Llosa: "El referéndum de Cataluña es un disparate absurdo"', *El Mundo*, 21 September 2017, www.elmundo.es/cultura/2017/09/21/59c2ce3546163f99058b4607.html.

Endwords

1. Conxa Rodríguez, 'Del carlismo al separatismo catalán', *El Mundo*, 16 September 2017, www.elmundo.es/opinion/2017/09/16/59bc1c8fe5fd eaf53f8b45e0.html.

2. Josep Fontana, *La formació d'una identitat: Una història de Catalunya*. Barcelona: Eumo, 2014, 427.

Appendix

1. John Berger, *Success and Failure of Picasso*. London: Penguin, 1965, 22.

Bibliography

This bibliography includes books and articles referred to in the text, plus general background books, with a certain bias towards English-language books.

General Books and Articles

Albareda, Joaquim. *La guerra de successió i l'onze de setembre*. Barcelona: Empúries, 2004.

Albareda, Joaquim, and Joan Esculies. *1714: La guerra de Successió*. Barcelona: Pòrtic, 2008.

Alexandre, Víctor 'Testigos del asedio de 1714', *Nabarralde*, 16 October 2014. https://nabarralde.eus/testigos-del-asedio-de-1714/ (accessed 25 May 2020).

Allison Peers, Edgar. *Catalonia Infelix*. London: Methuen, 1937.

Anderson, Benedict. *Imagined Communities: Reflections on the Origin and Spread of Nationalism*. London: Verso, 2016.

Anderson, Kevin B. 'What Marx Understood About Slavery'. *Jacobin*, 5 September 2019. https://jacobinmag.com/2019/09/slavery-united-states-civil-war-marx.

Anderson, Perry. *Lineages of the Absolutist State*. London: Verso, 1979.

Anderson, Perry. *Passages from Antiquity to Feudalism*. London: Verso, 2013 (1974).

Anguera, Pere. *Els precedents del catalanisme: Catalanitat i anticentralisme: 1808–1868*. Barcelona: Empúries, 2000.

Aragonés, Vidal. *Francesc Layret: Vida, obra i pensament*. Barcelona: Tigre de Paper, 2020.

Balcells, Albert. *Catalan Nationalism: Past and Present*. London: Macmillan, 1996.

Balfour, Sebastian. *Dictatorship, Workers, and the City: Labour in Greater Barcelona Since 1939*. Oxford: Clarendon, 1989.

Balfour, Sebastian. 'Nació i identitat a Espanya. Algunes reflexions'. *Segle XX: Revista Catalana d'història* 2, (2009): 13–23. https://revistes.ub.edu/index.php/segleXX/article/view/9760.

Bambery, Chris. 'Governments Can't Remain Silent Over Tamara Carrasco'. *The National*, 21 December 2018. www.thenational.scot/news/17315483.chris-bambery-governements-cant-remain-silent-tamara-carrasco/.

Bambery, Chris. *A People's History of Scotland*. London: Verso, 2018.

Bambery, Chris, and George Kerevan. *Catalonia Reborn: How Catalonia Took On the Corrupt Spanish State and the Legacy of Franco*. Edinburgh: Luath Press, 2018.

Batista, Antoni, and J. Playà Maset. *La gran conspiració: crònica de l'Assemblea de Catalunya*. Barcelona: Empúries, 1991.

Beevor, Antony. *The Battle for Spain: The Spanish Civil War 1936–1939*. London: Phoenix, 2007.

Berger, John. *Success and Failure of Picasso*. London: Penguin, 1965.

Blanco, Óscar. 'La vaga de Roca: autoorganització i conflicte a contratemps'. *Ab Origine* 70, February 2022. https://aboriginemag.com/la-vaga-de-roca-autoorganitzacio-i-conflicte-a-contratemps/.

Bonnassie, Pierre. *Catalunya, mil anys enrera: creixement econòmic i adveniment del feudalisme Catalunya, de mitjan segle x al final del segle xi*. Barcelona: Edicions 62, 1981.

Bookchin, Murray. *The Spanish Anarchists: The Heroic Years 1868–1936*. New York: Harper Colophon, 1978.

Boyle, Catherine. 'The Politics of Popular Music: On the Dynamics of New Song'. In Helen Graham and Jo Labanyi (eds.), *Spanish Cultural Studies: An Introduction: The Struggle for Modernity*. Oxford: Oxford University Press, 1995.

Brenan, Gerald. *The Spanish Labyrinth: An Account of the Social and Political Background of the Civil War*. Cambridge: Cambridge University Press, 1978 (1943).

Broué, Pierre. *La revolución española (1931–1939)*. Barcelona: Península, 1977.

Broué, Pierre, and Emile Témime. *The Revolution and the Civil War in Spain*. London: Faber and Faber, 1972.

Carr, Raymond. *Modern Spain 1875–1980*. Oxford: Oxford University Press, 1991.

Casals, Pau. UN Day Concert, 24 October 1971, General Assembly Hall in New York, UN Audiovisual Library. www.unmultimedia.org/avlibrary/asset/2362/2362972/.

Cases, Adrià i Ibàñez, Oriol Junqueras i Vies and Albert Botran i Pahissa. *Les proclames de sobirania de Catalunya (1640–1939)*. Sant Vicenç de Castellet: Farell, 2009.

Catà, Josep, and Antoni Muñoz. *Absolutisme contra pactisme: La Ciutadella de Barcelona (1640–1704)*. Barcelona: Rafael Dalmau, 2008. Also at *Història i Estat*. https://historiaiestat.cat/imposicio-militar-de-labsolutisme-1640-1736-3.

Chomsky, Noam. *On Anarchism*. London: Penguin, 2014.

Cirera Riu, Joaquim (ed.). *La Barcelona Rebelde: guía de una ciudad silenciada*. Barcelona: Octaedro, 2003.

Combate, paper of the LCR. At www.historialcr.info (and also on CD from the magazine *Viento Sur*).

Comellas, Pere. *Contra l'imperialisme lingüístic*. Barcelona: La Campana, 2006.

Crameri, Kathryn. *Language, the Novelist and National Identity in Post-Franco Catalonia*. Oxford: Legenda, 2000.

Desclot, Bernat. *Llibre del rei en Pere e dels seus antecessors passats*, known as the *Crònica*, Barcelona: Teide, 1997 (*c.*1285).

Déu Prats, Joan de. *Historias y leyendas de Barcelona*. Barcelona: Marge, 2010.

Diez, Xavier. *El pensament polític de Salvador Seguí*. Barcelona: Virus, 2016.

Dowling, Andrew. 'Catalonia, Spain's Biggest Problem'. *History Today*, 11 October 2017.

Durgan, Andy. *The Spanish Civil War*. Basingstoke: Palgrave, 2007.

Durgan, Andy. *Comunismo, revolución y movimiento obrero en Cataluña 1920–1936*. Barcelona: Laertes, 2016.

Durgan, Andy. *Voluntarios por la Revolución: La milicia internacional del POUM, 1936–1937*. Barcelona: Laertes, 2022.

Ealham, Chris. *Anarchism and the City: Revolution and Counter-Revolution in Barcelona, 1898–1937*. Oakland, CA: AK Press, 2010.

Eaude, Michael. *Catalonia, A Cultural History*. Oxford: Signal, 2007.

Eaude, Michael. *La transició: Moviment obrer, canvi polític i resistència popular*. Barcelona: En lluita, 2016.

Eaude, Michael. 'Kleptomaniac State'. *Catalonia Today*, September 2018.

Eaude, Michael. 'Gain Your Ends – and Damn Them'. *Catalonia Today*, October 2021.

Elliott, John H. *The Revolt of the Catalans: A Study in the Decline of Spain, 1598–1640*. Cambridge: Cambridge University Press, 1984.

Elliott, John H. *The Count-Duke of Olivares: The Statesman in an Age of Decline*. New Haven, CT: Yale University Press, 1986.

Elliott, John H. *Scots and Catalans: Union and Disunion*. New Haven, CT: Yale University Press, 2020.

Espinàs, Josep Maria. *Lluís Llach*. Barcelona: La Campana, 1986.

Fontana, Josep. 'Infrahistoria del presente'. *El País*, 14 July 2007.

Fontana, Josep. *La formació d'una identitat: Una història de Catalunya*. Barcelona: Eumo, 2014.

Forcano, Manuel. *Els jueus catalans: La història que mai no t'han explicat*. Barcelona: Angle, 2014.

Ford, Richard. *Handbook for Travellers in Spain and Readers at Home*, 3 vols, edited by Ian Robertson, Vol. 2. London: Centaur Press, 1966 (1845).

Fraser, Ronald. *Blood of Spain*. London: Penguin, 1981.

Fraser, Ronald. *Napoleon's Cursed War*. London: Verso, 2008.

Fuster, Joan. *Nosaltres, els valencians*. Barcelona: Edicions 62, 2016 (1962).

Gabriel, Pere et al. *Comissions Obreres de Catalunya, 1964–1989*. Barcelona: Empúries, 1989.

Gallego, Ferran. *Barcelona, mayo de 1937*. Barcelona: Debate, 2007.

Garcia-Soler, Jordi. *Crònica apassionada de la Nova Cançó*. Barcelona: Flor de Vent, 1996.

Harman, Chris. *A People's History of the World*. London: Bookmarks, 1999.

Harris, Simon. *Catalonia is not Spain: A Historical Perspective*. Barcelona: 4Cats Books, 2014.

Hill, Christopher. *The English Revolution 1640*. London: Lawrence & Wishart, 1979.

Hobsbawm, Eric J. *Industry and Empire: From 1750 to the Present Day*. London: Penguin, 1971.

Hobsbawm, Eric. *Bandits*. New York: Pantheon, 1981.

Huertas Claveria, J.M. *Obrers a Catalunya: Manual d'Història del Moviment Obrer (1840–1975)*. Barcelona: L'Avenç, 1982.

Hughes, Robert. *Barcelona*. London: Harvill, 1992.

Leon, Abram. *The Jewish Question: A Marxist Interpretation*. New York: Pathfinder, 1970.

Leval, Gaston. *Collectives in the Spanish Revolution*. London: Freedom Press, 1975.

Lloyd, Nick. *Forgotten Places: Barcelona and the Spanish Civil War*, self-published, Barcelona 2015 (nick.iberianaturemail.com). [Nick conducts excellent Civil War tours of Barcelona].

López Bulla, José Luis. *Cuando hice las maletas*. Barcelona: Península, 1997.

Low, Mary, and Juan Breá. *Red Spanish Notebook*. San Francisco, CA: City Lights, 1979 (1937). www.marxists.org/history/spain/writers/low-brea/red_spanish_notebook.html.

Macaulay, Rose. *Fabled Shore: From the Pyrenees to Portugal*. London: Hamish Hamilton, 1949.

Maragall, Joan. *One Day of Life is Life*. Translation by Ronald Puppo. Barcelona: Fum d'Estampa, 2020.

Maragall, Pasqual. 'Madrid se va'. *El País*, 27 February 2001. https://elpais.com/diario/2001/02/27/opinion/983228408.

Martínez, Guillem. *Barcelona rebelde: guía histórica de una ciudad*. Barcelona: Debate, 2009.

Maurín, Joaquín. *Revolución y contrarrevolución en España*. Paris: Ruedo ibérico, 1965 (1935).

Maurín, Joaquín. *La revolución española*. Barcelona: Anagrama, 1977 (1931).

Marx, Karl. *Revolutionary Spain*, articles from 1854. www.marxists.org/archive/marx/works/1854/revolutionary-spain.

Minder, Raphael. *The Struggle for Catalonia*. London: Hurst, 2017.

Nash, Mary. *Rojas: las mujeres republicanas en la Guerra Civil española*. Madrid: Taurus, 1999.

Nin, Andreu. *Els moviments d'emancipació nacional*. Barcelona: Editorial Base, 2008.

Nin, Andreu. *La revolución española (1930–1937)*. Barcelona: El viejo topo, 2007.

Payne, John. *Catalans and Others: History, Culture and Politics in Catalonia, Valencia and the Balearic Islands*. Nottingham: Five Leaves, 2016.

Payne, John. *Catalonia: History and Culture*. Nottingham: Five Leaves, 2004.

Peppe, Matt. 'Cuba's Operation Carlota 40 Years Later'. *Counterpunch*, 5 November 2015.

Pestaña, Ángel. 'El terrorismo en Barcelona'. Barcelona: *Calamus Scriptorius*, 1978 (1920).

Pla, Josep. *Salt Water*. New York: Archipelago, 2020.

Pons, Pau. *Catalunya per als treballadors*. Barcelona: Liga Comunista Revolucionaria, 1979.

Ponsatí, Clara (ed.). *The Case of the Catalans: Why So Many Catalans No Longer Want to be Part of Spain*. Edinburgh: Luath, 2020.

Preston, Paul. *Franco*. London: HarperCollins, 1993.

Querol, Jordi. *Joan Baptista Basset, militar i maulet*. Valencia: Alfons el magnànim, 1991.

Riera, Ignasi. *Els catalans de Franco*. Barcelona: Plaza & Janés, 1999.

Rodrigo, Antonina. 'La mujer en los frentes de las barricadas'. *La veu del carrer* 112, Barcelona, July 2009.

Rodríguez, Conxa. 'Del carlismo al separatismo catalán'. *El Mundo*, 16 September 2017. www.elmundo.es/opinion/2017/09/16/59bc1c8fe5fde af53f8b45e0.html.

Roig, Montserrat. *Els catalans als camps nazis*. Barcelona: Edicions 62, 2017 (1977).

Romero, Miguel. *La Guerra civil española en Euskadi y Catalunya*. Madrid: Crítica & Alternativa, 2006.

Rowbotham, Sheila. *Hidden from History: 300 Years of Women's Oppression and the Fight Against It*. London: Pluto, 1974.

Rudé, George. *Revolutionary Europe, 1783–1815*. London: Fontana, 1964.

Sánchez Soler, Mariano. *La transición sangrienta*. Barcelona: Península, 2010.

Sans, Joel. '1714: 300 anys de la caiguda de Catalunya. Mutacions d'una qüestió nacional no resolta'. *L'Heura*, May 2015.

Sans, Joel. 'Marxisme i qüestió nacional'. unpublished.

Sans, Joel. 'El republicanisme federal i el catalanisme en l'últim terç del s. XIX'. unpublished.

Santamaria, Antonio. 'Teresa Claramunt (1862–1931), líder anarquista y pionera feminista'. *Sabadell*, 13 March 2016. www.iSabadell.cat/Claramunt.

Sartorius, Nicolás, and Javier Alfaya. *La memoria insumisa: Sobre la dictadura de Franco*. Barcelona: Espasa, 1999.

Segura, Antoni. 'Catalunya, Any Zero'. In Josep M. Solé Sabaté (ed.), *El Franquisme a Catalunya, 1. La dictadura totalitària*. Barcelona: Edicions 62, 2005.

Slaughter, Valerie. 'How the Workers of Spain Battled the Spanish Flu'. *The Nation*, 17 December 2020. www.thenation.com/article/world/spanish-flu-unions/.

Sobrequés, Santiago, and Jaume Sobrequés. *La guerra civil catalana del segle XV*. Barcelona: Edicions 62, 1973.

Solano, Wilebaldo. *Biografía breve de Andreu Nin*. Madrid: Sepa, 2006.

Soldevila, Ferran. *Síntesi d'història de Catalunya*. Barcelona: L'Abadia de Montserrat, 1998.

Solé Sabaté, Josep M. (ed.) *El Franquisme a Catalunya, 1. La dictadura totalitària*. Barcelona: Edicions 62, 2005.

Song, H. Rosi, and Anna Riera, *A Taste of Barcelona: The History of Catalan Cooking and Eating*. Lanham, MD: Rowman and Littlefield, 2019.

Strubell, Toni (ed.). *What Catalans Want*. Ashfield, MA: Catalonia Press, 2011.

Subrat, Piro. *Invertidos y rompepatrias: Marxismo, anarquismo y desobediencia sexual y de género en el estado español (1868–1982)*. Barcelona: Ed. Imperdible, 2019.

Tortella, Gabriel. 'Catalanes, escoceses y Sir John Elliott'. *El Mundo*, August 21, 2019.

Tosstorff, Reiner. *El POUM en la revolución española*. Barcelona: Editorial Base, 2009.

Tree, Matthew. *Com explicar aquest país als estrangers*. Barcelona: Columna, 2011.

Tree, Matthew. 'Pork Pies in Bulk'. *Catalonia Today*, September 2021.

Trotsky, Leon. *The Spanish Revolution*. New York: Pathfinder, 1973.

Unamuno, P. 'Vargas Llosa: "El referéndum de Cataluña es un disparate absurdo"'. *El Mundo*, 21 September 2017. www.elmundo.es/cultura/2017/09/21/59c2ce3546163f99058b4607.html.

Vallès, Edmon. *La Generalitat de Catalunya en la Història*. Barcelona: Caixa de Pensions, 1978.

Van Paasen, Pierre. 'Buenaventura Durruti Interview – Pierre van Paasen'. *Toronto Star*, 18 August 1936. At: https://libcom.org/article/buenaventura-durruti-interview-pierre-van-paasen.

Verdaguer, Jacint. *Mount Canigó: A Tale of Catalonia*. Translated by Ronald Puppo. Barcelona/Woodbridge: Barcino·Tamesis, 2015.

Vicens Vives, Jaime. *Aproximación a la historia de España*. Barcelona: Salvat, 1970.

Vicens Vives, Jaume. *Historia de las Remensas (en el siglo xv)*. Barcelona: Edicions Vicens-Vives, 1978.

Vicens i Vives, Jaume, and Montserrat Llorens. *Industrials i Polítics: Història de Catalunya, Volum 11*. Barcelona: El observador, 1991.

Vila, Enric. *Què pensa Heribert Barrera*. Barcelona: Proa, 2001.

Vilar, Pierre. *Historia de España*. Translated by Manuel Tuñón de Lara and Jesús Suso Soria. Barcelona: Crítica, 1978 (1947).

Novels

Arquimbau, Rosa Maria. *Forty Lost Years*. London: Fum d'Estampa, 2021 (1971).

Aub, Max. *Field of Honour*. London: Verso, 2009. Translation by Gerald Martin of *Campo cerrado* (1943).

Aub, Max. *Manuscrito Cuervo: Historia de Jacobo*. Granada: Cuadernos del Vigía, 2011.

Cabré, Jaume. *Galceran*. Barcelona: Laia, 1978. [On bandits].

Cervantes, Miguel de. *Don Quixote*. Translated by Edith Grossman. New York: Ecco, 2005 (1605/1614).

Conrad, Joseph. *The Arrow of Gold*. London: Fisher Unwin, 1927. [On Carlism].

Falcones, Ildefonso. *Cathedral of the Sea*. London: Corgi, 2009.

Martorell, Joanot. *Tirant lo Blanc*. Translated by David Rosenthal. New York: Schocken, 1984.

Oller, Narcís. *La febre d'or*. Barcelona: labutxaca, 2019 (1892).

Orwell, George. *Homage to Catalonia*. London: Penguin, 2000.

Rodoreda, Mercè. *In Diamond Square*. Translated by Peter Bush. London: Virago, 2013.

Sánchez Piñol, Albert. *Victus*. Barcelona: La Campana, 2012.

Serge, Victor. *Birth of our Power*. London: Writers and Readers, 1977 (1931).

Solana, Teresa. *Octubre*. Barcelona: Al Revés, 2019.

Films and Videos

Buñuel, Luis. *Las Hurdes: Tierra sin pan (Land Without Bread)*. Spain, 1933.

Loach, Ken. *Land and Freedom*. United Kingdom, 1995.

Ortínez, Dan. *Dormir amb les sabates posades (Sleep With Your Shoes On)*. Aixina Produccions, 2020. YouTube: www.youtube.com/watch?v=2yIgcU jw5Mo?.

1-0 Guinardó – ni oblit, ni perdó (October 1, Guinardó – Unforgotten, unforgiven). 2018. YouTube: www.youtube.com/watch?v=Bh3gTfL2jxk&t=4s&ab_channel=CanalVisual.

Index